Mike Goodman's

Your Best Bet

Mike Goodman's
YOUR BEST BET

by

Mike Goodman

and

Michael J. Goodman

BROOKE HOUSE
Northridge, California

Library of Congress Catalog Card Number: 75-33446
ISBN: 0-912588-09-8

5678901234987654321

Contents

The New 21

The shoe isn't much to look at, a wooden box 9½ inches long and wide enough to hold a deck of cards. But this midget shoe box has revolutionized the game of 21 to the point where traditional betting methods, playing techniques, systems, and formulas have become obsolete. The world's casino operators have told the public as little as possible about the shoe and I really can't blame them. It has changed the game in favor of the club, not the player. After all, 21 has become the world's most popular casino game, and practically all foreign casinos and most in Nevada have switched over during the past ten years to dealing 21 from the shoe. In some casinos it's the only way you can play 21. Why should casino bosses tell those millions of 21 players that they've been had?

But I have no qualms. I'm going to tell it like it is.

The shoe had virtuous enough beginnings when it was first used on a widespread basis in Cuba during the 1950s, several years B.C. (Before Castro). The luxurious Havana casinos were owned and supervised by Americans, but the dealers and most other casino employes were Cubans, many of whom had put on their first pair of shoes to apply for the dealing jobs. They were raw and inexperienced, and cheaters flocked to Cuba to make their fortunes. And some Cuban dealers also were not known for their loyalty to the American bosses. The Americans quickly learned that some dealers wouldn't hesitate to help friends or agents win in return for big tips or a piece of the winnings.

The American bosses needed a dealing system that would allow the dealers and players to handle the cards as little as possible but wouldn't slow down the game. The Cuban dealers were becoming very adept at handling cards to help their pals. As an experiment, the bosses put four decks of cards in a makeshift wooden box with a roller inside to allow the dealer to slide the cards out one at a time very rapidly. The four decks were shuffled at one time and then locked into what became known as the shoe. During the play of those four decks, the dealer could touch only the top card with his finger. The cards were dealt face up so that the player had no reason to touch his cards either.

Results were immediate. Former casino bosses in Cuba have told me that cheating on both sides of the table, by the dealer and by the player, dropped sharply after shoes were installed. Cheaters posing as players, such as "hand muckers," "daubers," "benders," and "crimpers," were out of business. (Hand muckers conceal cards in their clothing or hands and switch them with the cards they get from the dealer to improve their hand or to give them instant blackjack. Daubers conceal a tiny bit of paint on a finger and dot certain cards, such as aces or 10s, so that they can be recognized when the dealer takes his hole card, which is face down, revealing the dot. Sometimes ultraviolet paint and treated sunglasses were used. Benders put a very slight bend on the corners of some cards, either high or low, depending on what they wanted to mark. Crimpers put a slight crimp on different areas of the cards to distinguish high or low cards.) But with the shoe the cards were dealt face up, so there was no reason for the player to touch them.

Dealers also found it much harder to cheat the club, because the only time they handled the cards was during shuffling, and then a supervisor was supposed to be watching. A 21 dealer still could reveal to an agent his hole card (the face-down card) by a secret signal, but now even that was harder. With face-up dealing, a supervisor could see each player's hand and could spot any erratic playing, one of the first hints of possible cheating.

Let's say that a player's two face-up cards show he has a hard 17, and the dealer has an ace or 10 face up. But then the supervisor notices that the player hits the 17 (calls for another card). Few players, even rookies, would hit a 17 against an ace or 10 showing— unless, of course, they knew beforehand that the dealer had them beat anyway. Now if the dealer turns up an 18, 19, or 20, the supervisor had better start checking the game as if his own pay check was at stake.

But perhaps the shoe's greatest deterrent value was to discourage counters, who were beginning to harass casinos in droves shortly after a flood of count books hit the public in the late 1950s and early 1960s. Counting is a technique to beat the dealer in 21 and other card games by mentally keeping track of the cards that have been dealt out so that you'll have a pretty good idea of what's left in the deck and can bet accordingly (see my later discussion on Counting the Cards). Most counters, even some top professionals, have enough trouble keeping track of a standard 52-card deck. The shoe, with a minimum of four decks, has proved to be too much for 99 in 100 amateur counters and many top pros.

Castro finally came up with the best solution to stop cheating altogether. He closed all the casinos and ran off all the Americans, who, with no other place to go, drifted to Nevada and brought the shoe with them. This was in the early 1960s and many Nevada clubs were also being plagued with counters and cheaters. A few casino bosses were quick to spot the shoe as the answer to their problem. Those were the days when all clubs had single decks. Even today there's no telling how much "leakage" or cheating is going on in clubs still using single decks. Some authorities estimate that ten million dollars a year is taken from Nevada by slot machine cheaters. You can be assured the "take" by counters and cheaters also runs into the millions. Gradually single decks have been replaced by shoes in casino after casino.

If the casino owners wanted to save millions of dollars a year at their 21 games, all they'd need to do would be to deal the shoe English-style, cards face-up, no hole card. The dealer does not take a hole card until the last player has acted on his hand. This would eliminate 99 percent of outside and inside cheating.

Cheaters and counters cornered the tranquilizer market trying how to figure out how to beat the shoe. They finally realized that the only way to beat the shoe was to switch the casino's four decks with four decks of their own which were already arranged so that the player would win. This is known as being "cold-decked." Cold-decking can be done only while the casino decks are being shuffled, and the dealer and floorman, of course, have to be in on it. That makes it a one-shot proposition because the dealer and floorman are fired immediately. Despite these drawbacks, shoes have been switched over and over, beginning a few months after the first one was introduced more than ten years ago, right up to now. The scores generally range from a few thousand dollars to more than $60,000, as happened to one Las Vegas club while I was writing this book. Once the phony decks are locked into the shoe, many hands can be played, or the whole shoe can be dealt, before the club realizes what has happened and the player has left with the money.

Because of this deck-switching problem and the natural resistance of old-time gamblers to try anything new, shoes at first were slow being accepted. Then casino bosses noticed that their 21 table volumes and winning percentages often were higher at tables with shoes. It didn't take long to discover that the shoe was the fastest game in the casino. Casinos, like insurance companies, are run on percentages and volume. With a single deck, the dealer had to stop and shuffle every few minutes, and since dealers are paid by the shift, they took their sweet time. With the shoe, the dealer shuffles only every four decks and then very quickly because a supervisor usually is watching to make sure the decks aren't switched. A single-deck dealer also has to wait for each player to mull over his hand. Often the player laboriously counts his cards to himself because nobody else sees them since they are dealt face down. But a shoe dealer doesn't have to wait for players to figure their hands. The cards are dealt face up, so often the dealer does the figuring for the player and quickly moves on to the next bettor. Bosses have discovered that the shoe increases player volume many times over single decks. Players who once lasted all evening on a single deck now can blow their money in a few hours with the shoe. Players don't realize that with the shoe you may play the same number of hands in one hour as you did in three hours with a single deck.

But the shoe can be as deadly against the house—if you know how to take advantage of it. Often cards will run in long winning or losing streaks in the shoe. Players have to react quickly to how the cards in the shoe are falling. A few veteran 21 players have adjusted, but most have not.

A typical example, the first of many, occurred not long after the shoe was introduced in Nevada. Two 21 players were sitting side by side at a shoe table in a club that I was supervising. One was a local clothing merchant who had been coming into the club once every few weeks to play $40 or $50 each time. He usually lost, but occasionally made a small score. This time he bought in for $40 and received eight $5 chips. He started to bet $5 a hand. Well, the dealer could not make a hand good. He went over or busted when he hit his stiffs (hands counting 12 to 16) and could not make better than 17 or 18 on his pat hands—which is bad for the club, especially with the fast action of the shoe. The action of the shoe was just as fast, but this time it was going against the club. The merchant bet faster and faster. He told me later he had been studying the shoe since it had been introducd and he was waiting for one to go bad. Before long he was betting two and three hands at $300 and $400 a hand. He played about two and a half hours and won $23,000, which he put into the cashier's cage for safekeeping before he left for the day.

The other player at the table was an attorney from New York who had been coming to Vegas for years and was a pretty fair 21 player with a single deck. He had a credit line of $10,000. When the shoe started to go bad for the club, the New Yorker bet much faster at first than the clothing merchant because he had a bigger bankroll. He won $30,000, but he should have won $50,000; however, he was just unsure of himself with the shoe. The New Yorker was still delighted with the $30,000 because it was much more than he had ever won in Las Vegas before. He was usually a quiet player, but this time he became outgoing and jovial, as many winners often do. Smiling and cracking jokes, the attorney gave the dealer a $25 chip each time he won a hand and a $5 tip to the cocktail waitress for each drink. It wasn't long before the dealer and the cocktail waitress were joking and smiling, too. The New Yorker then summoned the hotel jeweler to bring a ring tray to the table. He bought an $1,800 diamond cocktail ring for his wife, who had stayed in New York, and a $3,000 cocktail ring for his girl friend who didn't stay in New York. The only somber face in the club was the big boss, who stood fuming in the 21 pit next to me.

The New Yorker put his money into the cashier's cage and went to his room for a nap. But like most winners with money burning in their pockets, he returned a few hours later and started to play, this time for only $20 and $30 a hand. The shoe immediately turned against him, and it wasn't longer than a few minutes before he was down several hundred dollars. The New Yorker jumped his bets to try to get even. That's risky even when playing against a single deck, but against the shoe it can be fatal. Soon he was in $6,000. Then he started playing three and four hands at $400 and $500 a hand. Within two hours, he lost the $30,000. There was no tipping and joking now, and it was the boss who was smiling—discreetly, of course. The attorney played against his $10,000 credit line and promptly lost that. He wired home for $10,000 more and sold the $1,800 cocktail ring to another player for $1,000. His girl friend refused to give back her ring. By late afternoon, the $11,000 was gone. The attorney caught the next plane to New York while he still had a ticket.

From a $30,000 winner the New Yorker had become a $50,000 loser. Remember, the original $30,000 belonged to him. The local merchant, on the other hand, came back the next day, sat down at the same table as the New Yorker, and when the shoe started going bad left the club after only losing a few thousand dollars.

Before the attorney left, he asked me what he had done wrong. He conceded that he had never lost so much so fast in his life. All I could do was give him a quick lesson in money management. What he didn't realize then, and what most gamblers still don't realize, is that not only is the shoe faster, but it gives the casino a much bigger edge than a single deck. It's very difficult to determine the exact percentage, because every card dealt will change the situation. Also, casinos don't deal the shoe all the way to the end. They stop roughly about one deck from the end and reshuffle to foil counters (see the discussion on Counting later on). But there is no standard place to stop and reshuffle. It is left up to each individual dealer, and each of them does it differently at each table at each casino around the world. Try to figure percentages scientifically in that kind of situation.

But we do know for certain, after studying the shoe for years, that it gives the dealer a tremendous advantage at hitting his stiff hands (12, 13, 14, 15, and 16) because, though the game has changed, players still hit the same as they have since 21 was first invented by the French in the early 1700s. Most players with just a slight knowledge of the game will stop on a low hand (12 to 16) when the dealer has a small card (2 to 6) showing, because they know the dealer must hit his hand until he reaches a minimum of 17. That playing technique was fine with a single deck. There are more low cards than high cards, but the dealer had a limited number of low cards to draw from. If the low cards were bunched at the beginning of the deck or concentrated toward the middle and front of the deck as often happens, the dealer would have a tough time making his stiffs good as the deal progressed.

But with the shoe, the dealer has four times as many low cards to draw from. In a four-deck shoe, there are 128 lower cards (ace to 8) that favor hitting most stiff hands, compared to only 80 big cards (9s, 10s, and pictures) that will cause practically all stiff hands to go over 21. This means that there are nearly 50 smaller cards than big cards for the shoe dealer to draw from when he tries to make a stiff good. Even if some small cards are concentrated toward the beginning of a shoe, there still will be plenty left for the dealer to draw from as the game progresses. Shoe players must revamp their game to take this added advantage away from the dealer. The shoe produces many more hitting hands for the player and dealer than a single deck but, remember, the dealer must hit his stiff hands. Casino owners who have discovered this added advantage of the shoe are delighted when players use traditional playing methods and limit their hitting, because that just increases the dealer's chances of getting low cards to make his hand good.

If the casino wanted to cheat its shoe players, all the bosses would have to do is remove a few 10s or pictures from the four decks before they are shuffled and placed into the shoe. Each 10-count or picture removed from the shoe means that there is one less card that will make the dealer's hand go over. Remember, when the dealer makes a stiff good, he usually beats most of the players at the table because most traditional playing methods advise players not to hit stiffs when the dealer has a 2, 3, 4, 5, or 6 showing—which is fine if you're playing with a single deck. Don't think that removing cards hasn't been done. Before Nevada and England began cracking down on cheaters, I knew of casinos in Nevada and in England that removed pictures from shoes for years; some other countries still might do it. It's very difficult to spot because the shoes are not dealt all the way to the end, and players aren't allowed to check out the cards. Now, inspectors from the Gaming Control Board in Nevada periodically walk into a casino unannounced, randomly select a table, ask for all the cards in the shoe, seal them in an envelope, and later check to see if all the cards are in the deck. This is being done only in Nevada and England. Keep that in mind. It would be very foolish today for a multimillion dollar casino operation to risk its license just to remove a few measly cards.

Besides, casinos are making enough money now off the shoe because 21 players still play as if it were a single deck. The new 21 is a different game. The player, big or small, now has to learn to change his betting and playing methods to take away the dealer's hitting advantage with the shoe and to adjust to the increased tempo of the game.

STUFFED

This is a story about an eccentric old dowager in her late 60s who was a regular customer at a large hotel on the Las Vegas Strip. She would bring a maid, a chauffeur, and about fifteen stuffed animals: a lion, a bear, dogs, poodles of all different colors, cats, elephants, giraffes, a tiger, monkeys, and a squirrel. She would come down about 3 or 4 in the morning to play and bring four or five animals with her. When she sat down to play, she'd reserve a whole table. She would sit the stuffed animals in each of the empty 21 chairs and bet $500 in each spot, up to $2,500 total. As the dealer dealt the cards, she'd look at each animal and say, "Do you want to hit or do you want to stop?" Then she would say to the dealer, "Hit the lion." And the dealer would hit.

But if the hand "bust," she would slap the animal and say, "You dumb bastard; just for that you can't have a drink." If the animal's hand won, she would say, "Good baby; you can have a drink." Within a few hours the drinks would pile up in front of her and her nondrinking friends. When she wanted a drink, she would lean over to, say, a stuffed giraffe and say, "Do you mind if I take your drink? You don't seem to be enjoying it." There was never any argument.

After two or three hours she would make out a check for what she owed—she never won—and wobble up to bed with a security guard carrying her little stuffed friends. She would lose $40,000 to $50,000 every trip.

SHORT CHECK STORY

Casinos sometimes have trouble collecting gambling debts, especially when they are owed by nonresidents from other states or countries. One New Yorker came into a Nevada club and wound up losing $10,000. He had a $10,000 credit line and the club accepted his personal check for $10,000. The man acted nervous and one of the bosses smelled a rat. The check was sent to the club's New York office on the next plane. The New York representative learned that the player had only $8,000 in the bank and obviously had known the check would bounce.

The representative deposited the $2,000 difference in the man's account, cashed the check, and phoned Las Vegas with the news. The casino boss—a close friend of mine— walked to the pool where the New Yorker was sunning himself, handed him the bill for the extra $2,000, and whispered in his ear, "Naughty, naughty, but if you don't mind, this time skip the check and give us cash." The response was a gulp that could be heard across the pool.

How to Play the New 21 Against the Shoe

Every 21 player, whether beginner or veteran, must learn to play against the shoe. First of all, every casino in the world now deals 21 out of the shoe. The exception is Nevada, where some clubs still deal a single and double deck. Second, it is much more difficult and risky for a club to cheat the player with a shoe. (In the hands of a professional, a single deck can be manipulated to cheat the player in about a dozen different ways that only an expert could spot.)

A few major casinos in Nevada still deal the single deck, mainly because they think it will attract players who might not like the shoe's stronger house percentage. It is safe to play single-deck 21 in these big clubs, because they are carefully scrutinized by the Nevada Gaming Control Board, and no multimillion dollar gaming corporation would risk losing its license over what it could win by cheating a player. However, most other casinos have switched over to the shoe because it is faster, it increases volume, it is easier to deal, it gives the house an added advantage especially against inexperienced players, and it gives better protection to the club against counters and cheaters on both sides of the table.

Because of all of this, there is no legitimate reason for smaller casinos, such as you find in many foreign countries, to deal single deck unless they want to cheat the players. Except for England, no foreign government has qualified personnel to police the casinos. To make matters worse, most foreign governments are partners with the casinos and rake off a huge tax, sometimes up to 90 percent of the casino's winnings. If you walk into a casino outside Nevada and find the dealers using single 21 decks, do an about-face and head for the door. **DO NOT** play 21 there. It is not worth the risk.

I predict that even the few Nevada gaming corporations still using

single decks eventually will switch to' shoes as soon as their
stockholders realize these casinos are losing millions of dollars in
volume each year just because they think they are pleasing a few big
players. But once players learn how to knock down the casino's
advantage with my playing and betting method, they'll find the shoe
is a much faster, more exciting game. This chapter also is designed for
beginners, so experienced players should skim ahead to the new
advanced playing techniques.

The object of 21 is for you to play your cards so that you get closer to
a total of 21 than the dealer without going over 21. If your cards total
22 or more, you lose immediately. Most players, even experienced
ones, think they are playing a personal game or contest against the
casino or croupier. They think that the croupier plays his hand
differently each time so that he can beat the players. This is hogwash.
The croupier is really the same as a mechanical doll who's wound up
each night before work. He might just as well be a robot, because he
has no choice on how to play his hand. He must keep hitting his hand
(drawing new cards) until he makes 17 or better or goes over 21 and
"busts" (loses).

The game starts with each player and the dealer receiving cards.
The player always gets two cards. In Europe, the croupier
immediately takes one card face up and takes the second card after all
hands are completed. But in most other casinos, the croupier
immediately takes one face-up card, and one face-down card called a
"hole card." Look at your two cards right away so that you'll be
prepared when it's your turn. Picture cards (jack, queen, and king)
and 10s count as 10 points; aces can count as 1 or 11, whichever is the
best for your hand. That's up to you. The rest of the cards (2, 3, 4, 5, 6,
7, 8, and 9) count their face value.

For example, if you have two jacks, your hand is 20; so is a queen
and 10 worth 20; 9 and 9 are 18; and a 2 and 3 are 5, and so on.

If your hand totals 17, 18, 19, or 20 in your first two cards, then
you should not try to improve it because the odds say that you will
probably get a card that will make you "bust" (go over 21 and thus
lose). With such a stopping hand, you must just hope that you will
end up closer to 21 than the dealer. If it's a tie, nobody wins. If the
club should take your money on a tie, then leave the casino
immediately because you are getting robbed.

But if your first two cards total 16 or under, you must decide whether to try to improve your hand or stick with what you have. The dealer's face card will be the key to your next move. If the dealer has a 7, 8, 9, 10, ace, or picture card showing, you must ask for another card (called a "hit") until you get 17 or better.

All casinos, except a few Nevada clubs, deal your cards face up so there's no reason to touch them. If you want a hit, hold your fingers together about an inch over your cards and brush your fingers toward you several times, or say "hit." If you don't need a hit and want to stop, place your palm an inch or so over your cards and move it back and forth, or say "I'm good." If the club deals the cards face down and you have to pick them up, you can signal for a hit by brushing the cards toward you. To stop, just slide your cards under your bet (chips or money). Let's say your first two cards are 2 and 3. You ask for a hit and get a 6. Now you have 11. On the next hit, you receive a 7. Now you have 18, and this is a stopping hand. But let's say your first two cards are 4 and 9, and you are hit with a 10. Your hand now totals 23. That's too many; you've busted. If your first two cards are face down, as some Nevada casinos deal the shoe, then you must turn them over if you bust. This shows the dealer that you're over 21. You won't have to worry about that in clubs that deal all cards face up, because the dealer will be mentally adding your cards and will quickly rake in the money if you bust.

If a dealer has a 2, 3, 4, 5, or 6, face up, then you must hit your hand until you make 15 or better. For example, if you have a 9 and 3 (12), you must hit. If you then got a 4 (16), you would stop.

If you were playing against a *single* deck in this situation, I would advise not to hit any hand over 12 if the dealer has a low card showing because there is a good chance that the dealer would bust. But with the shoe, the chances are the dealer will make his hand good, especially if you don't hit your stiffs (low hands) more aggressively than against a single deck. You must hit against a dealer's low face card until you make 15 or better. The odds are in your favor that if you have 14 or less you won't bust on the first card. You have the same chance as the dealer to get the small cards in the shoe, so don't be afraid to take that advantage away from him. This often will make the difference between a winner and a loser against the shoe.

CIGARETTES

In most Strip clubs there are trays of cigarettes at the 21 tables for the players to smoke as they please. The boss of one of the major clubs heard that the dealers getting off the tables at their break would grab a handful of cigarettes to smoke during the break or to stash for later on. The boss told one floorman, hired a few weeks earlier, that his new job was to watch the cigarettes and make sure they went to the players only.

The boss came into the club a few days later and saw that a big player had stacks of $100 chips in front of him and nobody was watching the game. The new floorman, apparently ignoring the big player, was walking up and down the 21 pit looking at the cigarette trays. The boss asked how the big player was doing.

"I don't know," the floorman replied. "My job is watching the cigarettes. That's what you told me to do."

The boss was furious. "I pay you $65 a day to just watch cigarettes?"

"I was only following instructions," the floorman said.

The boss left and returned an hour later to give the floorman a white envelope. The word "INSTRUCTIONS" was typed on the front. The note read: "Walk to the north end of the casino and down the hall until you reach room 111. Open the door and ask for Shirley and tell her your name. She will give you another envelope. Open it and follow the instructions to the letter, like you are doing here."

The floorman did as he was told. The second envelope contained his paycheck and a piece of paper bearing two words: "You're fired."

The Ace and How to Play It

So far you have learned the basics of playing 21 anywhere in the world. You have been shown how to play against every situation except when you get an ace. Beginners have no trouble learning that an ace weighs heavily in getting the one and only bonus that a casino gives away in 21. And that's called a "blackjack." In the early years of 21, players were rewarded extra if they got an ace of spades and a jack of spades on their first two cards. It was called blackjack, which is how the game got one of its names. The blackjack reward has been expanded now to include an ace combined with any picture card or a 10. It's still called blackjack. If you get a blackjack on your first two cards, turn it over immediately. The standard payoff around the world is 3 to 2. For every two chips or units you have bet, you'll receive three in return. If your bet was $2, the blackjack payoff would be $3; a $10 bet would be paid $15, and so on.

But how do you play an ace if you don't have a blackjack? That question seems to boggle the minds of beginners, experienced players, and even many dealers (too many), because the ace has two values in 21. It can be worth 1 or 11, depending which value will best improve your hand. For example, if you are dealt ace and 2, you have either 3 or 13; with an ace and 8, you have 9 or 19, and two aces give you 2 or 12. These are called soft hands. When you're dealt an ace and another card, immediately make a mental note of both possible values. The next step is to use common sense. If you have ace-7, ace-8, or ace-9 (ace-10 is automatic blackjack), it would be sheer stupidity to ask for a hit because you are already assured of at least 18, 19, or 20. Why chance ruining your hand with a hit if you already have a good one? There are some soft hands you must hit, regardless of what the dealer has showing. They are ace-2 (3 or 13), ace-3 (4 or 14), ace-4 (5 or 15), ace-5 (6 or 16), and ace-6 (7 or 17). You must hit these hands at all times. You cannot bust the first hit regardless of what card you get. This is where soft hands become confusing unless you mentally note both possible values for each hit. Let's say you are dealt an ace and 4 (5 or 15), and you ask for a hit and get another ace. Now you have 6 or 16. Neither combination is a good hand, so, since you can't bust, ask for another hit. Let's say you receive a 3. Now you have 9 or 19. You could go on hitting, but that would be foolish because 19 is a good stopping hand. But let's say you were dealt an ace and 4 and hit that with a 10. You have just lost the double value of a soft hand, because the 10 gives you 15 and nothing else. You now have a hard hand. Whenever you hit a soft hand with a 9 or 10, you automatically have a hard hand. What you do next depends on the dealer's face card, as we discussed earlier. If he has a 7 to 10 or ace face up, you must hit your 15 until you reach 17 or better. If he has a 2 to 6 showing, you stop.

The only soft hand that differs from standard playing rules is the soft 17 (ace-6). I did say earlier that 17 or above is a stopping hand, so you might think that you would not hit a soft 17. Then, I was referring to a hard 17 so as not to confuse you any more than you already were. 17 and 18 are the worst stopping hands you can get. If you had 17 or 18 each time, you would eventually lose your money. There are 36 cards out of 52-card deck that will bust a hard 17 hand. So it just sneaks into the stopping hand category. It is no bargain. But with a soft 17, you can't go over on the first card, so you must try to improve it at least for one hit. Then let the dealer's face card decide what you do next. If you had a soft 17 and hit with a 5, you would have 22 or 12. You obviously would play the hand as 12. If you hit your soft 17 with a 3, then you would have 10 or 20. There should be no doubt what to do next. Your once mediocre hand of soft 17 now is 20. That is the best stopping hand you can get, except, of course, 21.

Many dealers and so-called experienced 21 players don't know their ace from a hole in the ground. So ignore other players' or dealers' suggestions, especially on soft hands. It's very important to know the game you're playing when gambling abroad, because often the foreign dealers can't speak enough English to help you find the bathroom, let alone advise you whether to hit or stop. If you study this chapter, you'll be able to play as well as any expert, and better than most.

Splitting and Doubling Down

Splitting and doubling down should be left to the experienced player who has mastered the basic playing techniques against the shoe. Playing a single hand against the shoe can be tough enough for a beginner without worrying about splitting or doubling down his cards. A player can double down at most casinos if his first two cards total 10 or 11. And many casinos will allow you to double on almost any combination, but I advise doubling down only with a 10 or 11. Never double down on soft hands, or 9 or under. Just stick to 10 or 11. To double, you must place your cards face up on the table (if you are playing where cards are dealt face down), and put down the same amount of money as your original bet. If you had bet $2 and wanted to double, you would put down another $2, making it $4. Then the dealer gives you one card and that's it. Traditionally, 21 experts have advised players to be cautious about doubling, and many experts have advised not doubling if the dealer has a high card showing, such as a 9 or 10.

But the shoe has changed all that. Don't be afraid to double against high cards if you are playing the shoe. Double down regardless of what card the dealer has face up. Professional counters who have been studying the shoe for years have confirmed my studies that, against the shoe, you'll win more double hands than you'll lose over a long period of play, regardless what the dealer has face up. But again, double only if you have a 10 or 11. And if you win a double hand, treat it as a bonus. Don't increase your bet at all just because you won a double-down hand. Play it as winning only one bet. Otherwise, it will throw your money management off kilter, and you will be betting far more than you should.

Splitting a hand simply means taking a pair, such as two aces, two 3s, or two 7s, and splitting that pair to make two hands instead of one. Just take the cards and place them face up next to each other in a face-down casino. You also must match your original bet for the second card. If you had bet $2 originally, drew a pair, and decided to split them, you must place $2 on the second card. Now you have two hands instead of one. The dealer will allow you to play each hand separately as you would any other hand.

The first rule of splitting against the shoe is always split aces and 8s regardless what the dealer has showing. You also can split 2s, 3s, and 7s against a dealer's face card of 2, 3, 4, 5, 6, or 7. But *never* split 4s, 5s, 9s, or 10s. And you should split 6s only if the dealer has a 4, 5, or 6 showing.

Money Management for the Shoe

All 21 players must change their basic money management techniques against the shoe. It is a much faster game. You must "press" (jump) your bets much quicker and higher against the shoe. This new philosophy will terrify many players, who already shake and tremble when they bet more than $10. But the shoe often runs in winning and losing streaks, so you must press your second bet if you win. That way you'll be in the right position if the shoe takes off on a streak. If you lose, revert to your original bet. If you win the second bet, my money management progression method will take care of you after that, in any country.

Money management will vary with the country. I have included a betting guide for each country separately because the foreign currency denominations and limits vary sharply and can have a drastic effect on how you progress your bets. But I've included money management for only certain games, and only for the countries where I think you should play. For some countries, I give no money management system, simply because I would not suggest playing there. For other countries I don't explain how to bet on some games because I don't advise you to play them. If you want to know how to bet, just turn to the pages discussing the country where you're playing and follow the specific betting method there. The $2 player doesn't have to worry much about game limits in foreign casinos, because it would be hard for him to get into trouble. It's the larger bettor who plays $10 or more each hand who must carefully watch the maximum betting limits and the foreign currency.

Many casinos outside Nevada, such as in Puerto Rico and the Caribbean, deal in American money. Usually there is a $2 minimum in 21. Even in Nevada, many clubs are dealing a $2 minimum on weekends and holidays. Soon the $1 bettor may vanish with the penny slot machines. Inflation. Inflation.

But even the $2 bettor must have a money progression system for the shoe. It's going to take guts to play, but whether you're a $2 player or a $100 player you must use the following progression method against the shoe.

$2 bettor—First bet $2, then $6 if you win; then $12 and $12 again; if you keep winning, $15 and then $15 again. After the second $15 bet, raise each winning bet $5 until you lose. I don't care if you keep adding $5 a hand until you're betting $500 a hand. Still add $5 a winning hand until you lose. Play the hands, not the amount of money bet. If you lose, revert to your original bet of $2.

$5 bettor—$5, $15, $30, then $30 again, as you keep winning; then $45, $45 again, then add $10 to each winning bet until you lose

$10 bettor—$10, $30, $60, $60 again, $90, $90 again, and then add add $50 a hand until you lose.

$20 bettor—$20, $60, $120, $120 again, $180, $180 again, and then $50 a hand until you lose.

$50 bettor—$50, $150, $300, $300 again, $400 and $500 (usually the maximum limit).

$100 bettor or higher—$100, $300, $500. If you are in a club with a $1,000 limit, bet $500 again. If you win, jump to $700. If you win, make your next bet $1,000.

High rollers who normally like to bet $50 or more from the start must use the $20 progression method outside Nevada in such countries as Puerto Rico and in the Caribbean where maximum betting limits often are $200 or less. You can't be a high roller with a $200 limit, and you may never get out if you get stuck.

BOSS STORIES

A player staying at a Strip hotel RFB is there with the hotel picking up the tab for his room, food, and beverages. This player had booked in for three days. At the end of his stay, he wanted to stay another day. He had lost $6,000. A floorman went to the boss and told him the player wanted to stay another day.

The boss said, "Tell him his time is up. He eats too much."

The player checked out. Now he stays at another hotel where he loses $40,000 to $50,000 a year.

A $10,000 credit line player was invited to a major Strip hotel as their guest. The hotel picks up RFB and plane fare on big players.

As the player was leaving to go back to New York, he handed the casino manager four first-class plane tickets: himself, his wife, his eight-year-old daughter, and his dog. He said to the casino manager, "Where do I pick up my money for the plane fares?"

The casino manager looked at the tickets. He said to the player very quietly: "I will be happy to pick up your and your wife's tickets. But if you can show me what games your daughter and the dog played, I will be more than happy to pick up their air fare."

Two fares were paid.

A big player coming out of the restaurant of a major Las Vegas hotel had a heart attack.

A boss walking by asked a floorman standing there, "Who is he?"

The floorman said, "That's Mr. S. He owes $7,400 in the dice pit."

The boss walked to the dice pit, came back with a marker check, said to the floorman, "As soon as he opens his eyes, make him sign this check to go through."

Money Management for Blackjacks, Double-Downs, and Splits

Count blackjacks and double-downs as one bet. If you win, treat the extra money as a bonus and use your normal progression. If you lose a double-down, start over and don't try to make up for the loss. On splits, if you tie one and win one, you break even, so continue with the same bet. If you tie one and lose one, you must start over again with your original bet. If you win both bets, count it as one bet so that you don't jump too fast. If you tie both bets, remain at the same bet.

Some casinos in Nevada and around the world will have cards on their 21 tables with the word "surrender." This means that if you don't like the total of your first two cards, you can throw the hand in and give up half of your bet. It is a sucker bet. Do not give up the hand. If you have a bad hand, play it out anyway.

If you are playing in a Nevada club that is dealing a double deck, play the same way you would play the shoe.

Insurance

This is going to be sweet and simple. Never take insurance. I don't care what dealers, kibitzers, and other players say. The percentages are against you, more so with the shoe.

The Secret of Betting

Winning at a gambling game depends on how much heart or guts the player has: can he take advantage of running into a streak? Most players today dog it or chicken out as soon as they are a little the winner. The most common expression of the player who has just won a few dollars is: "If I had only bet a little more, I would be even from yesterday."

A Jewish expression: *If* my grandmother had baytzim, she would be my grandfather.

It is too late after you have quit.

Ninety-five percent of the people gambling do not know how to take advantage of going good at the game they are playing. This is why hotels are always building new wings.

SUPERSTITIOUS BOSSES

Most gamblers, especially bosses, are superstitious, but sometimes it gets a little ridiculous. The boss of one big Strip hotel keeps a salt shaker in the desk in the crap pit. When the dice start passing, he grabs the salt shaker, walks over to the shooter, and sprinkles salt all around him and on the player's shoes, if he's wearing any. This boss has been doing this for years and the only result has been a dirty carpet. To the dealers his nickname is Salts.

The superstitious nature of one casino boss cost him about $50,000 a year. A high roller who often came into the club started shooting the dice one evening and they were passing. He would strike or click his chips with the dice just before shooting and it so happened he was making numbers. A boss standing there said, "You can't do that."

"Well, I am superstitious," the player replied. "It doesn't hurt anyone." He clicked the dice on his chips again and rolled another number.

"Well, I am superstitious also," the boss said. "You can't do that."

"You are being superstitious with my money," the player snapped. He picked up his money and walked out and has never returned to that club. Yet he had been losing about $50,000 a year shooting craps in that casino.

In the early days of Las Vegas gambling some of the clubs weren't doing very well. One casino was going very bad in the dice and 21 pits so the boss went to a fortune-teller. She read the cards and told him to erect a large light in front of the hotel, and that would change his luck. He did and two new partners bought in a few days later for two million dollars.

The superstitious boss of a hotel on the Strip was famous for changing dealers when the dice were passing. Sometimes he would change whole crews all at once to try to change his luck. One morning a fire broke out in one of the hotel's room sections. The boss's partner called him at 4:30 a.m. to tell him there was a fire in the hotel and the fire was burning real bad. The superstitious boss called back about fifteen minutes later to ask about the fire. His partner told him it was still burning fiercely.

"Change the firemen on the hose," the superstitious boss suggested.

We'll never know if it would have helped; the section of rooms burnt to the ground.

When one of the newer Vegas clubs opened recently, one of the point men (a point man owns a small percentage of a club) had the casino help scratching their heads over his actions. He would walk around the 21 and crap pits muttering and grumbling and staring at certain dealers. One day he came over to a shift boss and said, "I want you to take down the names of all the unlucky 21 and crap dealers."

Bewildered, the shift boss replied, "I don't know what you mean by 'unlucky' crap and 21 dealers."

"Well," the point man explained, "as I walk around this club I see some stickmen on these tables calling winners and some don't."

"We must have winners and losers," said the shift boss. "If the club won all the time, we would be out of business."

The point man insisted, saying "We don't want those type of dealers working here."

But the shift boss went to the major casino owner and told him the story. The owner assigned the point man to watch the food checkers in the kitchen.

One boss at a Strip hotel had the shift bosses tell him how the dice were acting as they changed on every shift. If the dice were passing, he would say, "Cancel out; don't use these anymore." But if the dice were cold, he would wrap them up with such notations on the wrappers as "You can use these dice today, they were very cold last night. Or "These dice were fair last night." This boss may consider himself the "keeper of the dice," but the casino help have a few less complimentary names for him.

Another superstitious boss tried to change the luck of a winning player by luring him away from the tables. This winner was playing 21 and was playing 3 hands—$500 a hand— and winning consistently. The boss, a little perturbed, watched the game for a while and then walked over to the dice pit. He picked up the phone and had the player paged, but when the player answered the phone the boss hung up.

The player returned to the tables. His luck had changed all right, but in his favor. The boss dashed to the crap pit again— this time to get some aspirin.

Counting the Cards to Beat 21—Fact and Fiction

One of the most discussed but least understood controversies in gambling today swirls around a playing technique called "counting the cards." The term "counting" is an often misused and abused catchall phrase for the dozens of schemes that have surfaced in recent years to beat the dealer in 21 by mentally keeping track of the cards that have been dealt so that you'll have a pretty good idea what's left in the deck and can bet accordingly.

There's nothing new about counting cards. It's a technique I'm sure began not long after cards were invented and people started playing for something more valuable than clamshells. I learned it from an old card hustler thirty-five years ago. He learned it from an older card hustler right after the turn of the century. We didn't have a special name for counting cards then. Now it's billed as The Count. Modern entrepreneurs have polluted the public marketplace with books, mail order systems, newspaper and magazine advertising, all professing that you'll never have to work again if you buy and master their own special counting methods.

Yes, it is true. You can beat 21 by counting, but only if you're allowed to play. Nobody with a quick mind and a good memory would ever have to work a regular job again if it weren't for that one phrase—*only if you're allowed to play.*

Most persons offering count systems for sale are doing so for one reason. They can't find a casino that will let them play. They have been barred. These count-system authors are like the guy selling treasure maps for five bucks each. He guarantees that you'll find a treasure if you reach the sunken ship. But he doesn't mention the mine fields and the fifty killer sharks you have to slip past first.

What these ex-counters don't tell you is that counting is like counterfeiting. It's not for amateurs. Amateur counters have a low success rate, between zero and one. They are detected very easily. It takes weeks of daily practice and memorizing to reach the point where your eyes can skim the cards dealt on a 21 table in a split second and have the count sorted in your head. Then you have to make the right bets, constantly keep track of the cards, act nonchalant, and while you're doing all this kibitz with other players and the dealer so that hopefully nobody will spot you. Try and you'll see why so many people are *writing* about beating the clubs by counting instead of doing it themselves.

What confuses me is that most count authors say in so many words that they have been barred from playing in Nevada. But suckers still buy a book and expect to do better. What does the person who buys a book expect to do after he has learned the count? If the author was barred, what do the readers intend to do—play among themselves?

Even the simplest counting technique requires intense concentration. All count systems, regardless how the author describes them, are based on a plus (+) and minus (-) factor. Each card in the deck is assigned a value, either plus, minus, or neutral (0). In most count systems the small numbers, such as 2, 3, 4, 5, and 6, are plus, and the larger cards, such as ace, 10, and the pictures, are minus. The remaining middle cards, such as 7, 8, 9, and 0 (no value), which means "Don't count them." As the deal progresses, the plus, minus, and neutral cards will cancel each other, keeping the count near zero, unless a larger percentage of high or low cards begin to show. Then the count will favor one side, revealing to the player what's left in the deck. But often the high and low cards will be distributed evenly to the end of the deck and the count won't favor either side. Then you have to wait for the next deal and start over again.

The cards and their plus and minus values vary slightly with each particular system, but the end result always is the same: when your count is minus, you bet less. The theory is that more low cards than high cards are being removed from the deck at that time, so you should jump your bet, because your chances of getting a good hand are much better. A plus count also means that you'll have a better chance of getting a high card with a double-down hand (10, 11), but it will be riskier hitting breaking hands (12 to 16) because there are many high cards still in the deck that will cause you to bust (go over 21). A minus count indicates the remaining deck is loaded with low cards, so drop your bet because it will be harder to get a pat hand or to get a high card when doubling down. But your chances of hitting a breaking hand (12 to 16) with a small card, such as a 4, 5, or 6, are much better.

Each author has his own value system. One technique gives the low cards +1 value and the high cards -1 value. Another system uses a +5 and a -5 on some cards, and a +10 and a -10 count on other cards. Some other systems use combinations of plus and minus values and vary as to which cards should be counted as zero. One system also has you counting how many 5s are left in the deck. The more 5s left, the more you bet. It is to the player's advantage when the 5s are in the deck because it is the *worst* card the dealer can have face up.

Those are a sampling of some of the simpler count systems offered for sale. For many you'll need a calculator. A few would confuse a computer. But you can be sure the casinos will make it as tough as possible, regardless what system you use. Most clubs around the world deal 21 from several decks (usually four) in a shoe. It's almost impossible for the amateur counter, and tougher than hell for most professionals, to count against a shoe and its four or more decks. Most counters have enough trouble with one deck (see Shoe chapter). Eventually the shoe will be used in nearly every casino in the world because it is the best protection against counters and gives the house a better advantage than the single deck.

The clubs which deal the shoe face down also won't turn a player's cards face up if the 21 dealer breaks and the player only has two cards in front of him. Clubs know the player with two cards must win that hand, so if those two cards are not turned over, the potential counter can't see them and will lose track of his count. Dealers also are instructed in most clubs to shuffle when there is at least one deck left in the shoe, so that, even if a counter has been able to do his figuring, the shoe will be shuffled before he can take advantage of the count.

If a counter is even suspected, a boss will order the shoe or single deck shuffled when it is halfway dealt out. But while these precautions are necessary, most amateurs give themselves away the moment they sit down at the table. They look as if they've just robbed a bank. I've seen amateur counters so nervous that their trembling fingers can hardly hold the cards. It's one thing to practice counting the cards on your kitchen table with your wife dealing, and quite another to try it in a casino with a professional croupier and bosses staring you in the face. Some amateurs bring crib sheets and pencils and paper into the clubs to help them. I've also seen amateur counters actually use their fingers to help count as if they were in grammar school learning to add, subtract, and multiply for the first time. Many clubs won't even bother these raw amateurs, because they'll often lose more money trying to act like counters than if they played their usual way. I've had several amateurs confess that they stayed longer at the tables, bet more, and lost more, just trying to make their count system work.

But don't think casinos treat all amateur counters as a joke. If casino bosses think they are getting the worst of it, they will tell the suspected counter to leave the game—and sometimes the casino. Believe me, bosses aren't ashamed or embarrassed to tell a suspected counter to hit the road. Casinos are private clubs and can deal to whom they please. They also aren't reluctant to take the counter, who might only be a weekend tourist, and turn his name into the local gaming authorities. In Nevada there is a "black book," which is constantly updated and is circulated among the clubs, with pictures and descriptions of known cheaters, counters, and undesirables. These black book members are kicked out of the clubs as soon as they enter, and sometimes they are just tourists who want to show off.

The consequences are much more serious in many foreign countries. Some count book authors claim that with a little practice you can travel the world first class for the rest of your days by playing their count method around the globe.

Nothing could be further from the truth.

It is true that in the late 1960s, when American-style gambling began booming in England, the Bahamas, the Caribbean, and other parts of the world, the professional counters and cheaters had a field day, especially in England. Counters swept through London casinos and their 21 games like Jack the Ripper through a streetwalkers' convention. It was slaughter, a massacre. The counters showed no mercy to the polite English chaps who were operating the casinos in such gentlemanly fashion. Many casino operators had installed 21 games only as a convenience for the hordes of American tourists they expected to crowd the tables with cash-filled pockets. The English thought that their biggest problem would be where to store the money they were going to win each night. But some of those tourists were professional counters who came over just to check out the new casinos. It took these pros about thirty seconds to realize that many English dealers and supervisors still weren't sure how many cards were in a deck, let alone how to spot counters.

The English learned some bitter lessons. Today you must register forty-eight hours before entering any English casino so that you can be checked out, and there are strict new 21 rules to hinder counters.

But the English reaction was mild compared to what happened in some other foreign countries. Practically all foreign countries are major partners in their casinos because they collect high taxes, often up to 90 percent of the winnings, as in Germany. These governments take a dim view of foreigners cheating them out of their money. That's exactly how casino owners look at counters. They consider them cheaters, though all the counter is using is his memory to beat the game. In Europe, you must show your passport at each casino before you enter. The passport number is written down, and if you're caught counting or cheating, your passport number is immediately sent to Interpol, the international police agency. Interpol then sends the passport number to all European casinos. Now you've made the European blacklist. If you're caught in one of those countries, especially in a casino, you're at their mercy. If they know you are a counter, they'll let you inside the club to play and then arrest you in the act. Then you'll have weeks, months, or even years, depending on the country, to practice your count system on fellow prisoners and guards, if they let you have playing cards. Professional counters are well aware of these dangers and take elaborate precautions to avoid them, including forged documents and expensive disguises. Let the professionals run the risk of cheating the clubs and save your amateurish counting attempts for church bazaars, stag parties, and private games. Then if you're caught being a wise guy, the most you'll probably receive is a black eye. Foreign casinos play much rougher. Your best bet is not to waste a penny on a count book. So far we've been talking about counters who beat the clubs, but the real bandits in this area are 99.9 percent of the count book authors.

Most systems are so muddled and confused I doubt that even the authors can understand them. They try to cover up their own confusion with an awesome assortment of graphs, charts, tables, diagrams, and gobbledygook. Many authors have the nerve to hustle readers into buying another system or book for more money. One author, after charging $7.50 for his regular book, says you can write for an "advanced" point count system for $200, and he offers another system for the four-deck shoe for an extra $250. Another writer, after making you pay $10 for one system, tells you it's not really his best one, which would cost $40 more. Some books offer you a secret "surrender bet strategy," which, of course, also costs extra. Save your money. "Surrender strategy" simply means that some clubs allow players who don't like their hand to throw it in immediately and give up 50 percent of their bet. These authors advise tossing in half your bet if the count is going against you. That doesn't make sense. I'd rather take a chance on winning the bet than give up half before I even know what the dealer has.

The saddest part is that some of these books actually work against the player. Who knows, maybe they were secretly written by casino owners. One author tells you to play differently with a big bet than when you make a small bet. This author does not say why you should bet differently other than that you have more money up. He suggests hitting certain hands on lower bets, but not to hit the same kind of hands on higher bets. That is ridiculous. How do the cards know the size of your bet? Another ex-counter advises raising your bet fifteen units (one dollar to fifteen dollars or five dollars to seventy-five dollars) in one jump if the count is favorable. Not only is that risking financial suicide, but it's like shooting off skyrockets advertising that you're a counter.

People who go for these systems just aren't using common sense. There are several ex-counters in Las Vegas who came to make a fortune but now are dealing because they lost their money and needed a job. They'll be glad to tell you about phony count systems, such as the one from the author who pledges out front that if you buy his advanced system for $50, he'll guarantee you'll earn $100 an hour with a minimum $5 bet. It's the old "something for nothing" come-on. But his system isn't much different than most of the others, and just as confusing. Some authors don't stop at giving the player a worthless or near worthless system. They want to make sure their readers don't have a chance of winning, so they give them other instructions. For example, there's the book that advises players to quit if the tables fill up, or if there are any bad players, or any other distractions. What this writer apparently really wants is for the player to find a casino with nobody in it but the dealer.

The classic bit of advice is from an author who suggests that players should quit if they don't like the dealers. No other reason— just the dealers' personalities and looks. Once we had a dealer in Las Vegas who was so ugly and grotesque that some of his fellow dealers secretly nicknamed him "The Wart." His nickname was an exaggeration. Wart didn't look that bad, but he was ugly as sin. Wart was harmless. He really was a nice guy. But he was also one of the unluckiest dealers I've ever seen. This dealer was known to lose steadily all night, night after night, but he was so ugly that players sat at his table only if the others were filled. When he started losing, I was always tempted to quote the book that advises you not to play if you don't like the dealer's looks. I could go on debunking other worthless tips offered by count book authors, but you should be getting the hint: stay away from count books.

If you insist upon learning a count system, then I'll give you one I learned from one of the smartest men in the business. It's simple, just requiring a quick mind and a good memory; but it's as effective as the complex plus-minus techniques that so many people have written so many books about. All you have to do is to keep track of the aces, 10s, and picture cards. When there is a high percentage of aces and high cards left toward the end of the deal, raise your bet a little. You don't have to be conspicuous. If you're a one dollar bettor, you can jump it to two or three dollars without alerting casino bosses. A five dollar bettor can safely go to ten dollars and a ten dollar bettor to fifteen dollars. If you're betting any higher, don't raise your bet more than 30 percent or you'll risk being spotted as a counter. There are sixteen pictures and 10's in the deck, and four aces. Once you have mastered keeping track of them with a simple flick of the eye around the table after each deal, you can add 8's and 9's, if you think your memory can handle it. Now all you need is a casino that doesn't deal out of a shoe, that deals the deck almost to the last card, and, most important of all, doesn't have suspected counters thrown into jail.

I learned this system in 1939 when casinos couldn't have you thrown in jail—because they were illegal also. I was in Florida, which had wide-open gambling then, when an old card hustler called Shimkey volunteered to teach me his system. Shimkey never worked a day in his life. He traveled back and forth across the country from town to town looking for 21 games. Gambling was wide open in the 1920s and 1930s, and for years Shimkey got all the action he could handle. But word spread quickly in the tightly knit gambling business, and as happens with most card hustlers and card sharks, the casinos and dealers began wondering why Shimkey always won. They couldn't catch him doing anything, but they figured he must be doing *something,* so, one by one, the clubs barred Shimkey from the tables. That's why he came to me. I also was hustling cards in those days, and our paths crossed several times. He wanted to teach me his count method, and then we would split the winnings.

Shimkey approached me five days before a new casino, the Terrace Gardens, was to open on 27th Street in Miami Beach. The casino bosses of the Terrace Gardens knew Shimkey from their other gambling operations, and he knew he wouldn't be allowed to play there. I spent the next five days in Shimkey's hotel room learning every trick and nuance involved in counting. I was scared stiff when I walked into the club opening night, but after a few hours I had everything under control. When the casino closed that evening, I had won $450, which was a pretty good score in those days. By week's end my winnings were $2,500. Shimkey and I got $1,250 each. It was the easiest money I had ever made. At $1,250 a week, it wouldn't be long before I would have my own casino. A nice dream, but the next night, which was my eighth night in the club, the top boss came over to a 21 table as I sat down and asked me into his office.

"Mike, my boy," he said, "you're a nice lad, but you're a little too lucky in here. We can't nail you doing anything to the cards, but I think you'd better play somewhere else from now on."

I insisted it was nothing more than a long luck streak and that I really was an unemployed 21 dealer looking for work.

"If that's the case, we'd rather have you working for us than playing," the boss said, and hired me on the spot. It was an offer I couldn't refuse: work or leave. That finished my counting career for a while, and almost my dealing career. Police raided the club two weeks later. Fortunately, it was my night off. As for Shimkey, he continued to live very comfortably off his count until 1963, when he died of a heart attack playing golf. He was sixty-eight.

Many old-time counters and cheaters were very secretive about their techniques and many of them died broke rather than reveal their secrets to a newcomer, as Shimkey did with me. But modern counters don't seem to have any qualms about teaching someone else their tricks for a piece of the action. With sophisticated anticheating devices, one-way mirrors in the casinos, and international police cooperation, counters and cheaters must share their knowledge with fresh, unknown faces to survive. Nevada counters were delighted when the University of Nevada opened a Las Vegas campus that has grown to several thousand students. The campus gave the blacklisted counters a steady supply of ideal recruits. College students generally have all the requirements of a good potential counter. Their minds are

trained for memorizing, they always need money, and they seem
willing, almost eager, to try nearly anything, especially ripping off the
big casinos. I know some blacklisted old-timers who have been
operating college-kid count rings for years now. They take a new
recruit and teach him to count, not by reading a book, but by sitting
down with him for several days until the trainee knows almost as
much as the old pro. Then they stake the pupil with a several-
hundred-dollar bankroll, send him out, and take half the winnings.
But this fifty-fifty relationship usually doesn't last long. Either the
rookie counter eventually is spotted by casino bosses, or he drops the
old pro and starts his own count ring, forcing the old-timer to look
for a new recruit.

The ideal setup, one that counters and cheaters dream about, is
talking a casino dealer into becoming their partner. It's happening
more and more as the gambling business continues to mushroom.
Reliable casino employees are becoming much harder to find. In
Nevada, it's safe to say that almost every large casino is being
victimized by one or more dealers who are working with agents on the
other side of the table. I can see where it would be very tempting for a
dealer making a couple of hundred dollars a week in salary and tips.
All he has to do is give the agent the "office," which is a signal
revealing the dealer's hole card (face-down card). If the dealer has an
ace, 10, or picture showing, he is allowed to check his hole card for a
blackjack. This process happens quite often during a 21 game. It
would give the counter a tremendous advantage if he knew whether
the hole card gave the dealer a stiff (12 to 16) that he must hit, or
whether it gave him a stopping hand (17 to 20). There are countless
natural movements and gestures a dealer makes while he works that
can be used as signals. The dealer and agent just have to spend a few
hours deciding on their signal system and they're in business.

Here are a few of the most popular. If a dealer has a stiff when he
peeks at his hole card, he'll look straight ahead for an instant and then
turn to the first player to see if he wants to hit or stand. But if the
dealer sees he has a stopping hand, he'll immediately turn to the first
player without looking straight ahead. The agent is looking for these
moves and can spot them instantly. To the agent, they stand out like a
red flag. But the move is done in a fraction of a second and is almost
impossible to detect because looking straight ahead is natural. Other
natural moves, such as eye movement, blinking, shifting the cards,
smiling or frowning, finger movement, and many others, are almost

impossible to detect. Watch a dealer for a few minutes and you'll see that almost everything he does could be a signal. The only way to catch an agent and a dealer working together is to get them to reveal their "office." Or watch the hitting and stopping of the player.

The standard agreement is that the dealer gets one third of the winnings, but if the counter loses it costs the dealer nothing. It's a hard proposition to pass up, because the dealer knows it's as easy as it sounds. This method of cheating would be almost foolproof except for such human weaknesses as greed and jealousy. Scores of dealers and counters have been blackballed from working in Nevada and many other countries because they got greedy. It's usually fine in the beginning. The agent and dealer readily agree to be very prudent and cautious about how often they will operate in the casino, maybe only once or twice a week and only for a few hours each time. They've told me how they do everything but sign blood pacts that they are just going to rip off a few hundred dollars a week and not try for anything higher. Anybody in the gambling business knows that if this agent and dealer were to grind out $100 each a week, it would be difficult to catch them, and the casinos probably wouldn't waste much time trying.

But as happens over and over, as soon as the agent and dealer have made a few good scores and get a little taste of the big money, they get greedy. They figure that it was so easy winning $100 apiece each week, why wouldn't it be just as easy to win $300 or $400? The casino visits increase, the bets increase, and for a while maybe they do get away with it. But eventually a boss begins to connect the agent, his winnings, and the dealer together. It doesn't take long for an experienced casino boss to spot a local or steady customer frequenting a certain dealer's table week after week and always winning. Experienced bosses learn to sense and look for these patterns.

Cheaters and counters also usually beat themselves through an indiscretion of some sort. It seems that many counters and cheaters have to brag to somebody else how they're beating the clubs. The word spreads quickly. A cheater is his own worst enemy. It seems he's got to tell everybody else how smart he is. Only those with an iron will, rigid discipline, and restraint survive. There are only a few of these top professionals who have lasted and already they have become legends in gambling circles.

THE OMAHA KID

Perhaps the greatest counter of them all was The Omaha Kid. That's only his nickname, but it's close enough so that every casino boss in the world who has ever met The Kid across a 21 table will know exactly who I am talking about. He probably has fleeced more casinos for more money than any other counter in the world. The Kid drifted to Nevada from the Midwest in the early 1950s. There were only a few casinos in the state then, but through the years The Kid consistently beat practically every one of them. He also would periodically make trips across the country to hit the places where 21 was still played. Then Nevada gambling started building up and he had his pick of the state.

Few casino bosses knew about the count then. They just thought The Kid was an extremely lucky player. He was more than lucky. He had a mind like a steel trap and almost a photographic memory. But as the years wore on, casino owners finally realized that nobody could be so lucky so often and so consistently. The beginning of the end came for The Kid in Nevada in the late 1950s. He had won more than $60,000 in a downtown Las Vegas club. The boss of the club told The Kid he was too lucky, and he didn't want him to play there anymore. But The Kid wanted to be a wise guy. He said, as the story goes, "I'll make you a proposition. Let me play and, if I lose, you can keep all my money, naturally. But if I win, and quit when I feel like it, I will still give you back half of my winnngs."

The boss mulled over the proposition for a few moments and then turned it down.

"I don't know what you're doing, sonny," he said. "I know you're not cheating, but you're doing something. You're too

smart for me, Kid. Take your business to the Strip and give
them the headaches."

It's a good thing the boss turned down the proposition,
because The Kid probably would have been the new
owner. But the boss was smart enough to spread the word, and
gradually The Kid was barred from club after club. Then when
the count became known to the masses through a flood of count
books on the market, the bosses finally realized what The Kid
had been doing all those years.

He started using disguises. He would bleach his hair, wear a
moustache, Vandyke beard, anything to camouflage his
appearance. It worked for a while, but soon the bosses
organized their own intelligence network to combat counters
and cheaters and The Kid couldn't play anywhere.

Then, like a gift from heaven, England opened large-scale
gaming. The Kid went to England, and you can guess what
happened. He annihilated the English casinos and was going
strong for about three or four years until finally the English got
"hip" to the count. And a few years ago, he returned to
Nevada. By this time, Nevada had a new generation of casino
employes mixed with the old-timers, and the rookies didn't
know about The Kid. He had grown a moustache and, as was
the style, his hair was long and curly.

A few days after he hit town, The Kid beat one club on the
strip in one quick sitting for $32,000. That was his mistake. He
had drawn too much attention to himself. When he cashed out,
an older dealer told a young boss about The Kid. Las Vegas was
no longer like the Nevada of olden days, where, if a boss didn't
like the way you played, he would simply ask you to leave. Now
the games were being policed very strictly, and many clubs were
owned by corporations. A few days later, The Kid went downtown and was about a $5,000 winner when another dealer
recognized him. A boss called the gaming authorities, who had
been trying to get their hands on The Kid for a long time. They
rushed to the club, but after much haggling and arguing they
realized there wasn't much they could do. The Kid wasn't really
doing anything wrong that they could spot. He wasn't bending
or marking the cards. He was just sitting there, and winning. No
crime in that. They even had to give him the money he won.
But The Kid was told that he couldn't play in Las Vegas
anymore and would be arrested as a vagrant. I know The Kid
very well, and now that gambling has spread across the world,
he *told* me he can pick his spots, because many casino owners

and operators in other countries have never seen or heard of
him. Occasionally he'll still come back to Las Vegas, sneak in,
make a quick score, and leave. But the grandaddy of all
counters may never again make the big scores of the old days.

MR. K

But The Kid has had the last laugh. Early in his career, he was
approached by a New York millionaire industrialist who had
been watching him play. The millionaire, even in those days,
was a very sharp gambler and he knew that The Kid was doing
something when he played 21 to give him the advantage. However, the millionaire, whom we shall call Mr. K, didn't know
what it was. Nobody is quite sure just what deal Mr. K and The
Kid made, because counters and cheaters, especially top
professionals like The Kid, are very hesitant about revealing
their playing secrets. Whatever the deal, he taught Mr. K how
to count. And Mr. K has terrorized casinos ever since.

Mr. K was, and still is, an established gambler with a huge
credit line in many hotels. He operated quite differently than
The Kid. Instead of sneaking into hotels to make quick scores
as The Kid did, Mr. K's specialty was to go right to the top
bosses and make them a proposition. It has been estimated that
Mr. K over the years has beaten casinos out of millions of
dollars with his propositions. Bosses have gone for his deals
because Mr. K is a millionaire and a well-known and respected
player. He just doesn't fit the stereotype of a hustler or counter.

Mr. K began making a name for himself in the late 1950s in
Cuba, where they were dealing the shoe and the cards were dealt
face down. But Mr. K had a keen mind and had learned how to
count so well from The Kid that the shoe was no problem. He
was $60,000 winner when Cuban government officials threw
him in jail. They thought he was cheating and couldn't figure
out how anybody could win so much against the shoe without
marking the cards. The government and casino bosses checked
all the cards and found nothing wrong. They didn't know much
about the count in those days. They had to let Mr. K go and
even give him his money.

But Mr. K wasn't done. He made the bosses a proposition.
He said he would play a $500,000 freeze-out with them. Either
he'd win the $500,000 or the club would win his $500,000. The
bosses knew that Mr. K was a multimillionaire, and they would

get their money. They were tempted, but they hesitated. That hesitation probably saved their club. Mr. K kept pressing, and the bosses realized that he was pushing a little too hard. They told him to leave and said they didn't care for his kind of business. Not long after, Mr. K was officially barred from Cuba. I'm sure he didn't lose too much sleep over it.

By the early and middle 1960s, Mr. K was having a picnic at the Nevada casinos. Again, because he was a millionaire and a big-time gambler, casino bosses thought he was just a big player and not a hustler. Mr. K had standard propositions for different clubs, depending how sharp the owners were. But Mr. K was devilishly clever. He would set up the owners with a little play-acting so that they would drop their guard. Here's a first-hand account how Mr. K operated. I'm sure the casino bosses involved in the fiasco are going to wince when they see it unfolding here.

Mr. K and another sharp card player—let's call him Mr. B— staggered into a large Las Vegas Strip casino about 2 a.m. They had a girl on each arm and were acting as if they were drunk, ordering drinks, laughing, joking, and sometimes even singing. They started shooting craps and won about $8,000. Two owners were in the club at the time and they hurried over to the crap table to watch the action. Mr. K, his speech slurred and jumbled, asked the owners if they would like a little proposition on 21. His proposition in horse betting parlance is called an "if-come" bet and is one of the strongest sucker come-ons around.

To the average player, the if-come will sound very confusing, but let me simplify it. Mr. K proposed that he invest $2,100 scattered on different playing slots around the 21 layout, but what he could win each time around was $6,600. Of course, he didn't explain it that way to the bosses. If he had, naturally they wouldn't have gone for it. It's pretty strong when you can invest $2,100, and the most you can lose is $2,100, but you can win $6,600. Plus you're counting the cards. Mr. K's proposition went like this: He would play six hands with $100 bet in front of each playing slot. Then, in addition, he would bet $500 on the first hand, $500 on the third, and $500 on the fifth hand. If the first $500 bet won, the total $1,000 would go on the second hand. But if the first hand lost, only $100 would go on the second hand. The same principle also applied to the third and fifth hands. That is, if the third hand won, the $1,000 would go on the fourth hand, and if the fifth hand won, the $1,000 would go on the sixth hand. The proposition varied for other bets such as double-downs, splits, or blackjacks, but it was all on the same principle. If you win, the bet increases on the next hand, but if you lose only $100 goes on the next hand. That's the kind of bet I would like to make every day of my life. I would never have to work again. The most I can lose is a little bit, but the most I can win is a lot. On top of that, I have the club against the wall because I'm also counting the cards.

Mr. K was not playing against the shoe at that time. He was playing against a single deck dealt to the end, which is like giving a counter the license to walk into your casino cage and scoop out the money with a shovel. The two owners went for the proposition right away. They figured that Mr. K and his friend were drunk, that their minds were foggy, and that they would have a chance to beat this loud-mouth millionaire out of a lot of money. Well, they started playing about 3 a.m. Mr. K was yelling that Mr. B was bothering him. Mr. B was yelling that Mr. K was bothering him. They would slapstick and clown around the table, pretending little concern for the game. But all that clowning was just a cover-up to signal each other who should count the cards in the next deal. They would alternate counting to further confuse the bosses.

By 9 a.m., when the day boss came in, Mr. K and Mr. B had more than $30,000 in front of them and they were just beginning. The day boss, a former hustler who knew Mr. K, walked over to the table, watched the game for about three minutes, and then asked one of the owners from the night before, "What the hell is going on?" The boss stuttered and tried to explain the proposition. The day boss said, "If you don't stop this game immediately, they'll be the new owners."

The game was closed. Mr. B and Mr. K miraculously sobered instantly, had breakfast, and left the casino with their girls and smiles on their faces.

But as soon as Nevada casino bosses figured out one proposition, Mr. K came up with a new one. By then it was the late 1960s and Mr. K took his latest proposition to one of the newest and most beautiful casinos in Las Vegas. I don't want to name the place, but if you drive down the Strip, I'm sure you'll figure out which one it was. When the club opened, he went to one of the owners and said that if the casino would remove the first fifteen cards from a shoe and then deal it to the end, he would play seven hands at $500 a hand. Few people in those days, even in the late 1960s, realized just how sharp Mr. K was and that he was not just a free-wheeling, swinging millionaire, but one of the shrewdest, toughest counters in the world. After all, the world's best, The Omaha Kid, was his teacher. The bosses figured that even if Mr. K were counting, taking fifteen cards would throw off his count and give him little, if any, advantage. Besides, they figured he would have enough trouble keeping track of the shoe's four decks, anyway.

It wasn't long before Mr. K was winning $20,000 or $30,000. But instead of continuing to play 21, Mr. K would go to shoot craps or play baccarat. He knew the casino bosses would let him win only so much at 21 before barring him from playing. So he pretended to lose his 21 winnings at craps and baccarat, complaining and moaning about his losses. He would eventually return to the 21 table. But what Mr. K really did was take his 21 winnings and stick it into his pocket. He had almost unlimited credit at the club, so he would get credit at the different tables as if he had lost his 21 winnings and needed more money. This casino is one of the largest and it is very difficult to keep track of how much players are winning or losing. The casino bosses only saw Mr. K take credit at the crap and baccarat tables, return to the 21 game, win another $20,000 or $30,000, and return to the baccarat and crap tables. This went on for four days. Insiders at the club told me that Mr. K was winning more than a quarter of a million dollars. Finally, the bosses realized that Mr. K wasn't losing that much money at craps and baccarat, but they were afraid to do anything for fear of offending him. Other gamblers in town had told them that Mr. K wasn't just a playboy gambler, but a topnotch counter as well.

Mr. K continued to frequent this club until a few years ago when the bosses had little choice but to tell him he couldn't play 21 anymore, though he could play craps and baccarat. Mr. K argued fiercely that he was a big player, that he lost fortunes at craps and baccarat, and that the club was getting the best of it. But it didn't help anymore. The club realized that Mr. K had conned them. He no longer plays there. Mr. K still frequents Las Vegas casinos and still finds casino bosses year after year that go for his propositions. Some casino owners are under the illusion that, because they own the casino, they can't be beaten unless they are cheated. They think that casino odds are so strong that they can go for propositions like those Mr. K dreams up and come out ahead. But I don't care if you're approached by Mr. K or a bum on the streets, don't go for the other fellow's proposition unless you have a long time to think it over, or unless you already know the answer.

"GOLDBERG"

One of the few counters who has remained undetected by the casinos is "Goldberg."

If you were to sit next to Goldberg, you would think he was just an ordinary player. Short, skinny, balding, and middle-aged, Goldberg appears to casino bosses like a businessman in for a few days to play a little golf, sit in the sun, and gamble a few hundred dollars. He often wears a gold hat with the name of the club where he is playing. In fact, Goldberg is a Southern California businessman who bought the business, a wholesale liquor distributorship operated by his brother, with the winnings from counting against Nevada clubs.

I know Goldberg very well. I spotted his moves several years ago in a Las Vegas club where I was working. He doesn't play where I work but always stops in to say hello. For the past five years, Goldberg has been winning an average of $1,000 a week playing the count against a single deck. He also plays the count against the shoe, but he prefers the single deck. Goldberg has even established credit in several clubs and uses the credit occasionally to make it look as if he is an ordinary player. His rounds include clubs from Reno to Las Vegas and occasionally abroad. He may play in one club and not return for a month or so. He knows exactly which clubs are soft and which are tough to beat. Goldberg has a routine he follows automatically. After playing the "circuit" (as he calls it) for a month or so, Goldberg returns to California for a few weeks' rest and relaxation with his family. He's said to me that his wife knows he is a counter, because in the early days she would go with him, but his two teen-age sons think he is a traveling liquor salesman.

If the average gambler were to watch Goldberg "work" for a few hours, he would be tempted to try his hand at counting; Goldberg makes it look so easy. He smiles and kibitzes with the dealer and other players, looks at his watch as if he was bored, yawns and stretches, and sips a glass of beer. But that's only on the surface. Actually, Goldberg is concentrating every minute he is playing. Sometimes he'll sleep for sixteen hours after a mentally exhausting session.

Goldberg's greatest asset is control. If he goes bad at one table, he'll get up and try another, or even another club. Goldberg has told me he has gone bad many times and has been a couple of thousand dollars loser in a few days. But he has confidence and control of his money and the know-how to overcome his losses. Goldberg's betting method is the secret of his not being detected as a counter. He will make only two types of bets. His opening bet is $20, and that is his smallest bet. If he wins the hand, he'll bet $40, and that is the largest bet he will ever make. He stays at the $40 bet until he loses a hand, then starts at $20 again. Of course, he will double down and split cards if the hand calls for it. And if he starts winning, he will take the chips and put them in his pocket instead of letting them pile up on the table the way most players do to show everybody how much they have won. Goldberg doesn't want to attract attention and will continue beating the clubs for years to come unless he becomes greedy like most other counters and gives himself away. It is a known fact in the gambling business that counters like to brag about the scores they have made in Nevada clubs and in foreign casinos. They become greedy and egotistical and start telling others how smart they are. Soon these counters are known and are run out of the clubs. Instead of limiting their bets to $40 and grinding out like Goldberg, they try for the big score and jump their bets drastically when the count shows the cards may fall in their favor. But any boss who knows anything about the game can spot this move and soon the counter realizes he's been nailed and leaves. Meanwhile, Goldberg could be playing a few tables away, smiling, yawning, and sipping his beer—and grinding out his $1,000 a week.

TOOTHLESS

Wearing an old wrinkled suit and a wrinkled sports shirt and carrying a small, old traveling bag, a toothless old man walked into a Las Vegas club a few years ago and started to play 21, betting $200 and $300 a hand. He would play a few minutes at a table, win a few hundred dollars, lose a couple hundred, cash out, come back, play at another table, and do the same thing over again. Toothless stayed about nine days and never changed his suit. About every three days he would buy a sports shirt at the men's shop. He said he was retired and had homes in California and Florida. At the end of his stay we figured he had lost around $20,000.

Three weeks later here comes Toothless again. Of course, this time they gave him a fancy suite. He had on the same old wrinkled suit and one of the sports shirts he had bought on the earlier visit. He started the same procedure: betting $200 and $300, cashing out every few minutes, more than a hundred times a day this would go on. But this time he was winning. After five days he was about $50,000 winner. He went to the gift counter and got a bag. He went to the cashier's cage, took all of his money out of safekeeping, and put it into the bag. The total was around $75,000, including the money he came with.

"Keep my room; I'll be back in a couple of days," he said.

They checked his room and found a small traveling bag with an old shirt and two pairs of old socks. Three days later here comes Toothless into the casino, same suit and sports shirt, holding a bag in his hand, and the betting started again.

After about four hours and $60,000 loser he dug down into the bag and it was empty. Toothless said, "Bet the bag." A boss standing there said, "Just a minute," to the dealer and told a floorman standing there, "Go to the gift counter and bring back some empty bags." The floorman went and got some. The boss said to the dealer, "Deal the cards."

Toothless lost the hand, got up and walked out the door. The floorman said to the boss, "What were the empty bags for?"

The boss said, "If he won, I was going to pay him bag for bag."

After three months the hotel took Toothless' bag and shirt and socks and threw them into the garbage bin.

ECCENTRIC PLAYERS

There is a wealthy Texan who loves to play roulette so much he calls his favorite club and makes bets over the phone. He bets five or six numbers at a time at $25 a number and hangs onto the phone while the roulette wheel turns. Often he wins a couple of thousand dollars and hurries to Las Vegas to collect. Of course, once he arrives he plays more roulette and usually loses what he won over the phone plus thousands of dollars extra. Unbeknownst to the Texan, the bosses let him win over the phone so he'll come to collect and play some more. This has been going on for years. The Texan is probably a million dollars loser by winning a couple of thousand dollars when he calls.

Howard Hughes doesn't like to be seen in public much these days but years ago he was not so modest and Vegas was one of his favorite haunts. About two o'clock one morning Hughes came into one of the largest Strip clubs—which he later bought —with a girl on each arm. He walked up to a crap table and asked to see the boss. The boss was sleeping but when they told him who was downstairs he jumped out of bed, dressed hurriedly, rushed into the casino, and embraced Hughes. Hughes said he wanted to shoot craps so the boss hurried over to the cage and brought back a rack of $100 chips—$10,000 worth. After all, one of the richest men in the world would hardly want to start off with anything less.

Hughes took a $100 chip from the rack and asked for change. The dealer gave him twenty $5 chips. Hughes tossed two of the $5 chips to the dealer and asked for more change. He received ten silvers, the lowest the club had.

Hughes told one of the girls to throw the dice, and he bet two dollars on the line. She threw a 9 and he took two dollars odds and bet two on the come line. She threw a 10 and he took two dollars odds. On the next roll, she threw 7 the loser. The dealer scooped up the money. Hughes gathered his $9,992 in chips, pushed them toward the owner, said, "Send me the bill," and walked out.

A big player in his 70s who had a very bad heart lost $100,000 recently at a Strip hotel. He told the boss he would send the money with one of his partners when he got back home. The partner left with the $100,000, but the big player instructed him to call and see if he was alive before paying the marker. "If I'm dead," the player continued, "then keep the money for yourself. You deserve it after being such a loyal friend all these years."

Upon arriving in Vegas, the partner discovered the player had died of a heart attack during the night. Grief-stricken, the partner sat in his hotel room for hours trying to decide what to do. He knew his friend had a reputation in Vegas as a very honorable gambler and that leaving the debt unpaid would tarnish his image. Finally, the partner decided the memory of his friend was more important than money and he paid the marker. A month later an audit of the company's books revealed that his gambling friend had been cheating him for years and that's how he could afford to go to Vegas all the time.

A little Egyptian fellow wearing a red fez with a gold tassel and sun glasses walked into the casino in a large Strip hotel and started betting $500 a time on the field—all cash. A crowd gathered and several of the casino employes and bosses remarked that the Egyptian looked very familiar, probably because they had seen his picture in the newspapers. Finally he went broke, losing $17,000, and asked a boss for something to eat.

"Certainly," the boss said. "But haven't I seen you some place before?"

"I don't think so," the Egyptian replied, and the club wined and dined him.

The next day he showed up again, this time through the employees' entrance, wearing a white busboy's jacket for the job he had been doing the last ten years. The story eventually leaked out and the casino employes learned it had taken the Egyptian ten years to save the money for that one-day fling. He's now working toward another one.

Systems

I am against systems. They are good for the club and bad for the player—and this is a book for the player. But I have been asked so many questions over the years, thousands of questions, about systems that I've finally come to the realization that many, many people are going to play systems in ever-increasing numbers regardless of what they are told. I see it every day in the casino.

For that reason, I've collected the top systems in the world for you to use. There are only a few but some are proven systems played by pros and hustlers throughout the decades and it's with the greatest reluctance that I make them public. Don't worry. The casinos won't be wiped out. Casino bosses know that even if everybody in the world were given a booklet containing some of the proven, winning systems in the following pages, only a handful at best would devote the time, patience, and hard work needed to walk away winner.

One of the first victims of "systemitis" was the Benedictine monk who invented the roulette wheel several hundred years ago. He had plenty of time on his hands, as monks usually do in between prayers. It took him twenty years to perfect the roulette wheel. The story goes that he then tried to find a way to master his invention and win enough money gambling with the other monks to buy a new bell for the monastery. After ten futile years of trying thousands of ways to win consistently, he went crazy and hanged himself from the steeple.

In the centuries since then thousands of systems have been tried unsuccessfully, but no one has ever come forward with a system that wins consistently. The only sure system player I've seen win over and over is the one who banks the game.

System players are a breed of their own. They are convinced that theirs is the only sure-fire system—until they lose their money. Then they go home and try to put together another way to beat the game. They never give up. They are worse than horse players.

There's one system player who's been around Las Vegas for 25 years—we'll call him "Lucky"—and he has collected thousands of systems, any type for any game. You want it, he has it. They are neatly filed in five large metal cabinets. Of course he doesn't have the money to play the systems himself, but every now and then he'll find some poor schmoe to give him money to try one of his many thousands of systems. Lucky's main problem in getting backers is his sloppy appearance: wrinkled threadbare clothes, unshaven, greasy stringy hair, holes in his shoes.

But occasionally he nabs a "live one." I was present a few years ago when Lucky won $3,000 playing one of his favorite crap systems. I suggested that he rush out winner for once and then advised, "Why don't you get cleaned up and look presentable? Buy some clothes and a wardrobe. That way you'll be able to pick up customers more easily."

He looked at me in amazement.

"How can you talk like that?" he asked. "I need this money for my system," he added, heading for the crap table again.

Well, that's the way system players are; they're dyed in the wool. You can't change them. The only thing that differs is the way they keep track of their systems. Pencil and paper is the most common device. Of course, system players make sure that they have plenty of paper. They have large pads, small pads, medium pads, large boards, blackboards, and ouija boards. In Monte Carlo I saw a fellow standing between two roulette tables keeping track of his system on rolls of toilet paper to make sure he wouldn't run out of paper to write on. His idea was to record 30,000 to 40,000 roulette ball spins and put a book out to show what numbers had hit on the thousands of turns he watched. I really don't know what any reader would learn by looking at the record of the thousands of spins, but I could have told him what to do with the roll of toilet paper, even though I'm sure he'd been told the same thing many times.

Another system player used two number clickers in his pockets, one for each side. His favorite game was craps. He would click one clicker when a field number hit and click the other clicker when a nonfield number showed. After fifty rolls of the dice he would look at both clickers. If more field numbers had showed, he bet $1 on the field. If more nonfield numbers showed, he wouldn't bet, but would wait fifty more rolls. Now that's a great way to spend the evening if you want to buy a couple of clickers and click yourself to insanity— like he is doing.

All I can tell you is that when you see someone with a pencil and paper playing a system, please don't ask him what he's doing because you'll fall right into the trap and it's going to cost you. Just walk away and let him enjoy himself in his own peculiar way.

Most systems are the progression type, where you have to bet more as you lose. Those are the worst kind. You must always have a fair-sized bankroll to play that type of system.

Don't fall for any of those phony, "sure-fire" ways to beat a casino that you read about in newspapers or magazines. Beating the casino is a difficult thing to do. Never listen to a stranger—or a friend—who starts a conversation and eventually brings up having a way to beat a gambling game by either being an expert or having a system. Be it either a male or a female, you must leave immediately. You are being conned. Eventually these characters will ask for money to play for you, or use some gimmick so that you put in with them as their partner. They'll swing their money to their other pocket and be playing only with your money without your knowing it. These leeches hang out in every gambling casino in the world. They're glib and convincing, and some of the world's smartest gamblers have taken the bait. In Europe a few years ago I was approached four times by people telling me they had a way of playing that was a cinch to win. I'd always ask them: "If you have a cinch way to win or beat the game, why do you need my money?" I've yet to receive an answer.

If these mooches had a sure fire way of beating a game, they'd be able to get their hands on a lot more money than you or I could supply.

There are some systems, however, where you really will have a chance. You can play them any place in the world and you will get a run for your money. I don't say that they're guaranteed or infallible when it comes to winning, but I do say you will finish winner more times than you will finish loser. All you have to do is study them and decide on which game you'd like to play. Practice and know what you are doing, know what game you are playing and how you play it, and you will stand a chance.

The World's Best Roulette System

In my forty years around gambling, this is the only roulette system I've seen that is almost infallible—and believe me I've seen thousands of systems. You could lose, remember that. It is very possible—and very easy—to lose, even with this system. But one friend of mine who has been playing this method over the years is about a quarter of a million dollars winner at this writing. He has been in the hole at times but he always gets out because he has the money to back him up. I don't suggest that some of you quit your job and just play the wheel as a living after you study this method. It's not that simple and it's not guaranteed. You will, however, have a very good chance to beat the roulette game if you don't deviate from my instructions and practice at home until you're a pro. Even my friend who has won a fortune does not try to make a living from the system because he knows he could lose. He just plays when he's around a resort area and doesn't frequent the tables that much. He does not make a habit or a weekly thing out of it. He spreads his business around and goes from club to club.

For the inexperienced wheel player I will explain a few minor details and basics of roulette. There are 38 numbers on the American-style roulette wheel used in Nevada, the Bahamas, the Caribbean, the Middle East, and European casinos. The numbers go from 1 to 36, plus zero (0) and double zero (00). The first 36 numbers (1-36) are split into what we call "dozens." It will state on the layout: first 12, second 12, third 12. The first 12 numbers are from 1 to 12, the second dozen from 13 to 24, and the third dozen from 25 to 36. You can play whichever dozen you prefer.

Precise placement of your money on the lines is very important. Where you place your chips will determine how many numbers you bet and your payoff. If you place your chips straight up, or directly on a number, you'll receive 35 chips if it hits. When you place chips on the line between two numbers (called "a split"), you are betting on either number to hit. If one of the numbers hits, it pays 17 to 1. When you place chips on a corner touching four numbers, that is called a "corner bet." Then you are betting on one of the four numbers to hit, which pays 8 to 1. Those are the only three types of bet you have to know in this system: straight up, corner, and split. Disregard any other bet or line on the roulette layout. (See diagrams.)

You will only be playing one of the three 12-number "dozens" (1-12, 13-24, 25-36). You don't bet on the 12 numbers at all times but you must stick with the same dozen numbers that you choose. You also must sit directly in front of the dozen you are playing so you will have easy access to placing chips on these numbers.

Playing this system can get pretty hectic. Let's use the first 12 numbers (1-12) as an example. The best way for the ordinary player to learn this system is to practice on a piece of cardboard with two-inch squares numbered 1 to 12. Then draw lines like you see in the diagram so that you will learn to make your bets swiftly and accurately, a very important requirement of this system.

This is one of the two systems that I'm putting in print where you progress when you lose. There's a very odd reason for this, because in this system you must be a loser before you can finish a good winner. This progression system is not like others where you continue to bet more as you lose. In this system you bet until you reach a maximum, then you start over again. The system is run on cycles and operates on two important factors: the number of cycles that have passed, and the time to bet your maximum chips.

The first step when you sit down at a roulette table is to buy enough chips to cover your early bets and when you go into the cycles. You must buy two kinds of chips. The maximum chip you buy must be five times the amount or value of the minimum chip. Again, you are buying two different sets of chips. For example, say you want to play with 10-cent chips. Buy 100 chips and place them in 5 stacks of 20 chips each. That comes to $10. Then buy 80 chips worth 50 cents each, which would be $40. The croupier will mark up the price of your chips because chips on roulette layouts are all the same unless priced differently. Players can increase the minimum and maximum value of their chips, depending on their bankroll—and guts. A higher betting player could buy 20-cent chips, then his maximum chip would

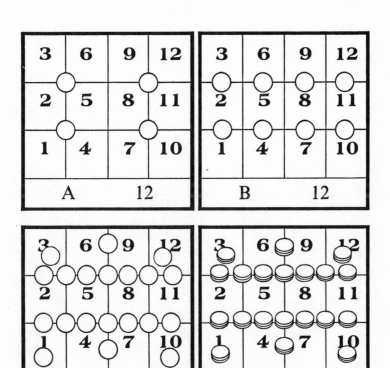

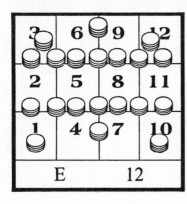

CYCLES IN ROULETTE

A - 4 chips
B - 8 chips
C - 20 chips
D - 40 chips (2 in each position)
E - 60 chips (3 in each position)

If you lose five minimum bets in a row, you are in the first cycle. Start over at A. Now, if you hit a minimum bet during the next cycle, you must immediately bet 20 maximum chips in the positions shown in C.

be a $1 chip. An even higher betting player could buy $1 chips as his minimum, which would come to $100, and eighty $5 chips for $400.

Regardless of the value, your first bet would be 4 minimum-value chips on the corners (see Diagram A). Look at the diagrams and note that there are only four corners in the dozen. If you win, you would still bet 4 minimum-value chips and you would stay at 4 chips until you lose a bet. If you lose (Diagram B), your next bet would be 8 chips on the splits. Note that there are only eight splits in a dozen. If a number hits, immediately go back to Diagram A and start all over again with 4 chips on the corners. If you lose the bet, your next bet (Diagram C) would be 20 minimum-value chips. You are now betting 14 chips on the first two lines. On the first horizontal line you are betting a split, corner, split, corner, split, corner, split. Do exactly the same on the line below. Now you place one minimum-value chip straight up on 1, 3, 10, and 12. Then place one chip between 6 and 9— that's a split—and the other chip between 4 and 7, that's also a split. You are now betting 20 chips. If a number hits, go back to your original bet of 4 minimum-value chips on a corner. If none of the numbers hit from 1 to 12, your next bet would be 40 minimum-value chips (2 chips as in Diagram C). Instead of betting one chip on each, now you are betting 2 chips in each position. If a number hits, take off all your chips and revert to Diagram A. You are starting over again. If a number does *not* hit when you are betting 40 chips, your next bet is 60 minimum-value chips (3 chips in each position as in Diagram C). If a number hits, revert to Diagram A and start over again.

If a number does *not* hit, you are in the FIRST CYCLE. At the start of your play you must lose five consecutive minimum bets to enter the first cycle. To keep track of the cycles, do not use a pencil and paper. Take 5 minimum-value chips and place them directly in front of you but in back of your playing chips.

At this stage you have lost five consecutive bets: four in the corners, eight in the splits, and 20, 40, and 60 chips placed in each position. Take one chip off the 5 and put it to your left. That shows that you are now in a cycle. (As you learn this system, you'll find yourself squeezing to lose at the start.) Now you have lost five consecutive minimum bets. You start all over again by betting 4 minimum value chips on the corners and play the same way. If it misses, bet 8 chips on the splits. But now that you are in a cycle, if at any time a number hits on your minimum amount bets (corners, splits, or 20, 40, and 60 chips), you must *immediately* bet 20 maximum-value chips as in Diagram C. Use the same positions: split, corner, split, corner, split, corner, split, straight up on the four outside numbers, and the two middle splits. Now if any number hits, you are out of a cycle. That means you have won a cycle.

That is the idea of this system: Get into the maximum betting amount of the chips so that you can hit the big ones. Now that you are out of a cycle start all over again—as if you were just sitting down at the table to play. If the 20 maximum-value chips did not hit, you would have to bet 40 maximum-value chips, 2 chips on each of the 20 positions. If that bet still does not hit, you would have to bet 60 maximum-value chips, 3 chips on the 20 positions. If that bet does not hit a number, you enter your second cycle.

To keep track of the cycles, take another chip off the original stack of five and put it on top of the one that you already have on your left from the first cycle. Then start all over again as if you just sat down at the table, and bet your 10-cent chips on the four corners. If a number hits with any minimum bet, you are now betting your maximum chips. If a maximum number hits, you would take a chip from your left and put it back on your stack of five, meaning you are down only one cycle; then start all over again with 4 minimum-value chips on the corners. If that number hits, go into your maximum-value chips immediately because you are still one cycle down. You would bet a minimum of 20 maximum chips on the 20 positions. You must know that when you have to bet your maximum chips. Your first bet must be 20 maximum chips as in Diagram C—not 4 chips in the corners or 8 chips on the splits. Only when you are in a cycle do you bet your maximum chips.

You could be three or four cycles down and hit your maximum bet every time. Just reduce the cycles until you have no cycles left except for the 5 "remainder" chips in front of you. That means that you are back where you started. You will be a good winner as this pattern goes on and you start over again. That is the idea of playing this method. I think it's self-explanatory if you practice and practice.

This system may sound complicated, but actually once you practice and know what you are doing you'll realize that there aren't that many bets to make. It's simply a matter of keeping track of the cycles and knowing when you must immediately go into betting 20 maximum chips.

You will notice you need much more money playing this system than most others in this book. Funny as it seems, you can't win any money unless you are loser, unless you are in the second or third cycle or so. You have to be down a few cycles to win any money playing this method. The idea is that you can go up and down on cycles; but by the time you get back even after clearing all the cycles off, you should be a pretty good winner. Of course, during all this you are still picking up the "in-between hits." You may hit 20, 40, or 60 minimum-bet chips as in Diagram C, which helps you accumulate money.

The diagrams will show you how to place your bets. You will have A, B, C, D, and E. They are self-explanatory. It may sound complicated but practice for half an hour or so on your cardboard layout and you will see that it is very simple. Again, this is one of the finest roulette systems I've ever seen.

French Roulette

If you are playing this system in Europe at a French roulette wheel, you have to be exceptionally careful because most players use the same type of chip on French wheels. The best places to play are where they deal with American-type wheels, which use chips of different colors for easier identification. That way nobody can claim one of your chips, because that color belongs to you while you are playing at that table.

This system has even a bigger advantage in Europe on the roulette wheels which have only a single zero. The double zero (00) has been removed and that helps the player using this system because it lowers the percentage against him. It's one less number you have to worry about.

One player who uses $1 as a minimum-priced chip and $5 as a maximum-priced chip has been in $4,000 or $5,000, but it didn't bother him a bit because he wanted to be loser at first. He had the bankroll and always got out. He has never once lost. It may seem hard to believe, but in the many plays that he has made at different hotels he has *never* finished loser. Now this doesn't mean that you cannot finish loser to a play. The numbers, after all, must show, and they usually do. You can also get caught in the switches, which is what happens when you alternate your bets while the numbers too alternate, but the other way. The odds are a little over 2 to 1 that one of your numbers won't show. Actually, when you are betting your maximum-priced chips, and you bet them three times, you are chancing that one of your numbers from 1 to 12 will show within three spins. That isn't a bad gamble for the sum you could win and the fast action you will enjoy. It's a game of concentration; you must know what you're doing. Keep track of the cycles and know when to bet your maximum-priced chips. But please don't quit your job thinking that you are going to make a living playing this. It is a good way to play when you are at a casino or traveling around the world. You can quit anytime—even right in the middle of the cycles. Look down to see if you're a winner, then forget about the cycles that you are down, and cash out.

One last tip. Many times when you hit a big number with your maximum-priced chips, the croupier will pay you off with even higher-priced chips. Just put them aside to use later if you run out of your smaller minimum chips. Tell the croupier "Change please," and give him one of your higher-priced chips. Do not be ashamed to hold the game up when you play for your own money. Speak right up.

If you are playing at a French wheel, tell the croupier which bets are yours and point to whatever bet you are making. When you get into the higher-priced chips, or when you are betting as in Diagram C, do not be ashamed to let him know which chips are yours, because there may be ten other people betting the same type chip with the same color right on top of yours, or yours may be on top of theirs.

The main principle is to study and practice. Go into a club and watch. Don't even play. In your mind, pick out one of the dozens and make "mind bets." You can't lost a thing (just your mind). You can stand there all night and practice mentally.

THE WHISTLE BLOWER

Of all the zany characters who gamble in Las Vegas, The Whistle Blower is one of the most flamboyant and is known by many club operators. He always wears a solid-gold whistle on a gold chain around his neck. Each time he wins a bet he blows the whistle as loud as he can so everybody knows who won. One time he walked into the club with a large shopping bag. He walked over to a crap table, turned the bag upside down onto the table. It was filled with $100 chips from a dozen different clubs.

"$1 goes on the field," he said. He lost the bet, took all the chips, put them back in his shopping bag, and went over to the casino cage. "Count these out and put them in safekeeping for me." There was $80,000 in the bag.

He comes to Las Vegas frequently with $10,000 or $15,000 but refuses to sit at a wheel table. He will go into the roulette pit and stand in the middle with four roulette wheels around him and bet $400 to $500 at a time on one or maybe two wheels. Or he may bet them all. He likes to star numbers, and when one hits he grabs the little gold whistle around his neck and blows it as hard as he can. Some nights the casino sounds like a train station. When The Whistle Blower wins, he rents a large safety deposit box from the casino cage, brings the box back to the wheels, throws all the chips into it, and returns it to the cage to be locked up. I've seen two hundred people around the wheels gawking at The Whistle Blower. Sometimes security guards must keep the crowd back. He always has a security guard or two with him as he carries his money. When he wants to play again, he goes to the casino cage and has the security guards carry the box for him to the wheel. Sometimes the box is so full of $25 chips that his hand disappears past the wrist, hidden by $30,000 to $50,000 in chips.

Another time The Whistle Blower walked into the casino pit with a dog leash in his hand. I looked down, and at the end of the leash he had a chicken walking around.

Then there was the time he came in wearing a chef's outfit, complete with a four-foot high white hat and white uniform, betting casually as if nothing unusual was happening.

Another time he walked in the club dressed as a conductor, with a cap and coin changer, and on his shoulder was a monkey.

One day a boss from another hotel called me to warn that a raja was coming over with a couple of his harem girls, and to take good care of them. A big limousine pulled up in front of the club, and The Whistle Blower stepped out in a turban and flowing robes. Behind him walked two harem girls. They stood at his side dancing while he played the roulette wheel. He never fooled anybody, since everybody knew who he was, but he had plenty of credit so everybody tolerated his actions and laughed when he put on the show. After all, he was paying plenty for it.

Several months later a man dressed as an Indian chief, riding on a horse, pulled up in front of the club with a woman dressed as a squaw on another horse. "Park these horses for me; I'll be right out," the "chief" said to the parking attendant.

He and the woman walked into the casino. He said to the squaw, "Sit." She plopped to the floor, folded her arms and legs, and just sat there. He started to play the wheels as if it were a common everyday occurrence. We quickly recognized him as The Whistle Blower. After playing for about half an hour, he said to the squaw, "Up." They left the casino and rode off down the Strip on their two horses. He tipped the parking attendant fifty cents.

Whenever The Whistle Blower played, hundreds of people watched, and we would always have a security guard hold them back. One time a woman slipped past the guard and asked The Whistle Blower who he was and what he did for a living. He whispered something in her ear. Red-faced, she ran out of the casino. I don't know what he said, but I can guess.

The Whistle Blower always wore a pair of custom-made glasses. The side bars that go over the ears were each made to look like a woman's leg, with one leg draped over each ear.

THE SIX-YEAR WAIT

A fellow walked into a large club in downtown Las Vegas in May 1974 and started to play the wheel with cash. He was $7,500 loser very quickly. He would cover the wheel layout with $25 chips, placing them at random. Then his numbers started coming up—almost at every spin—and within four hours he had $39,500 in front of him.

"I quit," he said and got up. The boss came over to the mystery player to help him cash out his money, but the player said, "I don't want it."

The boss said, "I'll give you a receipt and you can pick it up anytime you want to."

"I don't want it," the mystery man said again. "I just don't want the money. I wanted to play roulette and now that I have played I'm going home." He walked out of the club without taking even the $7,500 he came in with. The money is still in the casino cage. The club must wait six years before it can claim the money.

THE LAST LAUGH

Many players get nasty, especially when they are drinking and losing, but one of the worst was the owner of several California shrimp boats who loved to play the wheel. When he lost he would cuss out the dealers, often driving away other players with his foul language. He was a good player and many casino bosses were reluctant to ban him. He had a $5,000 credit line in most clubs and had no qualms about losing up to $5,000, but he never exceeded his limit.

One Saturday night he started to play at a Strip casino and was drinking heavily. He asked for $300, lost that, and became nasty and belligerent. He kept drinking, cussing and betting. He finally passed out at the table, about $1,000 loser. The dealer leaned over to wake him up, but the casino boss rushed over. It was the moment he had been waiting for. "Let him be. Just let him sleep," he told the dealer. "I'm going to teach him a lesson."

Several hours later, shortly before dawn, the shrimp boat

owner woke up with a groan. The dealer summoned the boss, who said to the still groggy player, "Well, Mr. B, how far do you want to go? You've lost $9,000 already."

The shrimp-boat owner leaped to his feet, trying to focus his bleary eyes on the boss. "How could you let me go that far? My limit is $5,000."

"Well, you know how you are when you are drinking, Mr. B. I tried to stop you, but I couldn't."

The shrimp-boat owner wrote a $9,000 check and told the boss to drag him to his room if he ever got that drunk again. "If you ever again give me more than my limit, I will not pay you," he added.

The boss, who later divided $8,000 among the casino help, replied—relishing every word—"Gee, Mr. B, if you had quit three hours ago when you were $8,000 winner, you wouldn't have to worry about paying me."

GREEN STAMPS, ANYONE?

The wife of one of Las Vegas' richest casino bosses doesn't know it but she owns the world's most expensive portable barbecue. She needed just a couple more pages in her stamp book for the barbecue, so one afternoon she asked her husband to fill the car with gas at a station that gave green stamps and bring the stamps home before the redemption center closed.

The station he picked was near the Stardust Hotel. The boss asked the attendant to fill the tank and have the car washed. Then he strolled into the casino to kill some time. Unfortunately he strolled a little too close to a roulette table, started playing, and lost $25,000. He checked his watch and rushed home—forgetting the stamps. Three hours had passed. His wife was furious. Not only did he forget the stamps but the redemption center had closed. The boss rushed back to the station, got the stamps, and went into the Stardust to buy his wife a gift at the jewelry store. He also tried to get even at the craps table and lost another $15,000. His wife is now saving stamps for a toaster. I wonder how much that will end up costing?

AM I BLUE?

A big wheel player at one of the large Las Vegas hotels always played late in the morning, about 3 or 4 o'clock, $100 chips scattered all over. He always liked music when he was playing, so he would hire a clarinet player from one of the lounge bands to play soft music for him at the roulette wheel. One time the high roller had to go to the men's room, so he took fifteen $100 chips ($1,500), gave them to the clarinet player, and said, "I want you to follow me into the 'can' and play for me."

It was a very funny sight. There was the clarinet player standing next to the closed door of a stall in the men's room playing, "Am I Blue?" the high roller's favorite song. And if you had peeked under the stall door, according to the men's room attendant, you would have seen one of the high roller's shiny pointed shoes tapping in unison.

The World's Best Crap System— Betting Wrong and Placing the Number

This is the only system in the world where you should always finish winner at the end of play. Those are strong words coming from one who doesn't believe that there is a guaranteed way to beat a gambling game. But this system is the closest gamble you can get for your money—and you'll never be in jeopardy with your bankroll. Of course, you must play correctly, and not become disgusted if you don't win right away. If you know exactly what you are doing, you can play all night at a crap game and finish winner. You can play this system anywhere in the world where a casino has a crap table. The system is more than fifty years old and was one of the best-kept secrets in the business. It was played for decades by some of the sharpest players and hustlers in their travels around the country. You'll soon see why it was never revealed to the public.

A person who knows something about place bets, or the 5% rules in the Bahamas, or crap games that deal a 5% game, will find this system easy to master. The most enjoyable part of this system is that it is ideal for a husband and wife, or any couple, to play. The husband won't have to worry where his wife is or what she is doing, and the wife, who usually doesn't have much to do, won't be able to keep nagging her husband at the tables. There's one husband-and-wife team that have been playing this system for years in the United States and in their European and Caribbean travels. They have always made travel expenses because they play the system exactly as it should be played, and they do not deviate, and they do not become disgusted. In your travels, if you play only this system you will be a winner at the end of the year.

There's a friend of mine who has been a top hustler for thirty years. He's very sharp at any game he plays, outside of one: poker. He thinks he is one of the greatest poker players that ever lived, but he very seldom wins a high stakes game. When he goes bad and loses at poker, he will borrow money (I have staked him many times) and play this crap system. Of course, he bets a minimum of $100 so he will grind out a good bankroll pretty fast; usually it takes about a week. Then he goes right back and loses it at poker again. This system has been his ace in the hole actually. He's never worked a day in his life and lives high on the hog. He admits himself that if he never played poker he would have a nice big farm and would be sitting on a rocking chair, just rocking up and back and watching his crops grow. But like anyone else, he has an ego. When you go up against sharp men, the sharpest poker players in the country, it can get a little tough making a living that way.

To play this system you must know what place bets are in craps. There are only six place bet numbers: the 4, 5, 6, 8, 9, and 10. The average player must understand that in order to win on any place bet, the place bet must be made before a 7 is thrown. Some numbers pay more than others on a place bet because they are harder to make. I advise using a $10 minimum on each number you bet, which can't hurt the $2 and $5 players. If you bet $10 and place the 4 and 10 and the number is made, you receive $28 in return. If you place the 5 and 9 for $10 and the number is made, you receive $24. The 6 and 8 are a little different. They are easier to make, so if you put up $12 you receive $26 if you win your bet. That is how place bets are paid.

You also have to know how to bet "wrong." All crap tables around the world have what is called the Don't Pass or Don't Win line. That means you are betting against the shooter—and that is called betting wrong. You must bet wrong all the time. You must NEVER bet the dice to hit or win.

Your first step is to bet Don't Pass (sometimes called Don't Win in Europe). The moment a place bet number is thrown, either the 4, 5, 6, 8, 9, or 10, you must place the number thrown. An example: Say you bet $10 on Don't Pass and the shooter throws a 10. Immediately give the croupier $10 and say, "Place the ten." He will take your $10 and put it on the 10. Now you *cannot* lose any money on this one bet you must either win or break even. If the shooter sevens out, you will lose your place bet. But, you will be paid $10 for the bet you made on Don't Pass and you'll be even. If the shooter makes the 10, you will lose your $10 on Don't Pass but you will receive $18 for the $10 place bet you made on the 10, for a total of $28. You have invested $20. You have won $8. The moment you lose your Don't Pass bet, you must ALWAYS take your money off the place bet. Just say to dealer, "Off the place bet" and he will give your money back. Now bet $10 again on Don't Pass. You are starting over again.

Let's say the number 5 is thrown. Give the dealer $10, and say, "Place the five." The dealer will go through the same routine: place the money on the 5. So if the 5 is made, you will receive $24. You have won $4.

The more numbers that are made, the more money you will win. If the shooter had thrown a 7 and did not make the 5, you would break even on the play. If numbers are thrown, you will continue to win. If numbers are not being made, you will never be in jeopardy because the worst that can happen is that you will break even. If you bet $10 on Don't Pass and a 6 or 8 is thrown by the shooter, you can still place it in most clubs for $10 and receive $11 in return. Or you could give the croupier $12. If the number is made, you win only $2 but if it misses you only lose $2. It is up to the individual. If he just wants to bet the $10 and place it for $10, that's fine. He would either break even or win $1. If a 7 or 11 is thrown on the comeout roll, you would lose your money on Don't Pass because they are numbers that are against you. If any crap (2, 3, 12) is thrown, you win your money on Don't Pass. All clubs in Las Vegas will bar what they call the two sixes on Don't Pass. If two sixes are thrown, you do not win or lose your bet. It's a standoff. Just let the bet stay there. If two aces, or ace-deuce are thrown, you win the bet, so bet $10 again. In Northern Nevada they bar the two aces, but it works the same as two sixes. If the layout says "Bar the Two Aces," and two aces are thrown, you neither win nor lose. It would be a standoff so let your money stay. You would win on two sixes and ace-deuce. In Europe they bar two aces in most countries, so it applies the same way.

The Advanced Place Bet System

Here is the betting method for experienced players.

After making a bet on Don't Pass, and a number is established, and you have placed the number, make another bet, this time on Don't Come. If a number is thrown, place that number. You now have two numbers. Then make another bet on Don't Come. If a number is thrown, place that number. Now you have three numbers—the more the merrier because, if numbers are being made, you will be winning money on your place bets. As soon as one of your place bet numbers hits and you are paid, bet again on Don't Come. If a number is thrown and you place that number, you still have three numbers. Continue to play this way until the shooter misses or sevens out. When the shooter sevens out, the dealer "locks up" your place bets, but he will pay your bet on Don't Pass and your two bets on Don't Come. Start again with the next shooter. Three bets are sufficient for the experienced player. It will keep you busy and on your toes—especially if you are making these bets by yourself.

This system is much easier for two people. They can stand either at opposite ends of the table or next to each other. When playing partners, I suggest a minimum bet of $25 to $50 each. The player betting on Don't Pass and Don't Come will only have to concentrate on betting wrong. The other player will only have to concentrate on placing the number his partner goes on. For example, the partner betting wrong bets $50 on Don't Pass. A 5 is thrown. The partner placing the numbers immediately gives the dealer $50 and says, "Place the five." The partner betting wrong then bets $50 on Don't Come. A 4 is thrown. The place bettor immediately gives the dealer $50, saying "Place the four." The partner betting wrong makes another bet of $50 on Don't Come. The shooter throws a 6. The place bettor at once gives the dealer $50 and says, "Place the six." They now have three numbers going. If any of the three numbers is made, the partner betting wrong makes a bet on Don't Come again. If a number is thrown, the place bettor places the number for the same amount.

Continue betting this way until the shooter misses out. When that happens, start from the beginning and repeat.

If the Don't Pass number is made (which means the shooter has made his number on the Pass line), the partner placing the numbers must ALWAYS tell the dealer, "My place bets always work on the comeout." This is done because odds automatically are off on the comeout in all casinos. Comeout means that the shooter has made his previous number or point. Now he is coming out for a *NEW* point or number. That is, if one of your numbers is thrown on the comeout you will be paid on your place bet. However, if you didn't tell the dealer that your place bets work on the comeout, and one of your numbers was thrown, the dealer would have locked up your bet on "Don't Come" and would not pay you on the place bet. Instead of winning a bet, you would lose a bet.

Remember, ignore whatever else is happening at the table. Just concentrate on three things: Don't Pass, Don't Come, and Place the Numbers.

With a $50 *minimum* bet on the 4 and 10, you would win $40; on the 5 and 9, you'd win $20; and on the 6 and 8 you'd win $8. If shooters are making numbers, raise your minimum bet to $100. If shooters continue to make numbers—and you have the guts—raise your minimum bet to $200, and so on.

When the dice cool off, however, revert to $50.

Disregard the 7s and 11s that are thrown, causing you to lose the bet. Make another bet. The shooter can also throw a crap. Then you win the bet.

Never bet more when you are loser. Stay with your $50 bet. The only time you raise your minimum bet is when you are winner.

Both partners must bet the *same* amount of money at all times.

When playing in Nevada and the dice are cold—of course you are not winning as much—you can always try another table. Lord knows, there are plenty of crap tables in Nevada! In other parts of the world, casinos usually have one crap table—so when the dice are chilly, take a break.

This system is especially good in England where they pay 9½ to 5 when you place the 4 and 10.

Some casinos in Europe and the Middle East do not have a Don't Come bet on their dice layout. In those casinos you can only bet Don't Pass and Place the Number. If you're playing partners, you can raise your minimum bet to $100.

If you are in a casino that bars the ace-deuce (3), it will state so on the layout. For example, the Monte Carlo Casino in Monaco bars the ace-deuce. Do not play; they are taking advantage of you. If you are in a casino that pays *even money* on the 6 and 8 (make sure you ask first), do *NOT* play—they are also taking advantage of you. Puerto Rico and some Caribbean Islands pay even money on the 6 and 8.

In the Bahamas, they do not have Don't Come on their dice layouts. They deal a 5% game (read the chapter on the Bahamas). In this case make only one bet on Don't Pass. You will have to *buy* instead of placing a number. For example, say you are betting $50 on Don't Pass and a 5 is thrown. Give the dealer $50 and say, "Buy the 5." The dealer will ask you for $2.50. If the 5 is made you will receive the full odds of 3 to 2, and you will win $22.50 on the total bet. It is the same as making a place bet, only you use the word "buy" instead of "place."

To make a place bet you must have a bet on the Don't Pass or Don't Come and a number then is thrown. Then you make a place bet. When a Don't Pass number is thrown, you will be paid on your place bet. You must *always* say to the dealer, "Off the place bet," as you are making a new bet.

NOVICE BOSSES

Just because someone buys into a gambling club and is considered a boss does not mean he automatically becomes an expert on gambling. In fact, many of these so-called "bosses" know as much about the gaming business as the cab driver who picks you up at the airport. One of these novice bosses came up to me several years ago and said he was convinced the hypnotist working in the club lounge at the time was hypnotizing the blackjack dealers. "Oh, really?" I said, trying not to alarm him. "What makes you think that, Mr. X?"

Mr. X walked like a pelican. That was his nickname behind his back.

Mr. X said he had been keeping close track of the hypnotist and he would win $200 and $300 between shows by hypnotizing the dealers.

"How is he hypnotizing the dealers?" I asked. "Is he calling the cards? Is he making the dealers pull seconds (second-card dealing)?"

Mr. X blinked a few times and said, "I don't care how he is doing it. All I know is he is hypnotizing the dealers. Call a meeting and find out what's going on here."

The cards beat me to it. The cards turned on the hypnotist a few days later and he lost several thousand dollars in one afternoon.

"Maybe his eyeballs are tired," I said to Mr. X.

He never mentioned it again.

Often, when some of the more experienced bosses discover one of the other bosses doesn't know too much about the business, they will try to ease him out of the casino without hurting his feelings. This all depends, of course, on just how much of the club he owns. One of the lesser bosses in a big Las Vegas club decided to let the other bosses watch the games while he kept track of the cigarettes, cigars, and drinks. Cigars, cigarettes, and drinks are usually given out quite freely in many clubs to the bigger players and this amateur efficiency expert was driving everybody crazy as he walked around with his little pad and pencil counting drinks and cigarettes.

Finally, one of the big bosses called Mr. Efficiency into his office and said there was trouble in the bakery department— someone was stealing the sweet rolls—so "You take charge of the bakery."

The sweet-roll leakage dropped to near zero but Mr. Efficiency gained about twenty pounds.

One big player in a Vegas club made the mistake of hanging around inside the dice pit with a new boss present. This new boss watched the big player for a while and then followed him when he went outside to sit in a chair by the pool. The player was wearing a black suit and tie with a white shirt. "You're fired," the boss said to the startled player. "You don't pay attention to any of the games," the boss explained and walked back into the club.

The player laughed and walked inside to one of the shift bosses. "I just got fired and I don't even work here."

They both laughed and the player went outside to the pool again with the first boss following close behind again. "I said you're fired," he told the player.

"You can't fire me," the player said.

"Why not?"

"Because I quit."

A credit manager told me about the time one boss came up to him waving a customer's hotel bill, madder than hell. The customer was a big player and would stay in the hotel for five or six weeks at a time. The hotel paid for everything, including room, food, and beverages, and the bill came to $7,600.

"This is a pretty big bill," the boss said. "Can't you do something about it? Cut this player off, or something?"

The credit boss answered, "Well, I just received a check from the player for the $105,000 he lost in the casino. If you want to call the debt even, I will pay for the hotel bill." That ended the conversation.

A club doesn't often give unlimited credit to players, and it can be pretty expensive when they give it to the wrong guy. One of the newer Strip clubs had given unlimited credit to an Eastern 21 player who frequented that club often—and for good reason. He would play the shoe and reserve the whole table for himself, playing $500 a hand. He often beat the club for thousands of dollars.

A new casino manager was on the job the next time this big player came to town. The new manager watched him play 21 for a while and then walked over to the dealer and told him to "break the deck down," meaning make a new shuffle. The player got up in a huff and complained to one of the big bosses who asked the casino manager why he was harassing one of the big players.

"My job is to run this casino," the casino manager said.

They had a few words, The boss is still there, the player still comes there, but the casino manager is looking for a job.

By the way, that big player is a well-known counter and has beat the club out of thousands of dollars since.

The crap table often confuses new bosses. One such boss walked into the dice pit and the dice were passing. He watched the shooters throw one "hard way" after another and promptly issued an order that the dealers should not hustle or encourage any players to bet the hard ways that day. I shouldn't have to point out that betting the hard ways happens to be one of the strongest bets—for the club.

"Follow the Dice"

This system also is very simple and easy to play. You can play it in any casino in the world.

All crap games will have either a Pass or Don't Pass line on the layout. Just bet the way the dice are going. If the dice are passing, bet with the shooter to win on the Pass line. If the dice are missing (meaning that the shooters are missing out and not making their points), bet the Don't Pass line or the Don't Win line. Just walk up to a crap table and wait for a decision on how to make the first bet. If the person shooting the dice makes the number he is shooting for, your first bet would be on Pass line with the shooter, and you'd keep betting that way as long as he makes numbers.

But if the shooter had missed when you approached the table (did not make his point), your first bet would be on the Don't Pass line. That means you'd be betting against the next person who was going to shoot.

The only flaw in this system happens when the dice start to "chop": pass, miss, pass, miss, pass, miss. That means you lose in both spots, because if the dice missed, your next bet would be on Don't Pass on the next shooter. Now if he makes the point you switch to the pass line. Then if he misses the point, you'd be "caught in the switches," and sometimes that can go on all evening, chopping up your bankroll.

But as long as you don't progress your bets when losing, you will not get into any real trouble. Make one bet and stay at that figure as long as you are losing. Also, do not switch if you are betting the Pass line and the shooter throws a crap (two aces, ace-deuce, or two sixes). Continue on the Pass line and disregard the craps. This also applies if you bet the Don't Pass line and a 7 or 11 is thrown on the first roll.

Switch only when you are betting the Pass line and the shooter misses his point (sevens out). Then you would switch to the Don't Pass line for the next shooter. The same formula holds when you bet the Don't Pass line and a point is made by the shooter. Then you would swtich to the Pass line and continue to bet with the same shooter until he misses the point. Never raise your minimum bet when losing; you're only defeating the purpose of this system. Raise your minimum bet only when you're winning. This will give you a chance to accumulate a little more money.

If you like to take or lay the odds on the numbers, that also is fine with this system. You should win a little more money if the dice are passing. But laying the odds takes a bigger bankroll. Once you start taking the odds, you must follow it through to keep in balance with your betting method. Some players guess they don't like the 6 and 8 because the odds—6 to 5—are too short. Other players don't like the 4 and 10 because they think the odds are too long—2 to 1. To eliminate the guesswork, you must take the odds at all times as long as you are on the Pass line betting with the player. The average player should not lay the odds against the point. This means you would have to put up still more money because you are laying the odds. If the point 4 were thrown and you were betting the Don't Pass line, you would have to lay $2 for every $1 you bet. Just let the Don't Pass bet stay. Then if the point is made and you switch to the Pass line, and another point is made, you can take the odds. You can play this method at any club in the world.

Placing the Six and Eight

This system is very simple once you know what a place bet is and what it means. You can play it at almost any crap table in the world but you have to be very careful in some countries, such as in some Latin American casinos where they pay even money on the 6 and 8. Always ask about placing the 6 and 8 wherever you go. If you're told it's an even money bet, do not play this method in that club. You are really getting the worst of it. *Never* bet the BIG 6 or 8.

You must give the dealer a minimum of $12 to place the 6 and 8. You should receive $7 for every $6 you put up. The correct odds are 6 to 5 on the 6 and 8 but that is only if you have a Pass line or a Come line bet. In making a place bet, the shooter must make the 6 or 8 only once for you to be paid. Actually, the true odds are $7.20 to $6, but you give up 20 cents to make your bet for the shooter to make it once. You are giving up about 1½ percent on every bet you make on a 6 and 8, which isn't too bad. It's the second best bet on the dice layout for a right bettor. All you have to know is for every $6 you put up you would receive $7 in return. Smaller clubs often deal a $3 minimum for the 6 and 8. In those clubs, you should receive $3.50 in return. You'll win your bet when the shooter makes either the 6 or 8 before a 7.

Again, never bet more when you lose. Too many people have a tendency when losing to try to catch up by betting more. Usually that just gets you deeper in the hole.

If you're not sure of yourself, try a minimum $6 bet on each the 6 and 8. If either the 6 or 8 is made, tell the croupier, "Press it." You will receive $1 back. This means you are now betting $12 on whichever number was made. If the $12 number (6 or 8) is made, tell the dealer, "Same bet." He will give you $14 in return and let $12 ride. Now you are betting with the club's money. Forget about the previous plays—

whether you won or lost—every shooter is a new play. Now, if 6s and 8s are being made, steadily bet it up, bet it up. You now can safely press your bets in varying amounts, depending on your nerve. If you say, "Press it again," your bet will go up to $24. Or, for example, you could press it $6, boosting your bet to $18.

At the start of your play you must tell the dealer, "My place bets *always* work on the comeout." This is a very important bit of instruction for the dealer in placing the 6 and 8.

In all casinos, when the shooter makes the line point and is coming out for a new point, all place bets are automatically off until the shooter has a point or new number. If the shooter makes either a 6 or 8 on the comeout roll, you will not be paid. It's a standoff. But if your place bets "work" on the comeout roll, you will be paid if a 6 or 8 is thrown. If a 7 is thrown on the comeout roll, you'll lose both place bets.

By placing the 6 and 8 and letting the place bets work on the comeout, you have the best of the bet, because there are ten ways to make a 6 and 8 with the dice and only 6 ways to make a 7. The odds are therefore 5 to 3 in your favor that a 6 or 8 will be made before a 7 is thrown.

If the shooters are making 6s and 8s and you're winning, raise your minimum bet to a higher level. Try to win more. You always can go back to your first minimum bet.

BOSS STORY

A stickman at the crap table called a twenty-minute hand and the club lost quite a few thousand to the hand. The stickman got off the table and started to cough. A boss who was rough on help was watching the dice passing. He said to the dealer, "What's the matter?"

The dealer said, "My throat hurts."

The boss said, "Here is a remedy for your cough." He took a penknife out of his pocket, gave it to the dealer. Said, "When you get home, use this and cut your throat."

The dealer quit that night.

Pass Line and Odds System

This method can be played by man or woman, Ms. or Mrs.—even a smart monkey. You don't have to be an expert or an Einstein at the crap table to play this way. All crap tables around the world have a Pass line on their layout and there is no law stating that you must bet all over the layout or make more than one bet at a time. You won't need as much money as the crapshooter who makes two or more bets. You will last longer, and if the dice should pass you'll have an enjoyable evening in a casino and possibly finish a big winner if you walk into a good hand. That means the dice are passing.

You cannot get into trouble playing this system. If you lose your money, the club will have to win it one bet at a time and that can be a slow process. But if the dice should catch on, that is, start passing, it is not a slow winning process for you, the player. It is a simple system of betting your money, not difficult at all. I must stress very strongly that you must never bet more when you lose. I suggest a $10 minimum bet for the small player, one who normally is a $2 player and makes two or three bets, takes the odds, all of which usually comes to more than $10 anyway.

Your first move naturally is to buy chips at the table. If the person shooting the dice does have a point (a point is 4, 5, 6, 8, 9 or 10), you must wait until he either makes the point or misses it. Either way, on the next roll your first bet is $10 on the Pass line. If a 7 or 11 is thrown, your next bet still is $10. If a crap is thrown, your next bet still is $10. You can take the odds only when the numbers 4, 5, 6, 8, 9, 10 are thrown. The numbers 4 and 10 pay 2 to 1 odds, which means that for every chip you place you receive two more—if you win. The 5 and 9 bet pays 3 to 2 odds, which means for every two chips you stand to win three. The 6 and 8 pay 6 to 5 odds, which means if you put up $10 you can win $12.

To take the odds, place the same amount of money about two inches behind the money you have on the Pass line. If you have a $10 bet on the Pass line, for example, and the point 4 is thrown, put another $10 directly behind your original $10 on the Pass line. This signifies that you are taking $10 odds. If the point 4 is made, you will receive $20 in return for the odds behind the line and $10 even money for your Pass line bet. That is a total of $30 winnings.

Anybody can play this method. Let the other players go through the hassle of trying to figure out what bet to make next and which bets on the layout are theirs. Your bet is right in front of you and in case the lights go out you won't have to reach far to pick up your money. That is all you have to do around a crap table. It is all that is necessary. Make one bet, take the odds, and you have become a very, very tough player, especially if the dice start to make a few numbers. I must emphatically state again: bet more only when you win. If you're a $50 or $100 bettor, play according to your bank roll. I cannot tell a player when to stop betting or how high to go; that's up to you. All I can say is continue to bet more if the shooter is making points on a Pass line. You must take advantage when the dice are passing and you are able to bet with the club's money. You must always take odds when a point is thrown by a shooter. It's very important.

If you ever have any doubt on what odds to take do not hesitate to ask the croupier. He must tell you.

The player also must disregard brooding or nail-biting about whether the dice will make the next number. It won't do any good. The dice don't know; neither does anyone else. Anyone can guess, and anyone may guess right, but guessing is not the answer. A player must take advantage of the dice passing because after a couple of numbers are made the player is not in trouble anymore. The more you bet as the dice are passing, the more money you will win. The moment you lose a bet, revert to the original bet of $10, or if you have been winning, raise your minimum bet accordingly. $25 is fine for a $10 bettor.

It is very important to start all over again on the next shooter. Never bet more when you are losing. The hotels keep building more and more rooms because the players do not take advantage when they are going good.

During the course of the play, if you're at the stage where you are betting $30 or $40 as a $10 bettor and a crap is thrown, it does not harm your betting momentum even though you lose. You must decide whether to make the same bet on the next roll or to bet less because a crap was thrown. Size up your bankroll and decide whether to make the same bet, or to go back to $10, $20, or $30. By playing this way you are considered a very, very tough crapshooter, and you'll have an enjoyable evening. Light a cigaret, have a drink. You don't have to worry about writing down figures and you will be very relaxed because you are not guessing like most other players that come to the crap table. Most of them are guessing practically all the time about what they should do next. Don't listen to any other players around the table or to the croupiers. Just do your thing, make your one bet on the Pass line, and always take the odds. Raise your eyes to the ceiling of the casino and pray that the dice make some numbers.

Losers always say after they lose their money that the dice are always cold, the dice never pass, the player doesn't have a chance for his money.

This is all baloney. Losers always are complaining. Dice do pass. It is the ignorant player who complains all the time. He never takes advantage of dice passing; he doesn't know how. We in the gaming business see dice passing all the time. Dice are constantly passing in scores of casinos around the world. In different hotels or different crap tables around the state all you have to do is be there when they pass and take advantage. Often I have seen dice pass for forty minutes—25 passes, 30 passes, many numbers being made by one player. Most of the time we pay no attention to players making 10 or 12 passes because usually they are betting $2 and wouldn't be a threat if 50 passes were made. It is only when the big players are at a table and dice are passing that we pay attention. So we in the business overlook hundreds and thousands of hands where 5, 6, and 10 numbers are made by small players.

I have had "wrong" bettors (players who bet the Don't Pass line) come to me and say, "Do dice always pass here? I never win." It works both ways.

If the dice are missing or cold, in clubs that have more than one table move to another. If there is only one table, take a rest. Come back later. Do not be stubborn and continue to play.

THE LARCENOUS BOSS

The big boss of a casino—we shall call him Moustache Willie—had a large moustache. He would play only when he was drinking, and he really could absorb some whiskey. He was very obnoxious and belligerent at the crap game no matter what club he played at. He would tell players at the table to go to his club and play, and he would belittle the bosses as they watched his play. The bosses at other clubs tolerated his behavior, knowing that they could do pretty well when they beat him. But they all hated his guts.

This one play he came into Larcenous' Club and started to play, behaving in his usual style. Moustache would never sign, as he took table credit. He would sign at the end of the play, if he lost. He would take from $5,000 to $20,000 at a time.

Larcenous was watching the play. The dice were missing and Moustache was taking marker after marker. Larcenous was entering the amount on the master credit card.

Before players were made to sign markers at a game, credit was kept on a large master card. At the end of the play the player was told how much he owed. There usually was an argument with some of the players, who didn't think they owed that much. But the master card was the last word.

The markers at that time were $45,000. Larcenous walked over to Moustache and said, "The amount is $45,000."

"Correct," Moustache said. "And listen, you S.O.B., don't tell me what I owe. I will tell you what I owe. I have a good memory."

Larcenous walked away plenty hot at being chewed out in front of everyone around the table.

The dice were still missing and Moustache was taking more markers. He now owed $65,000. Larcenous walked over and said to Moustache, "How much?"

Moustache said, "$80,000."

Larcenous' eyes enlarged about twice their size. He said, "You're right. I should have known better to tell you what you owe."

Larcenous skipped back to the desk and raised the amount to $80,000 on the master card.

Moustache lost $140,000 that night. $40,000 of the amount was Larcenous' bonus, just for saying "How much?" and having Moustache say, "Don't tell me. I will tell you."

After that, whenever Moustache came to Larcenous' club and lost, he paid a larger penalty.

The moral of the story: Don't drink when you're gambling.

Larcenous' greatest pleasure was beating a customer out of some money. His brain was always working on the larceny side. He didn't care how much a player won or lost. Even if he beat him out of only $5 he was happy.

One big player, who previously had a few arguments about how much he owed, decided to keep track of his markers at the crap table. Every time he took a marker for $5,000 or $10,000, he would make the floorman give him a marker button with the amount that he owed on it, and he put the marker in his coat pocket.

Larcenous asked the player, "What's the matter? Don't you trust us?"

The customer said, "I don't want to debate you on that. The markers in my pocket will speak for what I owe."

The boss looked at him, walked away, and stood in a corner meditating.

The player was drinking quite a bit. As the play went on, he would take a marker when he lost his checks. The boss left the dice pit, came back a couple of hours later. He said to the floorman at the master credit sheet, "What does Mr. Honest John owe?"

The floorman said $25,000.

The boss walked over to Honest John, put an arm around his shoulders, and said, "You're not mad at me, are you?"

"Of course not," said Honest John.

"Well, good luck. I hope you get even," said Larcenous as he walked away. He went to the floorman who was taking care of the master card, and said, "Make that $45,000 he owes; I just put four $5,000 markers in his jacket pocket. Let's see if he can talk his way out of this. After all, the markers speak for themselves."

When the law went into effect that all players had to sign a marker at the table whenever they took chips for credit, it solved many an argument. The signature spoke for itself. When a player paid a marker with either chips, cash, or check, he received his signed marker in return. For a club to tell a player what he owed, they would have to show him the marker with his signature on it. The player had to pay only the markers with his signature on them. No signature, no marker.

A big player was playing at Larcenous' casino, unluckily for him. He would take $10,000 in chips at a time, and sign the marker. He would play for hours up and back. Take and pay. If he ran into a little hand, he would push $10,000 in chips, ask for one of his markers back, and tear it up. The player had been playing a couple of hours with Larcenous walking in and out of the pit watching the play, checking on what Loudmouth owed. The boss called him Loudmouth because, being a little high, the player made plenty of noise when the dice passed.

As Larcenous was standing there, Loudmouth pushed in $10,000 in chips and asked for one of his markers. Larcenous brought a marker over and Loudmouth said to him, "Tear it up for me."

Larcenous' eyes opened and his brain started to click. He tore up the marker in front of Loudmouth.

The play continued. Larcenous never left the pit. A little hand showed, and Loudmouth as usual pushed in $10,000 in chips and asked for one of his markers back.

Larcenous took a marker over to Loudmouth. Loudmouth said, "Tear it up."

Larcenous tore it up and walked back to the desk.

He said to his partner, with a big smile on his face, "Just nipped Loudmouth for 10 big. I tore up a blank marker. Now I can go home."

The 31 System

This system, one of the easiest, has been played for over fifty years by hustlers and crossroaders around the country, especially during slack periods when there isn't much big action.

It is one of the best and simplest systems and can be played anywhere in the world where there is a crap table or a 21 table.

I knew one old hustler who died a couple of years ago at the age of eighty-six. He played this 31 System for over forty years in his travels around the world. He was forced to retire about ten years ago because his legs went bad and it became too rough for him to stand at the crap tables and work the 31 system. Because of that system he never did a day's work in the thirty years he spent in Las Vegas. His nickname was "31"; everybody called him "31." Many gamblers didn't know his real name. When he retired, he left a small fortune for his widow, most of it won playing this 31 system.

Of course, you must have patience and not be troubled if you lose—which can happen with any system. At least with the 31 system, if you lose you don't lose much. It doesn't matter what amount you bet in this system—25 cents, $1, $5, $10, $25, $50—that depends on your bankroll. It's called "the 31 system" because you start with 31 betting units. As an example, we'll use $1 as a unit, so you would start with $31. At a crap table you can either bet this system "right" (meaning you bet the dice will pass) or you can bet "wrong," hoping the dice will miss. Relax; you do not need a pencil or paper. To use this system you must bet the $31 (31 units) in the following progression or sequence: $1, $1, $1, $2, $2, $4, $4, $8, $8 —a total of $31 or 31 units.

The most important factor in playing this system is making the Bet Back (doubling up). After you make your first bet of one unit you continue to bet one unit as long as you win. When you *lose* the first bet of one unit, your next bet according to the sequence, is *still* one unit. If you win, you must bet the *two* units back on the next bet— that is the Bet Back bet. Now you must win two bets in a row and then start over. If you lose the Bet Back, continue, according to the sequence, until you win two bets in a row, or until you play out the 31 units. This is the secret of the 31 system.

Let's say you lose the first three bets ($1, $1, $1) without winning a Bet Back. You next bet on the progression table would be $2. If you win the $2 bet, you next wager would be the $4 Bet Back. If you win the $4 Bet Back you now have $8, but you only invested $5 (5 units). Then automatically start over at $1.

Let's say you lose five bets in a row ($1, $1, $1, $2, $2) without winning a Bet Back. Your next bet would be $4 (4 units). If you win the $4 bet, your Bet Back would be $8. If you win the $8 Bet Back, you now have $16, but you have only invested $11 (11 units). You must start over again at $1 no matter how tempting it is to continue with the bigger bets. You must stick to the rules of the system.

This is one system where you don't have to worry about losing the first several bets. In fact, you might make more money quicker if you lose the first several bets but win the big ones. Let's say you lose the first seven bets in a row ($1, $1, $1, $2, $2, $4, $4) without winning a Bet Back. Your next bet would be $8 (8 units). If you win, the Bet Back would be $16. If you win that you now have $32 (32 units), but your investment is only $23. Then you start all over again.

If at any time you lose the Bet Back, just continue with the next bet in the progression table. If you had *lost* the $16 Bet Back, for example, your next bet would have been $8, the final bet before starting the system over again.

The most you should lose in one play is 31 units ($31).

The longer you play, believe it or not, the more money you'll win. You will have ups and downs, but you could lose the 31 units and still be winner. If you should go through the 31 units quickly and still have money left over, start over again and play it out, but don't add any money to finish.

Most hustlers playing this system usually try to win only their original 31 units, such as $31, then call it a day after "making the nut." But I have found that if a system is working you must continue playing and take advantage until you lose the entire sequence (31 units). This could continue for hours. Nobody knows when the dice will stop passing, so the player must take advantage of his good fortune. It doesn't happen too often. During the play, you are grinding, grinding, grinding. You could be hundreds of dollars winner when you eventually lose your 31 units. If you are struggling with the system—almost reaching the winning side time after time— then the dice are not working your way and you should go to another table.

How to Play the 31 System at 21

This system is great for the average player traveling overseas, or in Nevada. If you are a 21 player and have learned in this book how to play 21 with a shoe (four-decker), you can play the 31 system very comfortably at any 21 table in the world. Play the units the same as in the crap system (1, 1, 1, 2, 2, 4, 4, 8, 8,).

But you do have to alter your 21 playing method slightly. Do not double down, do not split pairs   including aces—and never take insurance. This way you won't vary from the strict progression formula of the 31 system by betting odd amounts. If you should receive a blackjack, just put the extra winnings with the rest of your money and think of it as a little bonus. Aside from not splitting pairs or doubling down, play 21 as explained in the 21 chapter and the odds are in your favor that the 31 system will work for you anywhere in the world.

If you are going good and winning, don't be afraid to raise your betting units. A dollar bettor with a little nerve could raise his minimum 1 unit bet to 5 units ($5), that is a $155 opening stake. Play it out like a trooper. You can quit at any time, just as you can with $1. If you're going good, raise it to $10, which, at 31 units, would be $310. As long as you are going good, give yourself a chance to win enough to pay for the trip. It's been done many times with the 31 system. And always revert to your original one unit bet ($1) if you start losing.

Players who want to start their minimum bet at $25 or more must check the club limit before playing craps or 21. In Nevada most large casinos have a $500 maximum. That is fine for the $25 bettor. His biggest bet would be $400 on the Bet Back. For the $50 minimum bettor, the Bet Back would have to be $800, so the limit at that casino should be $1,000. Check club limits outside Nevada, because you could get trapped by not being able to progress high enough. If the limits are small in some countries, two people can play partners. By both playing the same way, you will get a higher limit.

THE DESPERADO

The desperado player likes to play fast and hard. He has one big asset that clubs fear. He bets like a madman with the club's money. Of course, you have to have plenty of guts and plenty of heart to bet this way. But the bosses know that a desperado, with a little luck and a short bankroll, can take an aspirin and run it into a drugstore. The average desperado comes to town with around $500 and bets it up as fast as possible in hopes that the dice are passing, or that the shooter makes some numbers.

We in the business see these desperados every day. One was a poker hustler, a very exceptional desperado. After winning at poker for a while, he'll pick up some chips, $800 or $1,000 worth, and take a shot at the crap table. If he loses, he just goes back to his poker game. One day last year in Las Vegas this poker player took $800 in poker winnings and walked into a "monster" hand at the crap table. When the storm was over, he cashed out $70,000. He had $1,000 bets all over the layout— place bets, buy bets, come bets—didn't even blink an eye when he cashed out, went back to the poker table, sat down, and very nonchalantly continued to play. He's what you call a real tough desperado.

But many players don't have the bankroll to be that kind of desperado. There was a floorman working with me who was more of the average man's desperado. He had a wife and nine children—four in college—and could only afford to invest $20 in a 25-cent crap game in downtown Las Vegas every so often. He'd bet 50 cents, 75 cents, a dollar or two. Sometimes he loses $20 and sometimes he wins maybe $40. One day the dice began to pass. He started off with 25-cent chips. When that hand was over, he cashed out $2,600, just enough for his oldest boy's tuition to college as he later told me. The next time he went downtown, he started with the same $20 but walked out of the club when he lost. It will take the casino an awful long time to win the rest of their $2,600 back.

A desperado from Los Angeles arrived in Las Vegas on the 8 p.m. flight September 22, 1974. He started to play baccarat at $20 a hand, lost $200, and went to the crap tables. He played at two different tables, lost another few hundred dollars, and finally settled on a table where an old Chinese sipping tea out of a paper cup was starting to shoot the dice. The desperado bowed politely toward the shooter, bought the 4 and 10 for $40 each, and placed the 6 and 8 for $30 each.

The shooter, calmly sipping tea with one hand and tossing the dice with the other, began throwing a monster hand that lasted over forty minutes. The only 7 he threw was when he sevened out.

The desperado would press his bets as numbers were being made. Finally he loaded all the numbers with $1,000 each. The only odds he took were on the line number. I watched the whole play. When the hand finally ended. I gave the desperado four empty racks to store his $40,900 worth of chips. If he had bet on the Come and taken the odds, he would have won at least $20,000 more.

But still, $40,000 isn't bad for about a $600 investment. After winning $4,000 more at baccarat, the desperado went to another hotel and cleaned them out of $15,000, and then he returned to our hotel where he won another $10,000. With the nearly $70,000 tucked safely in a money belt around his waist, the desperado took the morning plane back to Los Angeles with $70,000 more than when he arrived   that is why casinos hate desperados.

I'll never forget one boss who spotted a known desperado with about $15,000 in chips in front of him at a crap table.

"How much did that son of a bitch buy in for?" he asked.

"He bought in for $300 and is winning about $15,000," the floorman replied.

Commented the boss: "I hope that s.o.b. has a heart attack so I can carry his chips to the cage for safekeeping. I guarantee you he won't have $15,000 in chips when I reach the cage."

If that's how you want to be regarded by casino bosses, here's a betting method for an aspiring desperado with a short bankroll. You need at least $500.

Bet on the Pass line only and always take full odds. Make *no* other bet.

Start at $40 and $40 odds. If you win, bet $100 on the line and $100 odds. If you win, bet $200 and $200 odds and stay at the same bet if you win again.

By now the bosses are starting to sweat and you are in good shape. If you win your next bet, then wager $400 and $400 odds. If you win and it's a club with a $500 maximum bet, then bet the maximum. If the club has a $1,000 limit, then raise your bet to $600 and $600 odds and keep raising your bets $200 at a time until you reach the club limit. If you catch a few numbers, you'll quickly win a few thousand dollars. Don't be afraid to give the next shooter a chance, but start with $100 as your first bet and bet it up a little faster if numbers are being made. If the shooter fizzles out, hit the road. Quit. Adios. Amscray. Catch the next flight. Your desperado days are over for a while.

THE RICHEST DESPERADO

A South American horse breeder and rancher earned in a few short years the reputation of being perhaps the fastest-action gambler in Las Vegas history. As with other rich desperados, the bigger the limit, the better the South American liked it. Nothing fazed him. Money was of no value to him. The casino that dealt the largest limit was where he played.

It wasn't long before the casinos began fighting for his business. They would raise the limits and deal special limits that were even higher. If one casino found out that another casino was dealing a higher limit, the bosses would raise their limit just enough to beat the others.

The horse breeder would come to town with $200,000 to $300,000 in cashier's checks. He also had credit in four Las Vega casinos totaling $300,000. And he would stay until he lost the $300,000 cash and owed the $300,000 credit. Within a month or two after he lost—and this happened year after year from the late 1960s on—he would send someone up with a cashier's check to pay off the markers. A few weeks later he would be back again with his $300,000 cash and his $300,000 credit.

He bragged to me during one of his recent trips that he was determined to win a million dollars. This horse breeder would bet on anything and was known to go to the race track carrying a handbag with $200,000 in cash in it. Bet $10,000 and $20,000 on a race. Played all games: baccarat, backgammon, craps, and 21. His best game, though, was double-deck gin rummy.

Once he was challenged by one of Las Vegas' top gin players to a high-stakes game. The gin player was backed by six men who put up the bankroll. At the end of the first play the horse breeder had lost $120,000. The next play he won $90,000. And he won another $90,000 after that. The gin hustler had enough.

In 1974 two sharp Las Vegas hustlers followed the South American to France and tried to set him up in a gin game. The sharpies met him in a casino baccara room in Cannes and wined and dined him for three weeks. They even put in with him when he played baccara. Every move was made to set up the sucker. Finally, after spending three weeks and going $15,000 in the red in expenses, one of the hustlers brought up the subject of playing double-deck gin rummy for $5,000 a hand (the horse breeder played by the hand). The horse breeder said OK. They planned to meet at 8 p.m. the next evening at the hustlers' suite. The horse breeder decided it was time for him to leave. He checked out the next morning. As long as the sharpies were picking up the tab, the South American couldn't care less; they had made the proposition. The sharpies ran into him in Las Vegas several months later and were, as you would expect, very annoyed with him. He told them that one of his prize horses had taken ill and he had had to fly back to South America. What could they say? They were the cheaters.

In September 1974 the rich desperado returned to Las Vegas with $200,000 cash. In about one month, playing in four clubs, he won $1.2 million. He carried about forty safekeeping slips from four different hotels. But in the next six weeks he lost back a miilion. He still had $200,000. By playing marathon baccarat, craps, and 21, he worked his bankroll back up to $1.4 million.

He did most of his playing in one of the largest strip hotels, so the owners made him a propositon. If he would bet and play only in their hotel, they would let him wager $12,000 a hand in baccarat, $3,000 a hand in 21—and he could play seven hands at a time and double down for $6,000 if he had a legitimate double-down hand. At craps he would be allowed to bet $5,000 and $5,000 odds and place the opposite for $5,000. Also he could bet the Big 6 and 8 for $5,000. He liked big action and he would bet the Big 6 and 8 at even money. Of course, every time the 6 or 8 was made he lost $833 because of the odds, since he was getting even money on the bet.

Well, the horse breeder went for the proposition and he played in this club about the time the 1975 Super Bowl was on. He bet $200,000 on the Pittsburgh Steelers. It took ten bookmakers to handle his action, and he won the bet.

Six days later the horse breeder was broke. He lost the $1.6 million, mostly at baccarat. The club gave him a marker for $400,000. In all he lost $2 million and left town.

This is the same South American who told me he was going to win $1 million. He did—but after all, it was only money.

He'll be back in couple of months, pay off his markers, and start over again with $200,000 or $300,000.

And we'll be waiting.

The Sad Truth About Place Bets

The best way to bet the numbers (4, 5, 6, 8, 9, and 10) at craps is with a come bet, and the worst way is with a place bet. I've never considered this a deep, dark secret, so over the years I have expected place bettors to almost fade from the scene and the ranks of come bettors to swell as the public learns more about gaming.

In the early 1960s, I recall reading that the sophisticated American public was becoming narder to fool than ever, that Brooklyn Bridge sales had plummeted, that the bottom had fallen out of the Eskimo icebox market. I predicted to a few co-workers that several casino bets, such as place bets, would practically disappear from layouts through disuse as modern man shook more cobwebs from his head.

The early 1960s passed, but the flow of place bettors never slackened. It increased.

There was a noticeable decrease in the late 1960s, but it was among come bettors—not place bettors.

Place betting was becoming the rage among crapshooters, especially in England, where 98 percent of the crap players *still* place the numbers. English clubs pay 9½ to 5 on the 4 and 10, for example, so players I've talked to there assume it is the best bet because the payoff is higher than in crap games in any other country.

But even in England, if you bet the four outside numbers (4, 5, 9, 10), as many place bettors do, you still give up almost 4 percent in favor of the club. That's plenty strong.

If place bettors in England think they can beat the game while giving up that strong a "PC," they had better check their wallets at the end of an evening.

By the early 1970s, as international gambling began to boom, I learned that several casinos around the world were experimenting with crap layouts on which you could only bet the numbers with a place bet, or with a buy bet, which is almost as bad.

The experimental layouts had eliminated the come bet entirely, which made me, in the eyes of my co-workers, quite a predicter.

I can understand why some foreign casino operators want place bets only. You can bet your whole bankroll that Nevada's casino owners, for example, would eliminate the come bet tomorrow morning if they could ever agree to "get it on."

Luckily for crapshooters, Nevada casino owners are so fiercely competitive that they have enough trouble agreeing on anything, let alone such a significant layout change.

As place bettor ranks grew, I began quizzing the shaggy-headed younger bettors, the so-called "aware" generation, why they placed the numbers as their dumb daddies did before them. After all, they are our future players. We are well aware that today's younger generation views with cynicism anything the older generation does. But there they were, these bright young college-educated people, crowding the tables to make place bets.

Their answers, like the answers of their fathers' generation, were always the same: (1) It's a simple way to play; (2) There's no confusing come bets and odds to worry about; (3) No "seven the loser" gives you something to fret over as with come bet odds on the comeout roll; and (4) You only have to make the number once instead of twice as with a come bet.

To professional gamblers and expert crapshooters, that line of reasoning is good only for laughs. In my forty years of watching dice games, I've never seen a good crapshooter make a place bet. He knows there's little chance of winning.

Often my second question to place bettors was what they thought of buy bets.

The smart-alec answer from a sharp young Los Angeles attorney was typical: "Mike, any crapshooter with a brain larger than a parakeet's knows that you have to give up five percent on a buy bet."

I smiled, nodded, and walked away. Later, when the young attorney went for a swim, I sent a casino porter to town to buy a five-pound bag of birdseed. I sent the birdseed to the attorney's room with this note:

"Dear Mr. L, I thought you might want a little birdseed to nibble on if you shoot craps tonight.

"P.S. I forgot to mention during our chat this morning, Mr. L, that *yes,* a buy bet costs the player 5 percent 'vig,' but place bets average out costing the player 5 1/3 percent."

The attorney was red-faced that evening but eager to learn. First, to make sure he understood place bets clearly, I explained that six numbers on the layout can be placed: 4, 5, 6, 8, 9, and 10. These numbers average a fraction over 4 percent against the bettor. In most countries, the minimum place bet is equal to $5. You usually can bet $5 on one number or $5 on a minimum of four numbers, or $6 on the 6 and 8. Many players, such as the attorney, like to place what are called the "outside numbers," the 4, 5, 9, and 10. The player just hands his money to the dealer and tells him where to put it. If the shooter throws a 7, the place bettor loses all four bets, but if the shooter throws one of the four numbers the place bettor is paid on that single number.

It is in this payoff that the place bettor loses more than 5 percent, but he doesn't realize it. In a buy bet, the bettor has to come up with 5 percent of his bet in cash when he wins or loses. But a place bettor doesn't physically have to pay anything extra, so he doesn't realize he has paid through the nose a "hidden" percentage or commission.

For example, most casinos pay 9 to 5 odds if you place the 4 and 10, and 7 to 5 odds if you place the 5 and 9.

But a come bet gives you the *option* of taking the odds. The *correct* odds, and the odds you should be getting by making come bets, are 2 to 1 for the 4 and 10, and 3 to 2 for the 5 and 9.

A come bet is like making a second Pass line bet. You can make a come bet after a shooter throws a point on the Pass line. Just put your money in the area marked "come." If the shooter throws a number (4, 5, 6, 8, 9, and 10) on the next roll, your money moves to that number, and then you can take the odds on the number by giving your odds bet to the croupier and telling him where it should go. You can take odds up to the amount you have placed on the come. If the shooter had rolled a 7 or 11 before a number was thrown, you would win the come bet automatically. But if a crap (2, 3, 12) were thrown before the number, you would lose that one come bet.

The player who typically places the four outside numbers gives up 5 1/3 percent during an evening's play while the come bettor who takes the odds gives up less than 1 percent. Specifically, the place bettor gives up 6 2/3 percent on the 4 and 10 and 4 percent on the 5 and 9. Total the four numbers' percentages and divide by four to get the average loss (5 1/3 percent). Actually, it would be cheaper to buy the 4 and 10, for example, because you only give up 5 percent.

As I explained the pitfalls of place betting and the virtues of come bets to the young attorney, he came back with the standard argument: "But with come bets, you have to make the number twice and you only have to make it once with a place bet."

"That is true," I explained with fatherly patience. "If you put your money on the come and a 4 is thrown, your bet moves to the 4, and then you must wait until the 4 is thrown again before you get paid.

"But," I continued, "every roll of the dice is a new roll. It's like the expression 'Today is the first day of the rest of your life.' Dice don't have very large brains. They can't remember what number they turned up the last roll."

You could dream up a one-bet situation where the place bettor comes out ahead: if his one number hits on the first roll and he leaves. But I don't know many crapshooters who make only one bet when they visit a casino.

After a few minutes of play, the come bettor has the distinct advantage. The place bettor has the worst of it, regardless of what the dice are doing. If the dice are hitting and missing, then the place bettor will get slaughtered, as I'll explain later. But the come bettor is betting with the flow of the game. He has no choice. If numbers aren't being made, then his money remains in his pocket where it belongs until the dice are hot.

If a big hand does show, then both the place bettor and come bettor will have their bets spread across the numbers. During the hand, the place bettor will be giving up an average of 5 1/3 percent of each bet he wins, compared to less than 1 percent for the come bettor. The come bettor also is getting better odds. As each number hits, the come bettor will get paid more money than a place bettor standing next to him betting the same number. The hotter the dice, the higher the percentage mounts against the place bettor. I have watched come and place bettors play at the same table during thousands of evenings when the dice were hot, shooter after shooter. The results always are the same: a good, aggressive come bettor often ends up with twice as much money as his counterpart place bettor.

My attorney friend was getting a little green around the gills by this time, but he threw in one last argument, that a come bettor loses his odds if a 7 is thrown on the comeout roll.

I pointed out that when a typical place bettor has placed the four outside numbers and the next roll is 7 the loser, which happens often at a crap table, the place bettor has lost four bets compared to the loss of a single odds bet by the come bettor. And he almost broke even in the play, because he won the come bet.

A come bettor should let his odds ride on the comeout roll, because he has 5 to 1 the best of it that a 7 will not show on the next roll. This also applies to the place bettor.

Many crapshooters don't realize that there are thirty-six combinations on a pair of dice: six ways to make a 7, five ways to make a 6, five ways to make an 8, four ways to make a 5, four ways to make a 9, three ways to make a 4, three ways to make a 10, one way to make aces, one way to make sixes, two ways to make a 3, and two ways to make 11. If you had *all* the numbers (4, 5, 6, 8, 9, 10) covered, it would be 2 to 1 in your favor that the dice would make one of your numbers instead of a 7, 11, or craps on the next roll. That is why it's smarter to let your odds work on the come out roll. This also applies to place bettors with their money spread across the layout.

Gambling clubs decided to have odds off automatically on the comeout roll many years ago to avoid confusion at the crap table. So through the years, many players just thought that's the way it should be done, not knowing that they were taking a beating. But if you watch a smart crapshooter, he'll say, "My odds work on the comeout."

Sure, a 7 can show at any time, but players notice only when it does show and they lose, not how many times one of their numbers is thrown on the comeout.

What really kills the place bettor is that big hands with lots of numbers are not the normal state of affairs at a crap table. Otherwise, all casinos would go broke. Often the normal action at a crap table is for a shooter to make one or two or a few numbers, then throw 7 the loser. This can go on and on all night long. Any veteran crapshooter will attest sadly to that. After all, there are more ways (6) to make a 7 than any other number.

But when a place bettor typically places the outside numbers, for, say, $10 each, he has invested $40. The shooter must then make *three* of the place bettor's numbers for him to make any money at all. If he placed all six numbers with $10 each and $12 each on the 6 and 8, as some players do, the shooter must make five of his numbers to make any money. And if the place bettor presses his bets when numbers are being made, the shooter must make another four or five numbers for the place bettor just to break even, let alone make any money.

To put it simply, unless *every* shooter throws a nice hand, making at least five to eight numbers, the place bettor doesn't have a chance.

It is no wonder that I have seen casino owners actually wring their hands in ecstasy when the crap tables are loaded with place bettors.

According to the law of averages, a 7 should show once in every six rolls, and that includes the craps and 11s that are thrown. Put it all together and place bets are strictly for the birds—or maybe I should say for the birdbrains.

The best way to play in a casino that has place bets only is to bet just the Pass or Win line. You can apply the same betting and money management methods that I give for betting the Pass line in the chapter on 5% craps. The two bets are practically the same.

If you insist on making place bets, then my only advice is to pick out one or two numbers and progress your bets as I suggest in my 5% chapter.

But one thing is certain for "right" bettors, whether they bet the come or place bets, if the dice are cold and missing nobody will win, but at least the come bettor will last longer.

Placing the 6 and 8

If you are bound and determined to make a place bet, then at least bet the two numbers that best give the place bettor a chance, the 6 and 8. Next to the Pass line bet, the 6 or 8 is the best bet to make percentagewise, 1.5 percent.

Ironically, they are the two most unpopular numbers among place bettors. I guess the average place bettor figures that because the 6 and 8 do not pay as high odds as the 4, 5, 9, and 10, they are bad numbers to bet. Also, many players don't know how to place the 6 and 8, because you must put up an odd amount of money, and this confuses many minds.

To place the 6 and 8, you must give the croupier at least $6 for each number. The payoff is $7 for every $6 you put up. If you bet $5 and win, you'll only receive $5 in return. That is not a good bet. It is even money.

Here's a special money management and betting method for the 6 and 8 so that you'll last much longer, with a chance to make some money if the shooters roll 6s and 8s. The other "live ones" (place bettors) will be sweating it out as they spread across other numbers, worrying if they'll be made before a 7 wipes all their bets out. But you will be (or should be) calm and cool; no guesswork as to how you'll be betting.

You should bet a minimum $6 on each number. If you're in the minimum-bettor league, give the croupier $12 and say, "Place the 6 and 8 $6 each." If either a 6 or 8 is made, tell the croupier to press (double) your bet. This means you are now betting $12 on the number that was made. The croupier will give you $1 back, which is your odds bonus ($7 for $6). Let's say the number made was 6. If it's made again, tell the croupier, "Same bet" ($12), and you'll get $14 back. If the $12 bet wins a second time, press or double to $24. The croupier will give you $2 back. You are now betting with the club's money, so full steam ahead. If the $24 is made, tell the croupier to press your bet to $48. He'll then give you $4 back. If the $48 number hits, then bet $60. Say to the croupier, "$60 goes." He'll then give you $44 back. Stay at $60 as long as the 6 continues to show. Progress the same for the 8 as it's made.

For every $60 bet you win, you'll be receiving $70 in return. If a few 6s and 8s are made, you'll play all evening at the club's expense with no sweat or strain. You have only two bets to watch. You also must remember you can take your bets off at any time.

I don't advise quitting as long as the shooter is making 6s and 8s. Don't try to guess when the shooter will miss out. It can't be done. But when the shooter misses out, start again at your $6 bet.

A $10 bettor starts at $12 each on the 6 and 8. Let's say the 6 is made. Then press it to $24, $24 again, then $48 as it keeps showing. Just say "Press" or "Double." If 6 hits again, bet $60. You'll receive $70 in return. If a $60 number is made, bet $60 again, then bet $90. You have added $30. You will receive $105 if the $90 number is made. If the shooter misses out, start again at $12. Now you have become a tough player, especially at placing the 6s and 8s.

For a $25 bettor, start with the $30 minimum, that is, $30 each on the 6 and 8. If one is thrown, go to $60, then $60 again. Your next bet would be $90. If that number hits, jump to $120. You'll receive $75 in return. If that number hits, then bet $120 again. You'll receive $140 in return. Keep jumping each bet $30 until you reach the club limit, or until the shooter misses out. On the miss-outs, start over with your original $30 bet.

High rollers must know the limit of the game before making a bet. If the club deals a $200 limit, regardless of the size of your bankroll you must start at the $30 level. The limit is too low for a $50 or higher bettor.

Casino employees see dozens of high rollers each day, so you won't impress them by betting the maximum right off the bat.

You might attract a few gawking nickel slot-machine players and a hooker or two, but the gawkers and hookers will disappear as soon as your money does. And by betting the maximum, you'll cripple your chances of progressing to where you have a chance to play with the club's money and to stay out of trouble, especially if the dice should miss. By the way, if you've forgotten, dice do miss at a crap table.

If you do hit a casino which deals a $500 maximum to a number, as a $50 bettor you should start with $60 each on the 6 and 8 and progress your bet upward on the individual number as it is made. If a 6 or 8 is thrown, then jump to $120, and $120 again if you win; then to $180 and $180 again if you're winning. You'll receive $210. Then jump to $240, and, if you win, add $60 to each bet until you reach the club limit. On the miss-out revert to your original $60 bet.

For the $100 or higher bettor, start at $120, then $240, and $240 again if you keep winning, then $360 and $360 again and finally $600, which is $100 higher than the limit, but allowable for placing the 6 and 8. Stay at $600 until the shooter misses out, then revert to your $120 minimum, and watch the bosses groan. They know they've got a tough cookie.

When betting the 6 and 8, you must remember you're betting two numbers at all times. As each number is won, press it individually. Play the 6 and 8 each as a single bet.

All place bets are automatically off on the comeout roll, which is the next roll after a point has been made. So you must tell the croupier that your place bets on the 6 and 8 "work," on the comeout. You must specifically tell the croupier that your 6 and 8 bets "work" all the time, so there's no confusion during the play.

Having the 6 and 8 work on the comeout means that you are getting the best action for your money. If a 6 or 8 shows, you'll be paid the full amount, $7 for $6. If a 7 shows on the comeout, you'll lose both bets. But by having the 6 and 8 work on the comeout, you still have the best of it. The odds are 5 to 3 in your favor that 6 or 8 will show before a 7. So, as long as the odds are in your favor, you must take advantage. There are more 6s and 8s thrown than 7s on a comeout roll.

The betting methods that I have described for the 6 and 8 are for casinos that deal place bets only. There are also a few countries with clubs that pay even money on the 6 and 8. *Never bet a 6 or 8 in those clubs.* You're giving up over 9 percent on each bet. Always ask what the place bet on the 6 and 8 pays before you start playing. If the answer is "Even money," forget it. Don't make a bet. You're giving away too much.

Many casinos, in Nevada and other parts of the world, display on the crap layout what is called the "Big 6 and 8." It is there in very large numerals and is very easy to see. Casinos haven't made the bet so visually attractive because they *don't* want you to bet it. They *want* you to bet it because it is one of the biggest sucker bets on the layout. The Big 6 and 8 pays even money. Why should you bet the Big 6 and 8 for even money, when you can get 7 to 6 or 6 to 5 odds by placing the 6 and 8, or by making a come bet?

But, walk up to almost any busy crap table and you'll see somebody betting the 6 and 8 corner on the layout.

Right away you know this person doesn't know the first thing about a crap game. I don't care if he has a diamond pinky ring, fancy gold watch, beautiful suit, and a gorgeous dame hanging on each arm. I don't care what the guy looks like, if he's betting the Big 6 and 8 he doesn't know the first thing about a crap game. The size of the bet doesn't determine whether the player knows what he's doing.

We had one player betting $200 on the line, who said to the dealer: "$200 on the 8, please. Buy it." The dealer put the $200 on the 8 and asked the player for the $10 vigorish. The player shook his head and said he didn't want to pay the $10. The dealer said, "Well, sir, would you like to place it instead?"

The dunce again shook his head. "Give me my money back! I'll put it over here on the Big 8." The player just lost $33, because he could have gotten $33 more by placing the 8, and he would have gotten even $30 more by buying the 8. But during the evening the player continued to put his money on the Big 6 and 8, and he continued to lose $33 a pop. By the end of the evening, he was broke, but he could have played for several more hours on the hundreds of dollars he gave away by betting the Big 6 and 8.

WRONG BETTORS

In some casinos that deal place bets only, the wrong bettor (a person who bets that the dice *won't* pass) must lay the box numbers, and this gives him much the worst of the action. The club's advantage is even stronger against him than if he placed the numbers.

On laying the 6 and 8, for example, the wrong bettor must lay $5 to $4, which is like playing in a 5% game. On the 5 and 9, the wrong bettor must lay $8 to $5. The right price in a 5% game is $7.75 to $5, so the wrong bettor is giving up an extra 25 cents. On the 4 and 10, the wrong bettor must lay $11 to $5, but in a 5% game the price is $10.25 to $5. The wrong bettor has given up an extra 75 cents.

If you're a wrong bettor and play this type game, you should have your head examined. You don't have a chance for your money; the game will grind you out. The longer you play, the worse it's going to be.

But if you must play and insist on betting wrong, then make one bet only. Just bet the Don't Pass line. It is free.

Conservative players do not have to lay the odds. Just make one bet and enjoy the game. Progress as you win, but progress very slowly.

Using $5 as a base amount, your first bet would be $5, then $10, and $10 again, then $20 if you keep winning, then $30 and $30 again, and finally $50. Stay at $50 until you lose and then revert to your original $5 bet.

Higher bettors should adjust this progression method to their bankrolls.

Just making a single Don't Pass bet won't satisfy many players who want more action and like to lay the odds on a number. I can't really fault that; you just need more money than a right bettor, because you are laying the odds instead of taking them.

My basic advice is to bet faster than right bettors and don't play as long. If you catch four or five miss-outs in a row, you're in a good position to quit, or start with the next shooter and continue to bet the same way if the dice are still missing.

Let's use $5 as an example. Start with $5 and lay the full odds. If you win, bet $15 and lay the odds, then jump to $25 and lay the full odds, then to $40 and then $60, laying the full odds each time. If the dice continue to miss, add $20 to each winning bet until a number is made. Then start over, or quit.

A wrong bettor, sometimes called a "don't player, must have more control and patience than a right bettor. The ruination of many a wrong bettor is chasing the dice when they are passing. He bets more when numbers are being made, thinking that the shooter can't possibly make the next number. But the smart wrong bettor will back off after the shooter has made one or two numbers and wait for the next shooter. The smart wrong bettor won't put himself in a position to go broke on one hand.

I have been at many fading games through the years where if one number was made, the wise wrong bettors would lay less on the next number, or not bet at all, and just wait for the next shooter. This was their way of money control and many of these wrong bettors made a living playing that way. They always had control of their money and never tried to break anyone. They were satisfied to grind out a few hundred dollars a day.

A gambling casino likes nothing better than to have players betting right and wrong at the same table. The bosses know the percentage is working for them on both sides. One will offset the other.

We used to have five wrong bettors who flew in once a month for two years without ever hitting it big. Then one evening the dice grew cold and stayed that way for hours.

The cold dice finally drove off all the right bettors and the five wrong bettors had to shoot the dice themselves. They would shoot and bet the dice would miss. The dice continued to cooperate, and when the smoke cleared the game had lost $125,000. The five players cashed out and left that night. They're still probably pinching each other to make sure it wasn't a dream. They only made one type of bet, the Don't Pass line, and then laid the odds. If they had made a couple of Don't Come bets at the same time, they would have won $300,000. I hope they read this and learn.

Another problem with wrong bettors is they'll call their bets off a number at the merest whim. A wrong bettor should *never* take his bet off a number, though I've seen thousands of players do it.

Casinos will allow a wrong bettor to call his bet off at any time, but a right bettor cannot do this. The reason is simple. Once a wrong bettor's money is on a number, he has the best of the bet. But every day I see wrong bettors calling their bets off the numbers. Typical was the player betting $250 on the Don't Come. The number thrown was 4. After a couple of rolls, he took his money off the 4, and then a couple of rolls later he said the shooter "can't make a four now" and laid $500 to $250 against the 4 and paid the $12.50 vig. You guessed it: the 4 was made on the next roll. Then the player said, "I guessed wrong." He tilted his head as he spoke, and I swear I could see the overhead light shining in one ear and out the other. This brainless player had 2 to 1 the best of it by leaving his money on the 4 originally. He lost $512.50, when he should have lost only $250, but he decided to try and outguess the dice.

The worst offenders are the wrong bettors who take their bets off the 6 and 8. Apparently, they don't like the 6 to 5 odds in their favor I don't know about you, but I would rather have the odds in my favor. If you take the bet off, you have to start over again with the percentage against you on the comeout roll. But if a 6 or 8 is thrown, you now have 6 to 5 the best of it; on a 5 or 9, you have 3 to 2 the best of it, and a 4 or 10 gives you a 2 to 1 advantage. For God's sake, don't be foolish enough to call off a bet when the odds are to your advantage.

Origin of Craps

Players constantly ask me who conceived and designed the modern crap table.

It didn't happen all at once. The original game, a simple 7 the winner versus 7 the loser exchange, has been traced to the black sections of New Orleans, when the dice were carved out of bone and wood. They would bet only on the number the shooter threw. It was a nice simple game. Then the whites picked it up and it gradually evolved into the game it is today.

As for place bets, their origin also has been traced to New Orleans, but after whites had discovered craps. Many players were complaining they lost their bets when a crap would show, and if they were late on getting down on the pass line they didn't have a bet to make.

One smart boss who knew percentages told players they could bet $1 on the line and take $4 odds (or $1 and $5 odds on the 6 and 8) *after* the point was thrown (also any other numbers they cared to bet on), and the same ratio would apply to higher bets. This way, the boss told the players, they wouldn't have to worry about losing their money to a crap.

The players thought this was great, another monster was born, and the boss got rich.

HUNTZ

This is the story of the granddaddy of all eccentric players. I shall call him "Huntz," though many gambling men in Las Vegas will quickly be able to give him his right name. Huntz first checked into a Strip hotel, a "walk-in" as they call one with no reservations, with one small traveling bag in one hand, an attache case in the other, and wearing an old red shirt, brown pants with a rope as a belt, no socks—and sneakers. He looked like a bum just off a freight train.

The clerk gave him a cheap room in the rear and made him pay four days' rent in advance. (This is the usual procedure when the guest has no identification and very little luggage.) Huntz checked into his room, then went to the casino cage with the brief case.

"Will you give me a receipt for this money, please?" he said, opening a case filled with $100s and $10,000 bills. A boss came over pretty quickly and asked Huntz where he got the money. "You start to count the money," Huntz said to the cashier. "Don't make any mistakes; I know exactly how much is there." He turned to the boss and said, "Write this number down. It is my banker's phone."

The boss called a large bank in the East, explained to the banker what was happening, and described Huntz. The banker emphatically advised the boss that Huntz' checks were good, if he wrote any, and to handle Huntz very carefully and to humor him.

There was $700,000 in the attache case.

A security guard helped Huntz carry $100,000 in chips to the crap table. The guard was told never to leave Huntz alone. Then Huntz started to bet the $500 maximum on the line and took $500 odds. His next $500 bet was on Don't Come and laid full odds. Then he bet on Come $500 and $500 odds and he kept on betting this way every roll of the dice—one bet right, then one bet wrong. The boss watched, his eyes and mouth wide open. He and two bellhops ran to move Huntz' luggage to one of the finest suites. All they found was the little bag, which they handled as if it belonged to the President.

Huntz was at the crap table in a chair with his feet propped up on the rail, eating a cheese sandwich he had taken out of his pocket. He kept telling the dealer to make the same bets. The boss gave Huntz the new room key, told him he was the guest of the hotel, and returned the four days' rent Huntz paid in advance. "You shorted me forty cents," Huntz said after counting the money. The boss quickly reached into his pocket and gave him the forty cents.

Huntz would play for hours at different times of the day or night. He changed his style of play constantly. He probably had been cheated a few times in his life and must have thought that by playing crazily he would confuse any crooked dealers. A couple of hours he would bet wrong, then a couple of hours later he would bet right and wrong at the same time. And he would change to betting win for a couple of hours and continue to do this jumping around.

He could never win, as he always bet every roll of the dice a different way.

He always wanted to bet more and kept asking if they would raise the $500 limit.

After playing a couple of days, he changed clothes—to a pair of bib overalls. Sometimes he came down to play in the casino around 4 or 5 in the morning in his pajamas and sneakers. Nobody would say a word, as if it were an everyday occurrence for players to gamble in their pajamas. After all, in Las Vegas the motto is "Come as you are." And most of the help had been warned not to be surprised at whatever Huntz did. Within a week many casinos in Las Vegas were aware of Huntz. One morning about 4 o'clock the outside security guard making his rounds saw a man in his pajamas sitting in a chair with a pole and a string attached to the pole, apparently fishing in the swimming pool. When the guard saw who it was, he hurried into the casino. The casino boss rushed outside.

"Mr. Huntz, you're wasting your time fishing there; that's the swimming pool."

"I know," Huntz replied. "I don't have any bait on my line."

(It's such an old joke even Henny Youngman has stopped telling it, but the casino boss swears it's the truth.)

A few days later Huntz learned that a club a couple of blocks up the Strip dealt a high limit. One windy morning about 3 o'clock police watched in amazement as Huntz sauntered up the Strip with a white bedsheet draped around him and over his head, his favorite rope tied around his stomach, the end dragging along the pavement. Looking like an Arab heading into a dust storm, Huntz walked up to the crap table and said, "My name is Huntz and I'm betting $1,000 they win."

"Just a minute, sheik, where did you park the camel?" a boss snapped, thinking Huntz was just another kook. Las Vegas gets more than its share of kooks.

But when the shift manager heard the name "Huntz" he said, "Go right ahead and bet," then immediately rousted one of the casino owners at home. The owner hurried down, rubbing the sleep from his eyes. Huntz took off his bedsheet and started to shoot craps in his pajamas. He played for six hours and lost $200,000. At 9 in the morning Huntz, followed by the boss and two security guards in a Cadillac, walked back to his hotel wrapped in his sheet and paid the $200,000.

The next morning about 4 Huntz returned, dressed in his bedsheet, and lost $100,000. The boss again followed as he walked down the street to the other hotel, collected the hundred thousand dollars, and left.

The next afternoon Huntz checked out of the first hotel— traveling bag in one hand, brief case with $100,000 in the other—and walked up the street to check into the other hotel where he quickly was given the master suite.

A few days later Huntz asked if it was okay for a secretary and a chauffeur to come out for a while. His secretary came out the next day and the chauffeur drove the Huntz car to Las Vegas. But during Huntz' entire stay in Nevada, he never once took a drive in his car. It was parked all the time, except when the chauffeur drove by himself so the battery wouldn't go dead.

Huntz quickly lost the hundred thousand dollars he had in safekeeping at this hotel, so he asked one of the owners, "Can I have 500? I'll give you a check."

"Sure," said the boss and walked to the casino cage with Huntz. "Give Mr. Huntz $500."

Huntz leaned over and whispered to the boss, "You misunderstood me. I mean $500,000."

Before the boss could recover from the shock, Huntz gave him his banker's number. The boss called and was told, "Whatever amount the check Mr. Huntz writes, it will be good."

The boss stammered, "Well, this one is for $500,000."

"That's fine," the banker replied. "Even if he wrote one for $10 million it would be good."

Here are a few of the gems about Huntz during his stay. Some I witnessed myself, other stories were told to me by other casino bosses.

One evening Huntz came into the casino with his attache case and told a boss to watch it. The boss put his foot on it and never left the spot, thinking it was full of money. About an hour later Huntz came over, thanked the boss, opened the attache case, took out a pair of pajamas, shook the pajamas for about thirty seconds, put them back into the attache case, and told the same boss to please watch it for him again. The boss' foot never left the attache case. When the boss went to the rest room, a security guard took over.

Another time Huntz brought his old traveling bag into the pit and opened it. Inside was an old, torn, broken umbrella. A boss standing there remarked, "Why the torn and broken umbrella? It's not usable."

"Why waste money on a good one?" Huntz replied. "It doesn't rain here in Las Vegas."

One afternoon Huntz walked into the coffee shop, sat at a table, took a raw hamburger patty out of his pocket, and said to the waitress: "Will you have the chef heat this up for me—medium-rare, please."

After playing a few hours at the crap table one day, Huntz walked into the coffee shop, put his feet up on the table, and fell asleep.

No one dared disturb him. He woke up about an hour later and asked the hostess how long he had been asleep. She told him about one hour. Huntz took $3 out of his pocket, "Here, give $1 to the waitress, $1 to the chef, and you keep the other dollar. That's for the time I used the table."

One evening Huntz was shooting craps and was about $200,000 loser. (He was always loser.) He pulled a chair up in the middle of the crap pit, pulled an old cheese sandwich out of his pocket, ordered a glass of milk, and told the dealer to keep betting $1,000 every roll and take the odds "until I eat this sandwich."

He liked cheese sandwiches. He would order them by the dozen from the kitchen and kept some in his room. But he always carried a sandwich or two around with him. He also was very fussy about what he ate, and never ate too much.

Huntz would order oatmeal at least once a day. It could be at any time, evening, morning, afternoon. Each and every time he would call and tell the chef personally what temperature it must be. The oatmeal had to be delivered the moment it was done. Then he would take a little taste and, if it wasn't just right, he would send it back and the chef would have to make a fresh order. Each time the waitress would ask if he wanted a tablespoon or teaspoon of sugar on the oatmeal. Huntz would always answer, "I don't care. It makes no difference as long as the spoon is level." So the waitress would use a tablespoon one day and a teaspoon the next. She also would ask every time if he wanted cream or milk, hot or cold. He would answer, "I don't care—hot, cold, cream, or milk, as long as it is tepid." She would bring warm milk one day, and warm cream the next day. And each time Huntz put his finger in it to see if it was okay. If it wasn't tepid enough, he would send it back and tell the chef to use a thermometer.

Toward the end of his stay at this hotel, Huntz was on the telephone daily talking with the head engineer about designing a special spoon to be used only by him and only for his oatmeal. A design engineer was hired to make the spoon, but Huntz moved to another hotel before it was done.

Every time Huntz lost $500,000 he would write a check for $500,000 more, sometimes for $750,000. The hotel would immediately send a man on the next plane to cash the check at the bank back East. The checks were always good.

Huntz never drank and very seldom tipped, and never fooled around with women. He just gambled and seemed very happy in his own little world—not the least bit concerned about the crowd that always gathered when he played, especially in the mornings when he wore his pajamas or bib overalls.

One day Huntz was playing his peculiar way of betting right and wrong every roll and laying or taking the odds. The other players around the table all started to do exactly as he did, figuring Huntz had to know what he was doing because of all those chips he had. In the middle of all this Huntz said to the dealer, "All my wrong bets are off." The dealer gave him his wrong bets back. The players, of course, would repeat exactly what Huntz did. Take all their wrong bets down and the dealer would give them their money back on the Don't Come. The bosses would laugh—to themselves—when this happened at the stupidity of people who follow someone who has quite a few chips in front of him. Anyone with a fair knowledge of craps knows that you never take the money off a bet on Don't Pass or Don't Come. Once you are on a don't number, you have the best of the bet and you never take your money off. But day after day the sheep would follow Huntz to the slaughter.

Early one morning, after playing a few hours, Huntz told the dealer to continue betting for him and he would be right back. A half hour passed but Huntz did not return. All the bosses started to look for him. He was found in a corner propped up against two slot machines fast asleep. "What's the matter, you need more money?" Huntz asked, and went back to sleep.

Huntz had an elaborate suite and a king-size bed, but he would never sleep on the bed. He would tell the maid to make up his bed on the floor. Huntz didn't like to sleep in the same spot every night, so he would have the maid move the blanket about twelve inches from the position it was in the night before. He did that every night.

After a few weeks of wearing the same outfits, either the bib overalls or pajamas in the morning, and red shirt and brown pants with the rope tied around it, Huntz asked a boss where he could buy another pair of bib overalls, since his were getting a little shaggy. The boss said, "Don't worry, Mr. Huntz, just give me your size and I'll get you another pair in a jiffy." The boss' secretary called every store in Las Vegas and surrounding areas, but no one had bib overalls, or they didn't have Huntz' size. The hotel chartered a plane and flew a man to Los Angeles for the overalls.

Huntz' traveling bag or his attache bag sitting in the dice pit became a common sight. One evening, after playing a couple of hours, Huntz opened the bag, took out his bib overalls, shook them a few times, put them back inside, and continued playing. A couple of hours later he said to the shift manager, "Please bring three or four men here; I'm going to change." Huntz opened the bag, took out his bib overalls, shook them a few times, and said, "Gather around, men. I'm going to change." He took off his brown pants, put on the bib overalls, folded the pants neatly and stuffed them into the bag, dismissed his human dressing room, and went back to the crap table.

After being at the hotel a little over six weeks—writing checks from $500,000 to $750,000—Huntz was over $2 million loser. He heard, or probably somebody told him, that a downtown club was dealing a higher limit. The owner, of course, had heard of Huntz and told him he could bet $3,000 and $3,000 odds, either right or wrong. Huntz asked the owner if he had a room for him. Shown the room, Huntz then complained that the entrance to the room was too narrow; it was immediately enlarged. "I would like a toaster and a hot plate in the room. Take the bed out and just put an extra rug on the floor. I like to sleep on the floor."

The owner later told friends he would have ripped the whole top floor to any specifications Huntz wanted. Huntz stayed at this hotel around five weeks, and he kept writing checks. He also had his custom-made cheese sandwiches to eat when he wanted them.

When Huntz left town, he had lost over $4 million. This happened around four years ago. No one has heard of him since. But all front-desk clerks in all hotels have been told—or they should have been— to keep a sharp eye out for a man in his middle 60s wearing either bib overalls or a red shirt and brown pants, sneakers, rope tied around his pants, and carrying an attache case in one hand and an old battered valise in the other. If any of them should see him, they are to call a boss immediately.

Baccarat (Punto Banco) and Its *Deadly* Deceptive Relatives, Chemin de Fer and Baccara

Baccarat, the new monarch of gambling, is an offshoot of baccara, the parent card game created in the 1500s as an idle diversion for French aristocrats. Baccara still is popular in many countries, along with its other offspring, chemin de fer. You'll find both games in casinos around the world. But I advise *against* playing baccara or chemin de fer for several reasons, one being their resemblance to the Venus flytrap.

But first let's talk about baccarat (called punto banco abroad), which has become the fastest, most exciting, and highest money stakes game in the world.

More money is being won and lost in baccarat than in any other casino game in modern history.

Even the most grizzled, blase Las Vegas professional gamblers, many of whom weren't sure how to spell or pronounce baccarat a few years ago, now agree that they've never seen so much money change hands so fast as over a baccarat table. Casinos in Europe and England brag about their high stakes baccara and punto banco games. Often, rightly so; but the big action is in Las Vegas, which boasts the highest baccarat limits in the world and the money to book any action.

As this chapter was being written, five Japanese businessmen had finished making a historical play at baccarat. They had checked into one of Las Vegas' oldest Strip hotels, now owned by billionaire Howard Hughes, and said they wanted to play high stakes baccarat. They placed a million dollars in cashier's checks in the casino cage to back their words. The club had a $2,000 maximum bet per person, but to speed up the game for the Japanese the bosses allowed them to pool their bets and play one hand at a time for $30,000. The first night they won $240,000. The next night they lost the $240,000 plus the million dollars in cashier's checks. The Japanese wanted credit. The club quickly investigated their background, found that all five were millionaires, and gave them a total credit of $1 million. The million dollars was lost within a few days.

The five businessmen had enough and left for Japan. But right along with them was a casino representative to make sure that they didn't forget about the million. It's one thing for a casino to win money on paper and quite another to collect it. Nevada casinos often have little legal recourse on collecting gambling debts outside Nevada. But the casino representative returned with the $1 million, all in cashier's checks, plus a message from the Japanese that they'd be back for another try. Sayonara.

The Japanese never revealed how much money they wanted to win. It must have been plenty. After all, at one time they were nearly a quarter of a million dollars ahead. Casino executives like myself, who have watched the biggest players in the world come and go for nearly a half-century, often wonder just how much high rollers must win before they'll be satisfied. Sometimes it seems that no sum will make them happy. But at least one of the world's biggest baccarat players, an Arab prince, has made his goal clear. He told me he wouldn't be content until he won a million dollars in one sitting.

"I'm going to be the biggest winner ever in Las Vegas," he said during his last visit. He wasn't kidding. He is one of the calmest, coolest players I've ever seen, winner or loser. If anybody is capable of winning a million dollars, he is. But he will have to wait until next time. His last trip didn't turn out so well.

He followed his usual practice of bringing between $150,000 and $200,000 in cash to town to place in safekeeping among his three favorite Strip casinos, the only ones where he'll play. Those clubs give him a special limit of $4,000 a hand and extend liberal credit on his name. He also rents a room in each club so that he won't have to leave when he's tired of playing.

For the next eighteen hours, he played baccarat nonstop, taking time only to change clubs. At one point he was $190,000 winner, but at the end he was $330,000 loser, including what he borrowed. He may yet win a million dollars in one shot, but I'm afraid he's going to lose a few million first.

He'll be back again and again. There is something about baccarat that lures the world's richest gamblers, such as the five Japanese, our

Arab friend, and many other legendary baccarat players I'm going to tell you about. Baccarat seems to represent the mystique and glamour of gambling. The game is usually set apart from other casino games in a roped-off area. Even baccarat croupiers and bosses dress in blue or black tuxedos to match the exclusive atmosphere, while other casino employes often only wear shirts and ties or blouses. Baccarat tables truly have become the haunts of the gambling elite, though anyone can gain entrance past the thick velvet ropes if he can come up with the minimum baccarat bet. It can vary from a few dollars to more than $20, depending on the country. Don't be afraid to play. You'll be hobnobbing with royalty, movie stars, and millionaires. It may be the highlight of your trip.

Baccarat moves at a breathless, almost hypnotic pace, but the player, big or small, doesn't have to worry about taking odds, keeping track of bets, hitting and stopping, doubling down, insurance, splits, propositions, and all the other rigmarole of 21 and craps. Baccarat requires no thinking except how much money you are winning or losing. Just put the money in front of you and the croupiers handle the rest. They'll tell you when to hit or stop. Printed cards at the table present the rules. Your only choice is whether to bet on the banker or the player.

The object in baccarat is to achieve a total of 9 with two cards or an additional third card. If 9 is not attained, the next highest hand wins. The game is played between one individual (player) and the banker. All other participants bet on the hand being played, either with the banker or with the player. The club books both sides of the bet (player or banker) up to the house limit. Players are seated around the table. The game begins with the bettor in the number one position drawing cards for the player and banker from a small box known as the "shoe."

Bettors around the table can place a wager on the banker "with" or on the player "against" the bank. If the bet "with" (for) the banker wins, the bettor pays a 5 percent commission of the bank's winnings to the club. If the bettor player wins against the bank, no commission is involved. Baccarat odds favor the bank, so the 5 percent commission is to offset those odds.

Cards in baccarat have values quite different from those in most other card games. Picture cards and 10s have no value. All other cards count face value, including the ace, which counts as one point. If your hand totals 10 points or more, you must subtract 10 points. If your hand totals 20 points or more, you must subtract 20 points. For example, if you received a queen and 9, you would have 9, which is an automatic winner unless the other side also has 9. Then it's a tie and nobody wins. If you had a queen and 10, you would have zero. And if you got an 8 and 5, you would have 3. You must take a third card if you have certain combinations. The croupier will do this for you automatically. All casinos have rule cards—free to players.

Mini-Baccarat

A mini-baccarat table has been devised by the casinos in Nevada for the small player. That is the $2 and $5 player who cannot sit in on the big games with their $20 minimum bets. Mini-baccarat is played exactly like regular baccarat. Some clubs have limits from $2 to $500 and $2 to $1,000, a very nice limit for any type of bettor. The mini-baccarat tables are usually found in the 21 area, since the layout is placed on a 21 table. It can accommodate seven players very comfortably and is dealt much faster than the larger game as there are fewer players. Play mini-baccarat in the way I recommend for the larger baccarat.

Bet with the Banker

According to the consensus of opinion of the sharpest baccarat players, so far as percentage is concerned the best way to play baccarat is to bet on the banker all the time. Make one type of bet and stay at this bet throughout the play. Never bet more; never bet less. At the end of the evening the bank should finish three to four bets the winner. By betting on the banker you have the best of it over the player's side. But the house has an overall percentage of 1.25 over both the banker and the player. In this way, a player can enjoy himself in Nevada or in his travels without the hassle of trying to figure what his next bet should be.

BACCARAT STORIES

A Chinese gentleman and his wife checked in to a major Las Vegas Strip hotel. The man went to the cage and asked the cashier if he could play against a cashier's check. It was for $100,000. The casino manager was called and he told the player that as soon as the check was OK'd, he could play against it. The San Francisco bank on which the check was drawn was called; the check was good. The club told the bank they would send a man out to pick up the money.

The Chinese gambler was cleared for the $100,000. He lost it all in a week. By this time the hotel had moved him to their best suite. The man called the casino manager, told him he had another cashier's check; would he okay it?

The casino manager met with the player, who handed him a cashier's check for $1,100,000, and said, "This is also good. But I would like a larger limit." The check was good, and the casino manager gave the player a $12,000 limit.

The player was $600,000 loser in two weeks. The owner of the hotel told the wife to go to the jewelry store and pick out some trinkets for herself and her husband. She did, and it came to $32,000. The store called the owner and told him the amount. He couldn't say no.

The Chinese gambler lost the balance in three weeks. So he lost $1,210,000 in six weeks. He asked the casino manager if he could get some credit, for which he would give him a check for $50,000. As they didn't know the Chinese, they told him they would cash the check but he would have to play somewhere else. The club didn't want to give him money not knowing if the check was good; if the player should get lucky, the club didn't want to be playing against a piece of paper.

The player said OK, took the money, went across the street to another hotel, and lost the $50,000. The check was put through immediately and it cleared.

An Arabian oil prince who comes to Las Vegas quite often was staying at a major Strip hotel. He played all games and played them high. The club let him bet $600 straight up and star any number for the same amount. If a number hit straight up, it was an $81,000 payoff At the crap game he could bet $1,000 on aces and sixes—a $30,000 payoff if one of them hit. Baccarat he could bet $12,000 a hand.

The prince played two weeks, lost $2 million, most of it at baccarat, made out four checks for $500,000 each, and they went through.

Following the Shoe

Another way to play baccarat without outguessing yourself is to "follow the shoe." This means bet on whichever side is winning at the time, player or banker. Most casinos will explain in English on the layout where to bet on the player or banker.

When you sit down, your first bet would be on the side that won the previous hand. For example, if the banker won the last hand, you would stick with the bank until it loses. Then you would switch to the player's side. Keep betting on the player's side until it loses, then switch back to the bank.

Bettors around the table take turns at being the banker. Each time the banker loses, the shoe is moved to the next bettor and he officially becomes the banker. But just because you are officially the banker, you still can bet on the player's side. You are the banker in title only. If the player's side won the last five hands, it would be foolish to switch your bet to the banker just because you now have the shoe. In baccarat, cards can run in lengthy winning or losing streaks for one side or the other. For centuries, mathematicians have been trying to figure why cards and dice fall the way they do. It is not uncommon for the player's or banker's side to win six or seven hands in a row. By following the shoe, you have eliminated the guesswork and have a chance to catch a winning streak. This is how you should play baccarat and its identical twin, punto banco, anywhere in the world.

Most foreign casinos use six decks for baccarat and punto banco. In Las Vegas they use eight decks. In an eight-deck shoe, there are between eighty-five and ninety decision hands dealt in which somebody wins or loses, not counting ties. It takes between thirty and forty-five minutes to deal an average eight-decker; but the more big bettors, the longer it takes, sometimes up to ninety minutes. Still at roughly eighty hands or more an hour, a gambler, whether he's betting $5 or $2,000, can win or lose a bundle before the ice melts in his drink.

Baccarat players usually don't leave until the shoe is played out and reshuffled. That's why they run up such high losses and wins. In craps, winners usually walk away from the table when the shooter finally misses out (throws a 7 loser). In 21, players who have been on a winning streak often will leave a table when the dealer pauses to reshuffle. But in baccarat, the reshuffling break may happen only once every hour. Often players sit there shoving out their money as if they were hypnotized, hoping the shoe wll turn in their favor and make them rich.

It can happen. Anyone who hangs around a baccarat game knows that small fortunes are won and lost every day. In 1972, I witnessed one of the longest and largest winning streaks in gaming history.

A well-known New York gambler, whom we shall call "Moskowitz," started playing at a Las Vegas Strip hotel with a $20,000 bankroll. He bet $1,000 a hand on the player's side only and would raise it to $2,000 a hand when he won. The first night he won $50,000. He asked the bosses to raise the $2,000 limit, but they wouldn't. Moskowitz quit for the evening, went to his room, called a friend in New York, and told him to catch the first plane out.

The next night, Moskowitz bankrolled his friend and both started betting $1,000, and then $2,000 each if they won, which they did again and again. They still were betting on the player's side only. For every hand they lost, they won ten. By bringing in his friend, Moskowitz had raised his betting limit to $4,000 each play. There was nothing the club could do about it. Within six hours, the two men had won $190,000. The bosses again refused to raise the limit. Moskowitz put the $190,000 in the cashier's cage, along with the $50,000 winnings from the night before.

He called two more friends who arrived the next night. He bankrolled them. By giving them money to play with, Moskowitz unofficially raised his limit to $8,000 a hand. Still, there was little the club could do. Everything seemed on the up-and-up.

Moskowitz and his crew didn't have to win. The shoe could have gone against the player's side also, but it didn't. The amazing lucky streak continued. The player's side would win nine times in a row, lose once, then win twelve times, lose once, and win another dozen hands in a row. The casino had me check the game to make sure everything was legitimate. The cards, and how they were dealt, were checked and double-checked closely, but nothing was wrong. It was just one of those streaks players dream about and owners stay awake quivering about.

The game continued all night. By 6 a.m., Moskowitz and his crew had more than $240,000 from that one play. His total winnings were now $480,000. He decided enough was enough. I watched as he and one friend stuffed nearly a half-million dollars in their pockets and caught the early morning flight to New York.

Moskowitz has returned four times since, hoping to catch another winning streak, but he has lost each time. The club has won about $200,000 back and may eventually get the rest. As sure as God made little green apples, Moskowitz will keep returning until he runs out of money or makes another score. But if $480,000 didn't satisfy him, what will?

"WELL DONE"

Some Nevada clubs try to attract big players by letting the word get out that they will raise the stakes according to the players' bankroll.

One Las Vegas club allowed twenty-eight high rollers from New York to reserve two baccarat tables for the weekend. The limit was $4,000 per player, which meant that $56,000 was riding per table on each play, one turn of the card. On two tables they were all betting on the banker. The club lost two million that weekend.

Several weeks later, a Mideast oil prince playing baccarat, craps, and roulette lost $600,000 after playing twelve hours. He told the casino manager he wanted to eat and that there were six people with him. The manager called the maitre d' of the gourmet room and told him to set up two tables with wine and appetizers to start with. The prince came down, and two captains and four waiters seated the party. The prince, as he was sipping some wine, called the maitre d' over and said, "While we are having a little wine, please send one of your captains over to McDonald's and have him bring back thirty hamburgers—well done and no onions."

Money Management

Maximum and minimum baccarat bets vary greatly around the world, so here's a standard money management system that can be used in any country. Nevada did deal baccarat with cash until the summer of 1974 but now uses chips, as is the world-wide custom.

First, decide what denomination chips you can afford. Then buy chips of the same value so that you don't get confused. For beginners, I advise starting at the minimum bet until you get the feel of the game.

Using the "following the shoe" method, your first bet would be 1 chip on the side that won the last hand. Your next bet is 2 chips, then 4 chips, then 4 chips again, if you keep winning. The next bet is 6 chips and then 10 chips. Then bet 10 chips for two more hands. If you continue to win, raise your bet to 15 chips and keep raising it 5 chips at a time until you lose or reach the club's maximum limit. Don't worry. The bosses will let you know very quickly when you have reached the limit. Stay at the club limit until you lose. The moment you lose, regardless of what stage you're betting at, revert to the original bet of 1 chip. Watch the bosses run for Alka-Seltzer. Now they know that it is going to be like pulling teeth to get their money back.

It's very possible for you to catch a streak in baccarat, but I don't want to raise your hopes too high. Often the player's side will win one bet, then the banker's side will win the next bet, then the player's side, and back and forth, back and forth. This is called "crisscrossing." It can go on all night, gradually whittling away at your bankroll. But those are the hazards of gambling and you must be ready for a baccarat streak; they can come and go in a flash.

Tourists who never won more than $100 in their lives have seen their wildest dreams come true and vanish in one evening over a baccarat table. Typical was the sailor who sat down at a baccarat game late one night and started to play with $100. About daybreak he was $25,000 winner. A boss told him to put the money in the casino cage for safekeeping, adding that it wasn't safe to walk around with that kind of money. The sailor was tired and asked for a room. The bosses scurried around, made several phone calls, and put the sailor in one of their finest suites. He was served a gourmet breakfast, compliments of the club, and a bellhop personally escorted him to the suite.

The sailor slept for a couple of hours and returned to play. By early afternoon, he had lost the $25,000. He went to one of the casino bosses and said, "I'm a little weary now. I think I'll go back to my suite and take another nap. When I awake I'd like to have a little lunch sent up." He then gave the boss a list of what he'd like for lunch. The boss checked with the baccarat supervisors, learned that the sailor was now broke, and told him, "I'm sorry sir, the suite has been reserved for someone else and we're all booked up. I'm afraid you'll have to go elsewhere."

It's lucky for the sailor that he had brought down his small duffel bag full of clothing and toilet articles, otherwise they might have been thrown out by the maid.

Another novice at baccarat sat down early one evening and lost $30 very quickly at $5 a hand minimum. He looked like a college student traveling through on spring vacation. There was another young fellow who also looked like a college student sitting next to him betting $5 a hand. They didn't know each other, and it was apparent they didn't know much about the game. The player who lost the $30 asked the stranger next to him if he would cash a check. They had become friendly at the table. They both left. A few minutes later the player who had lost his money and needed the check cashed came back with $200 cash and started playing.

Several minutes after that the other young fellow returned with a policeman and said that his new friend had stolen his wallet. There was a terrible row in the casino. The two youths, the policeman, and the bosses were ushered into a private office. But as it turned out, they couldn't find a wallet, there was no actual proof, so nothing could be done. The one young fellow stormed out $200 lighter and wiser. The other youth continued playing. This was around 10 p.m.

By 5 in the morning he had won $60,000. The youngster was in shock. He bet the maximum $2,000 a hand, was betting for everybody at the table—players, shills, and dealers. Of course, they were all happy because, every time one of their bets won, they "locked up" the money for themselves.

Then the shoe turned against the young man. Within three hours, he had lost $58,000. Much of that had been given away to the shills, cocktail waitresses, dealers, and a few other players. I'm sure this youngster had never seen $60,000 at one time in his life, and he may never see it again. But that's typical of baccarat action. At least he walked away with $2,000. And the club was around $30,000 the loser, the money he had given away and never got back into play.

Sometimes even bosses get swept up in the baccarat action. A good friend of mine, a boss at one of Las Vegas' largest hotels, had an experience recently that still gives him nightmares. One of the regular baccarat players, who came to the club several times a year, had lost $6,000 in cash on his latest three-day trip. He asked my friend, the supervisor in charge of the casino, for $300 to return home. He told my friend he would pay him on his next visit. My friend okayed the $300. This player had lost possibly $50,000 in the club over the years. But the boss made the player vow that he would not play baccarat or any other game with the money.

"Oh, yes, I promise I won't go near the tables. I'm going just to stick around the casino until it's time for my plane, and then I'm going to take a cab right to the airport. I promise I will not touch a card."

That's what my friend says the baccarat player told him.

But the moment my friend went to dinner, our player rushed to the baccarat table and the shoe turned in his favor. By the time my friend returned from dinner, the player was betting $2,000 a hand. The supervisor was furious. Not only had the player gone back on his word, but now he was winning, and winning big. Of course, like many gamblers, now that he was winning the player couldn't care less what the supervisor thought. And he kept right on winning all evening. By the time my friend's shift was almost over, this player was winning $80,000. One of the hotel owners was called to the club. He was madder than hell because someone had told him that this big winner had been mooching around the casino earlier for plane fare home. The owner called my friend over and demanded to know who staked the player. My friend confessed that he had given him the money, "but only $300 to get home." The boss looked him in the eye.

"If that player leaves with $80,000 or more from this club, you're going with him."

My friend told me that he doesn't know to this day if the boss was kidding or not, but he had such a cold look in his eyes that he wasn't going to take any chances. As soon as his shift ended, he hurried over to the baccarat table, sat down next to the player, and started talking to him, anything to keep him in the club. He ordered him drinks as fast as the player could down them. They talked about everything under the sun.

As they talked, the shoe changed against the player. My friend told me that he talked to this player about anything that came into his mind: girls, horses, golf, fishing, hunting, the weather, the player's shoes, ring, tie, haircut, the brand of cigarettes the player smoked, the brands of cigarettes he didn't smoke, his marital problems—and that's when my friend hit pay dirt. It seems the player's marriage was on the skids. Half-smashed with the free booze, he started to blubbering about his personal woes. My friend sympathized profusely and draped his arm around the player's shoulder. They went on and on about how tough it was being married. As they talked, my friend made sure the player kept putting out another $2,000 each hand because the shoe still was going against him.

For three hours they talked about what he could do to save his marriage. My friend advised the player in a grand finale of tears that he should go home and give it one more try. The advice came conveniently just as the player lost the last $2,000 of the $80,000 and was broke again. My friend guided him gently from the table, took him to the airport in his own car, gave him $500 out of his own pocket, watched him as he bought a ticket, took him to the airport women's shop to buy a $150 outfit for his wife, and put him on the plane. My friend's parting words were: "You don't owe me a dime. The $500 is a gift."

As for the player's wife, well, you can be sure the marriage would have endured if the player had come home with $80,000 instead of a canceled plane ticket and an overpriced, out-of-style pantsuit.

Punto Banco (Foreign Baccarat)

In England and many European countries, baccarat is called punto banco, but it's the same game as the baccarat of Nevada and the Caribbean. "Punto" means "player" and "banco" means "banker." Play punto banco the same I have advised for baccarat. Just make sure you don't accidentally sit down at a chemin de fer or baccara table. Many casinos will have all three games, and they look similar. Most clubs will have signs above the tables; but if they don't, then ask. It could save you a thick wad of traveler's cheques.

Money management for punto banco is the same as in baccarat. Let's say you are playing punto banco in England and you're going to start at the standard minimum of £1 (about $2.30). If the bank (banco) won the last hand, your first bet would be £1 on banco, then £2, £4, and £4 again if you keep winning, then £6, and £10. If you win, bet £10 for two more bets and then raise your bet £5 each time until you lose or reach the club limit. But the moment you lose, regardless what stage of betting you're at, revert to your original £1 bet.

Baccara

Baccara is the glamour game of European casinos. But it is not all peaches and cream. The percentage is too strong against the player. Maybe that's why foreign casinos have baccara tables with high limits. Players sometimes think that because the casino has a game with high limits it is a good game to play. Wrong. You can be assured that, if the percentages weren't so strong in favor of the club, there would be fewer baccara tables and much, much lower limits.

Baccara is very popular among Europeans. Why, I don't know. They would have a much better chance for their money at punto banco, which is the same kind of game and often can be played in the same casino. Europeans are very tradition-oriented and baccara is the oldest game of this type. Maybe they think that because it's been around a long time it is okay to play. Fortunately for these European sheep, their ancestors didn't also originate Russian roulette as a pastime.

Read closely and you'll see why baccara is a game for the club, not the player.

In baccara, there are usually fourteen chairs at the table, numbered 1 to 14. The table is divided into two sides: 1 to 7 and 8 to 14. The croupier deals three hands of two cards each face down. He deals two cards to the 1 to 7 side, two cards to the 8 to 14 side, and two cards to himself. Players are called "punters" and the bank is the "banker." Players *cannot* bet with the bank in baccara. They can only bet against the bank.

After the hands have been dealt, the representative of the 1 to 7 side acts on his hand, either hitting or stopping, according to the card combination rules, which are similar to baccarat. Then the player representing the 8 to 14 group acts on his hand. You are allowed to hit only one card in baccara. The player's side has only one decision. If the player representing either the 1 to 7 or the 8 to 14 side receives a total count of 5 in his first two cards, he can choose whether to hit or stop on the hand. That is the only decision the player's side makes. It is called an "option." It is really a matter of guesswork. It all depends on how the player feels, because he cannot see the banker's hand. After both players' hands are completed, then the banker turns over his cards. Now he must decide what to do. Remember, the banker represents the casino. You cannot bet *with* him.

Here comes the catch in baccara. The banker has three options on how to play his hand. The player has only one. That is the strength of the game for the banker—and it is pretty strong. I wish I could fill a casino full of baccara tables in Las Vegas if I could get the action. The banker must quickly survey how the two sides played their hands. Then he chooses from his options.

If the banker's hand totals 3 and one of the players' hands was hit with a 9, the banker has an option to hit or stop at 3. Or if one side had said "No card," meaning that side could have a 5, 6, or 7, then the banker, if he has a total of 6 in two cards, again can opt whether to hit or stop. Also, if the banker turns over his hand and has a total of 5 in two cards, and one of the opponents had hit with a 4 earlier, the banker has another option. He can either hit or stop. The final decision for the banker is which hand he should play against. It may be the one with the most money bet, or the hand that's easiest to beat. It's his choice.

These bankers *are not ordinary* croupiers. Baccara bankers are real pros. They have a very important job. They are experts at picking the options. Their decision is the final one. They've had years of experience, and many have memorized hundreds of hitting and stopping combinations. They also carry a small card in their inside pocket with numerals on it. These are combinations. They won't show these cards to anyone, for it would reveal how they figure when it is best to hit and stop. You can bet that these bankers don't make many mistakes or they would be looking for new jobs. The bankers usually have a percentage of the winnings, which stimulates them to make right decisions. The little card is their textbook. Stay away from these experts and their baccara domain.

Baccara is so strong for the club that large gambling syndicates scramble for baccara concessions in some of the major world casinos. In the exclusive Casino Municipal de Cannes, one of the biggest casinos in France, the baccara game is leased from the casino by a Greek syndicate. The syndicate pays the casino rent by giving the casino 1¼ percent of each winning bet, that is, each bet that the banker wins. That is how confident the baccara concessionaires are of the strength of their game. The syndicate also pays for the croupiers' salaries and other overhead on the baccara game. The casino does not have to worry about the losing bets because the syndicate pays them. But that 1¼ percent is just the casino's piece of the action. The syndicate also has to make money. When you add it all together, baccara is the cheese in the mousetrap, and you are the little mouse.

A very strong factor is that all the casinos in Europe deal only two shoes a night, six decks. That way, if the players should, by accident, get lucky it won't last long. They'll have to wait until the next day to see if their luck holds.

Chemin de Fer

DO NOT play *chemin de fer* in any casino in the world. It is easy to get butchered in this game, especially if you are a higher than average bettor. Chemin de fer is based on the same card combination principle as baccarat and baccara. The main difference is that chemin de fer is a game where the players bet among themselves. The house does not gamble at all. The casino just supplies croupiers that deal the game. The croupiers see the game is run properly and, most important of all, collect 5 percent of each bet the banker wins. This 5 percent is for the "privilege" of playing chemin de fer in that club. Isn't that dandy! All the club does is supply you with a table and some chairs and they get 5 percent of the action. The person who has the shoe is the banker. He sets the size of the bank. Then the other players decide individually how much of that bank they want to fade. For example, let's say there are five players at the table. You decide to sit down; you become the banker and put up $500. But the other players take only $20 apiece of your action, so only $100 of the $500 has been faded. You win the hand and the house takes its 5 percent. Now you have $595 in the bank. But this time the five other players want to fade you only $10 apiece. Let's say you win the next four or five hands in a row with the other players fading you from $5 to $20 apiece each time. You have won a few hundred dollars. Whoopee! Had you been playing baccarat or punto banco, you would have won several thousand dollars. In those games the casino fades all bets up to the house limit (usually $2,000 or more). That should be reason enough never to sit down at a chemin de fer table.

But I'm going to give you another reason, and this one is just as important.

Let's start all over and say you sat down, became the bank, put up $500, the other players faded you $20 apiece, but you lost the first hand. The five other players would be paid $20 apiece out of your bank and the bank would move on to the next player because you lost. The bank moves to the next player whenever it loses. Now let's say the next player puts only $10 in the bank. That's his privilege, and it's often done by smaller players who want to nip away at the big fish. (That's you!) Now you are stuck with $100 with little chance of getting it back unless another big player sits down and gets the bank, or you win one hell of a lot of hands. Okay; you fade the new banker his $10 and you lose. Now he has $20 in the bank, but instead of letting the $20 ride he puts $10 in his pocket, leaving only $10 in the bank. In chemin de fer, the banker, if he wins, can put as much as he wishes in the bank again. He does not have to let the money ride. Now let's say that the bets seesaw back and forth around the table as the other five players take turns at being banker and put up only a small sum, as often happens. Finally the bank gets back to you. You are still stuck around $100 because you have won a few bets and lost a few bets. You put $200 in the bank, hoping to get the money you lost and maybe a little to boot. But the five players at the table all look at their watches, say they have to catch a bus, and leave. The table is empty except for you, sitting there with your $100 in their pockets and no way to get it back. Now the only way to get even is stick them up in the parking lot. There is no law requiring them to stay and play.

Many times I have seen a big player stuck for thousands of dollars after a turn at being the bank while the small players around the table smile happily as they nibble away at him.

Nevada casinos tried chemin de fer before they installed baccarat and found out the hard way what a poor game it is. At first they thought they only had to take their 5 percent cut of the winnings and let the players worry about getting faded. But the owners quickly found out that the games didn't last long enough for the clubs to make any money. The small players collected at the tables waiting for the big fish to enter the game, and then they all took shots at him. If the small players lost a few hands, they would get up and leave. The big player never could get even or win much. The games would quickly break up, and the Nevada casino owners realized chemin de fer was becoming a nuisance. That's when they replaced it with baccarat.

Americans traveling in Europe find chemin de fer games everywhere. It's strictly a grind game for the club. If you sit down, you will be the live one. You will be the sucker at the table. If you get involved and lose, believe me, you'll never get out. If you happen to walk by a chemin de fer game and the supervisor says, "Sir, there is one chair still open," keep walking and don't look back. That seat has been reserved for any American walking by. The trap is being sprung. Don't get caught. Fly away.

In Nevada, baccarat games are open 24 hours a day. A player going good can win as much as he has the heart for. That's the difference in gambling. Any time a club can close a game, you the player do not have much of a chance. I have seen and heard of tremendous scores made by baccarat players in Nevada.

Every now and then you read of big winners and losers in clubs in Europe. I have been to quite a few clubs in Europe—never saw a very large baccara game—or any other game. The biggest action in casinos is done in Nevada on a continuous basis. This includes the whole world. This includes baccarat against baccara.

In Europe you see spasmodic play. In Nevada you can walk into clubs and see tremendous games at all hours of the night. In Europe when the two shoes in baccara are played out using six decks, the clubs will be very obliging and let you play chemin de fer all night amongst yourselves. Where in the whole world can you walk into a casino and bet as much as you want on the pass line and $10,000 a card at 21—only in Nevada. There are two clubs in downtown Las Vegas that will handle your action. Just bring the cash.

ECCENTRIC BOSSES

In the gambling business, some bosses, like employees and players, do things that don't make sense. A polite way to describe them is to call them "eccentrics." One big boss was driving the employees and fellow-owners crazy with his long distance phone calls. He would travel to Europe quite often to look for entertainment acts for the club. But he would constantly call the club during his tour to find out what was going on and to get details on winners and losers. Only, he wouldn't stop there. He would kibitz over the phone with his friends, fellow-owners, and employees and would call around to different departments just as if he were around the corner instead of 6,000 miles away. The phone bills began piling up and one particular boss who was accepting most of the calls got fed up.

The next day, just like clockwork, the big boss called the irritated boss in the dice pit from London. "How are we doing?" the owner in Europe queried. The boss in Vegas put his hand over the phone and gazed around the casino. It was almost empty and the crap dealers were standing around yawning.

"There is a big hand going on. Quite a few passes are being made and the blacks ($100 chips) are piling up on the table," the boss said in a grave tone.

There was a moment of silence. "I'll call you from Paris," the faraway voice snapped.

About an hour later the phone in the dice pit rang again. "How are we doing?"

The boss in Vegas surveyed the empty casino again. "Believe

it or not, the same fellow is still shooting the dice." The traveling
owner hung up immediately.

There wasn't a peep out of him for about a week, but then, on
a busy afternoon, "How are we doing?" the familar voice asked
the boss who answered the phone.

"There is a big hand going on and a shill is shooting the dice."
He says he could hear the owner sputter.

"When the hand is over fire that shill." The shill, a retired
shoemaker who had been working in the club for years, is
probably still walking around trying to figure out why he was
laid off.

One boss in the blackjack pit of a Strip club was nicknamed
"The Toe," a few years ago because he would walk over to 21
dealers who went busted and kick them in the shins. The dealers
couldn't say anything for fear of their jobs, so they bought
shin guards. The Toe, who liked to wear $175 handmade Italian
shoes, had a choice of buying football shoes or stop the kicking.
He stopped and the shin guards gradually disappeared.

A big hand was showing early one morning at a large casino.
The employees began frantically looking for the boss on duty
because he had left strict orders to notify him anytime the dice
were passing. Finally one of the dealers found the boss in the
hotel kitchen feeding bread into the big toasting machine.

"The dice are passing and a big hand is showing. The shift
boss is looking all over the place for you," the dealer said.

The boss ignored the dealer and kept feeding the revolving
belt with bread, taking the finished toast from the other end and
stacking it in neat little piles for the waitresses.

The dealer repeated his urgent message, but the boss cut him
off. "I can't go. Can't you see I'm very busy. The other
machine broke down and I'm helping them with this one. How
would you like to have eggs with no toast for breakfast?"

Now the dealers call him "The Toastmaster" behind his back
and there's a standing wager on what will happen if the
dishwashing machine breaks down.

The dice were passing in one club and the shooter was a little
old woman. She held the dice about forty minutes, betting a
dollar at a time, and was making number after number. She
finally sevened out, but the club had lost about $60,000 to the

other players. The elderly woman watched everybody else filling their pockets with chips and said,"Is this all I win—$15— after shooting so long?"

A boss, who was standing there fuming, glared and walked over to the two racks of silver dollars at the crap table. "Here, my dear lady, take as many silver dollars as you think you should have won." With that he took both racks, containing about $200, and dumped them in front of her on the table.

Some bosses have moods that change as quickly as the dice. One boss stood in the dice pit puffing his cigar happily as he watched a big player, who was betting $500 and $500 odds, lose about $15,000—all cash. The boss turned to a floorman and said, "Look at the nice player. He lost $15,000 and never changed the expression on his face." The floorman quickly nodded in agreement.

A few days later the same player returned, a big hand showed, and he cashed out $25,000. The same boss and floorman were standing there, but this time the boss was chewing on his cigar angrily. "Look at that dirty s.o.b. He won $25,000 and never changed the expression on his face."

Backgammon

About four years ago a sharp young dealer in Las Vegas came to me one morning and asked if he could speak to me privately during lunch. We went over to a vacant 21 table at the casino I was managing. To my surprise he asked me quite bluntly if I knew how to cheat with dice. I reminded him that that was a very risky thing to say in this day and age of legalized gambling and with state gaming commissioners lurking about. But after several minutes of talking I realized that he wasn't interested in cheating at dice at the crap tables. He and several of his friends had stumbled on a new game—at least a new game to them—called backgammon.

The dealer had just returned from a trip to the East Coast and had discovered that backgammon was the current craze. In his home town of New York he found backgammon quickly replacing gin rummy and bridge as the local social game. In New York, Miami, and Chicago there were even some commercial backgammon clubs springing up. This young dealer had found out from some of his friends that there was plenty of money to be made in hustling backgammon, especially if you took advantage of certain aspects of the game, such as the dice cup and the dice themselves.

I advised him that I wasn't in a position to teach anyone how to cheat with dice, though I had learned almost every technique during the several decades I worked the East Coast when craps was the big money game and dealers had to learn all the cheating moves to protect the club.

I did give this young dealer the names of a few old-time dice hustlers who might be willing to teach him. About six months later this dealer left the club and I didn't hear from him for two years. Then about a year ago he came into the casino looking very spiffy and over lunch he explained that he had been doing very well hustling the backgammon circuit.

The backgammon circuit, it turned out, very closely resembled the old circuit that dice and card hustlers of the 30s and 40s used to travel: Miami, New York, Los Angeles, Chicago, and several cities along the East Coast. Now, of course, you would have to add Las Vegas and other resort areas. Hustlers also work cruise ships and try to infiltrate the increasing number of exclusive backgammon clubs that have cropped up in major cities.

Because I had steered the former dealer to an old-time dice hustler, he was willing to show me some of the dice moves that he had learned from the old craps hustler and had transformed into good hustling moves in backgammon. We went into the main showroom of the casino where, because it was well before noon, everything was nice and quiet and nobody was there. We sat down in one of the big booths in the back. He produced an attache case containing a backgammon set, which consists of the game board, thirty men resembling oversized checkers, a pair of dice, and a cylindrical cup to throw the dice from.

I knew the basic fundamentals of the game, so we started to play. Within a few minutes I realized that the young former dealer was moving in and out with loaded dice. He was good but I could tell by his hand motions, and had it been at a crap table we would have stopped the game immediately. But I let him continue. Soon we quit playing the game because he knew my curiosity was killing me.

Crooked dice in backgammon can be rigged with weights or shaved to favor certain sides, or magnetized. It was the same kind of stuff used in dirty crap games in the 30s and 40s. My companion said that a good set of loaded dice today cost about $50. Magnetized dice were a little more expensive. The kind of dice he was moving in and out of our little make-believe game were loaded dice, meaning that platinum had been inserted in certain sides of the cube so that numbers more favorable to him would show on the opposite side. He kept two or three sets, fixed to favor different combinations of numbers, hidden along his belt line in what was known in the old days as a "holdout box" or "snap box." It is a spring-loaded box about the size of a match box. You quickly insert the dice you want to exchange and the others pop into your hand. He explained that the most sophisticated method used today is to rig the board and dice with magnets, or rather electromagnets, which can be turned off and on by applying pressure, say with an elbow.

Sometimes called the "juice gaff," this kind of device was used on many crap tables when gambling was wide open and unregulated on the East Coast in the 1940s. But crooked dice are useless in backgammon if the cheater cannot match the color and shape of his rigged dice with the dice already in use on the board. But, as I was beginning to learn, the rules of backgammon help the cheater immensely. Wealthy backgammon players often invest hundreds of dollars in their boards and pieces, but the dice invariably are the cheap drugstore variety, the easiest to match and rig. Backgammon also is played in a sitting position with the two opponents seated at a table facing each other. This makes moving crooked dice in and out of the game almost too easy to resist. Half of the player's body is concealed under the table, even to bystanders. Another hustler told me later that he attaches his holdout boxes underneath the table by using a suction cup arrangement, and easily moves the dice in and out as the game goes on. To remove the boxes, he leaves the table for a legitimate reason, such as going to the toilet.

But I knew enough about backgammon to question this young hustler's reliance on crooked dice. Unlike craps, in which rolling a special number like a 7 is guaranteed winner or loser, dice combinations in backgammon can help at one stage and hurt at another. I questioned my friend very closely on just how much he could rely on the dice, since all the crooked dice in the world might not help his position no matter how sure he was that certain combinations could be rolled.

Then he showed me other techniques. And again they are techniques that have been used in many other forms of hustling.

The most important technique, of course, is to find players who think that they know how to play the game well but really don't. Backgammon can be very deceiving. A good player can teach a person who has never played before the basics of the game in thirty to sixty minutes, just enough so the newcomer thinks he knows what he is doing. And after a few months or weeks of playing, the newcomer often mistakenly believes he knows enough about the game to get into some heavy action.

Backgammon is a game of ego. Many people, when they lose, attribute it to bad luck—not to bad playing. There is a story among professional backgammon cheaters of one pro who set up a rich European count in one of the classic rip-offs. This professional hustler formed a syndicate of four partners. Each partner put up $50,000 cash. The hustler went to Europe disguised as a retired businessman. He had all the credentials and gained entry to the club to which the Count belonged through a friend who was a legitimate member. The hustler put on a classic show. He was very liberal with his money, played constantly in the club, but avoided the count as if he were the plague.

He'd watch the count and would make some clever remarks on how well the count played backgammon and how tough a player he would be. The hustler played a very loose aggressive game when he played. After a couple of weeks, and after the hustler was a few thousand dollars loser, he became known as a fair player who didn't mind losing—he just liked to play. It wasn't long before the only person the hustler hadn't played was the count. And with just enough subtle conversation and remarks tossed about, it became known in the club that for some reason these two men hadn't faced each other. When this word gradually filtered back to the count he was intrigued.

A few more weeks went by but the count still wouldn't approach the hustler. The hustler's backers were getting nervous because their money was disappearing at a rapid rate. The hustler also liked to have a good time and was a man known to have many girl friends with whom he was very generous. Naturally, his girl friends never won when he brought them to play.

One night the hustler decided to bring things to a head and he let the word get around that he was going to the Mediterranean, where he heard there was some big gambling action. The trap was set and the count walked into it.

The next night the count approached the hustler. "How come you never ask me to play? You've played everyone else."

The pro, in the sweetest voice, informed the count that he had watched him play and that the count played an excellent game but that the count's stakes were too high. But the hustler reluctantly agreed to play a few games. The hustler lost $10,000 cash. The next evening the count was waiting, and the hustler lost $15,000, promptly paying the minute the session ended. This went on for five nights. The hustler had lost $60,000 to the count. Actually, the hustler had tossed the games because he wanted to lose. He was building up the count's ego.

The sixth night the professional said to the count, "You've been very lucky (as most suckers usually say when they are losing). Let's raise the stakes. My turn should come soon to have some of the luck." The count eagerly said yes, and the fly was now firmly in the spider's web. The hustler went to work. By the end of that night he had won $100,000 and said, like a little boy who has found a shiny penny, "Oh, goody, my luck is changing." This put the furious count into the mental position of a born loser and sucker. The count could not stand to lose to both a bad and a lucky player, and he demanded that the stakes be raised. To make a long story short, they played for two weeks. The pro beat the count out of more than a million dollars. The count still thinks that the sloppy American businessman was just too lucky.

After the hustler paid his partners off with $600,000, he took the $400,000 and returned to the States. And according to several friends who knew him well, he promptly blew it in Las Vegas and at the race tracks, and is now back hustling the backgammon circuit. This hustler simply had outplayed the count and didn't resort to loaded dice, or any of the crude hustling techniques. He couldn't afford to offend the count by using many basic hustling maneuvers.

For example, one favorite technique among cheaters is simply to "false move" the men (pieces) around the board. This is easily done by the simple sleight-of-hand technique of moving one piece in one direction and nudging another piece in another direction with your thumb, or by just falsely counting the number of times you have moved. It's very easy to do. There often are many pieces on the board at one time, and often they are bunched in one area.

Another favorite technique is not to spell out before the game potential areas of dispute, such as rule variations. In every locality, as with many other games, there are local variations. These change as one travels across the country, or into different countries. The hustler finds out what the local variations are before he starts to play, but then he makes sure that he and the sucker do not discuss the variations with each other. That way, if the game takes a bad turn for the hustler, he can always protest that that's not how he learned to play and the game will have to be canceled or started over again. Now this may not sound like much, but when your whole living depends on winning the game and you are losing, a little thing like that can give you a fresh start.

Another favorite tactic is simply not to discuss how the bet will be paid off. Remember, the hustler cannot afford to have pride, heart, or soul. His job is to hustle, and it's a very tough, ruthless, cold-blooded business. By not spelling out how the bet will be paid, the hustler, if he should lose, can always say, "Ah, I'll send you a check." Of course, he never plans to send one but then, what does he care; he's a hustler and will be moving on. Or he can say, "I don't have the money right now. I'll pay you tomorrow." Any excuse will do and, unless his opponent is the type of person who can, shall we say, impress upon the hustler that not paying his bet could be very unhealthy, the hustler couldn't care less if he has offended somebody or is called a welcher. The name of the game is survival.

A good backgammon hustler also knows a person in the area who can be called over to settle any disputes. Naturally, that person is in with the hustler and calls the disputes in his favor. Another technique is simply to rattle your opponent by talking to him all the time, making fun of him when he makes a mistake, spilling drinks, acting drunk, blowing smoke in his face, whistling at the girls—just being a loud bore.

All these techniques are pretty crude but they are used by hustlers in almost every game. Backgammon is ideally suited for them because traditionally it is played among the upper crust who pride themselves on their manners and etiquette. That kind of attitude is a hustler's dream.

In backgammon the hustler also doesn't have to worry too much about building the sucker up to make big bets. The secret of hustling is to get the person you can beat to bet a large sum of money. But backgammon has what is known as the "doubling cube," which was introduced in 1925. This doubling cube permits the stakes in a single session to be multiplied by as much as 64, though normally it never goes that high. The cube has, displayed on each of its six sides, the numbers 2, 4, 8, 16, 32, 64. A player wishing to double must wait for his turn, and flip the cube so the 2 faces up. His opponent must accept the double, or drop out and pay the stakes. Or he may turn the cube so that the 4 faces up, redoubling the opponent. The other player can redouble again by turning the 8 up, and so on until the cube reaches 64. Each time a double is accepted, the stakes are multiplied by the number showing on the cube. Hustlers like to wait for the sucker to offer a double, accept it, and then immediately redouble. The doubling cube has allowed hustlers to quickly raise the limit of the game before their opponents realize what is happening. It is the doubling cube that has made backgammon such a temptation for hustlers. A game that starts off with $5 or $10 can very rapidly turn into a nightmare for the sucker. Once the hustler has the stakes up that high he no longer has to worry about the true skill of his play.

The No. 1 rule in backgammon (as well as any other game) is to be extremely careful about who you play with. In backgammon this is more than usually true because the game is held in very high social esteem and a legitimate player can quickly drop his guard. In playing craps, poker, or 21 the average American is normally very leery of his opponent. Those games have a long colorful history—radio, movies, television, books, folklore—as favorite haunts of card sharks, cheaters, and all sorts of disreputable characters. Movies, books, and legends have been built around cheating at cards and dice. But backgammon remains the game of the elite. It's very easy to be deceived into thinking your opponent, that distinguished looking gentleman with the monocle and woodbriar pipe, wouldn't dream of pulling any shenanigans, when in fact he might be one of the world's greatest cheaters and you are about ready to get fleeced.

Here are some tips on how to avoid being cheated:

1) Be sure of all rules, options, and stipulations before you begin to play.

2) Determine the amount of the bet, and when and how the payoff will be made.

3) Always use a dice-rolling cup that has a lipped outside edge, or in which the interior is rimmed, thus forcing the dice to roll and tumble freely so they can't be set up inside the cup. And make sure that your opponent uses the same kind of cup.

4) Before the game starts, determine what will be considered "cocked dice" (dice which are on a tilt or slant because they are leaning against something on the board, such as a piece).

5) When moving your piece, use only one hand and don't make moves that are "smart-alecky" or "show-offy."

6) Determine immediately if an outside arbitrator or judge is going to be used, or if an outside person will roll the dice. Then make darn sure that person is neutral and isn't your opponent's cousin.

7) Remember that your turn doesn't legally end until both dice are back in your cup, and that the same goes for your opponent. A favorite hustler's trick is to put only one of the dice back in the cup and hold the other one in his hand so if his opponent rolls a good

combination the hustler can say, "Hey, I haven't finished putting my dice back in yet. I'm not done. You'll have to roll over."

8) When you are ahead or in position, be particularly aware of being doubled or being redoubled and accepted.

9) Always show good manners.

10) Remember, if you are being hustled or conned, almost all of your doubles will be accepted and usually returned by a redouble.

11) Watch very carefully what dice combinations are being thrown by your opponent. If favorable combinations for your opponent continue to crop up, start thinking very carefully about what is going on. Loaded dice may have been brought into the game.

12) You must eliminate a lot of the guesswork from backgammon, as in any other gambling game. Learn the combination odds and percentages needed to make decisions on each roll. They are available in any basic backgammon book.

13) You should switch colors and sides after every single game so a player can't use the same dice and rolling cup game after game.

14) Master the back game and running game.

15) Try to keep the doubling cube on your side of the board as much as possible.

16) Try not to be forced into a back game as this is an all-out gamble and can result in a backgammon, which doubles and triples the bet.

17) If at any time you feel or sense that you are being cheated, quit as quickly and as gracefully as possible. In most cases, a cheater or con man has his moves perfected to the point where you do not see what he has been doing and how he has been working you over.

Most backgammon players blame themselves when they lose or think that the opponent was too lucky. It's the old ego thing again. They refuse to accept that they have been suckered into the game by a pro who watched them play in previous games and knew just how far to go.

EXPERT

A cocktail waitress was showing a diamond ring to a boss in a club I worked in a few years ago. He looked it over. "It's a very pretty diamond, well worth the money you paid for it," the boss said.

I asked the boss, "What do you know about jewelry?"

"I was in the business years ago," he replied. "I used to stick up jewelry stores."

He wasn't kidding.

THE BANKER

A few years ago the president of a bank on the West Coast began coming into town quite frequently. He played all games and was one of the biggest tippers in Las Vegas history. He gave money away like water while he was playing, win or lose. If he liked a dealer or cocktail waitress he would give a fifty-dollar gold piece as a tip, which wasn't bad considering the price of gold. He was a born gambler, especially when it was somebody else's money. Then we found out that his bank closed, and now he is in a very secure place—rent free—and will be there for a few years to come. A lot of dealers and cocktail waitresses are hoping he opens another bank when he returns from his little "vacation." They don't plan to be depositors, however.

5% Craps Bahamas Style and Some Advice For the Thousands of Suckers Who Play It

The 5% crap game, which is the only way craps is dealt at a few popular resorts such as the Bahamas, is one of the worst gambles in a casino today, yet each year another wave of tourists can't roll into those casinos fast enough to plunk down their bets.

What these doomed lemmings don't realize is that the 5% crap game is stronger for the club than a ton of freshly grated horseradish.

The crap dealers should be wearing bandit masks.

It's a bigger heist than the Brink's robbery, only nobody's going to get arrested.

Tens of thousands of crapshooters, especially those who learned to shoot dice East Coast style, will find these facts about 5% craps very distasteful, maybe even a little nauseating. But it's about time they learned the truth. To put it very bluntly, if you fail to heed my advice and betting suggestions on 5% craps after reading this chapter, then either you're an idiot or you're stealing your money someplace.

Originally called "New York craps," the 5% game was started around 1910 by a veteran gambler and bookmaker named John Winn. He died long before he could see what a monster he had created.

Most crap games were called "loft" games in those days, because they were held in the deserted, after-hours stock rooms of the New York garment district and on rooftops and in the back rooms of pool halls, candy stores, and restaurants. They were strictly "fading games" in which the players bet among themselves and had to cover each other's bets.

Winn was an avid crapshooter, but he was also a shrewd odds-maker and an expert on crap game percentages. On one fateful night, Winn, who was watching a particularly big game, noticed that several players were complaining because they couldn't get bets faded on certain numbers. The other players already had enough action on those numbers and didn't want to put up more money. I was still a gleam in my father's eye at the time, but an old-timer at the game recalled that Winn, during a brief lull in the action, said in a loud, clear voice so that all could hear, "I'll take your bets. Just give me 25¢ for every $5 you bet." Winn went on to say that he would book action for both "wrong" bettors and "right" bettors, and pay full odds. The players were delighted. Winn's offer would allow them to lay or take the odds, such as 6 to 5 for wrong bettors laying the 6 and 8, plus they did not have to worry about having other bets covered, because Winn would fade them also. All they had to do was give up a paltry 25¢ for each $5 bet.

Soon other smart gamblers realized the strength of Winn's proposal, and they opened "book" at other fading games. At these games a player knew he could always get his bet covered by the "book" as long as he paid the 5% "vigorish," as it was nicknamed. New Yorkers grew up shooting craps the 5% way and didn't know any better. I know, because in the 1940s I was dealing to them.

As the years passed, illegal gambling flourished along the East Coast, and fancy casinos opened from New York to Miami. Naturally, they opened with 5% crap games and the club booked all bets. These were called "banking games." In some clubs, players could make a Pass line bet and take the odds without paying vigorish. In other clubs, only the Pass line bet was free; players had to pay to take odds behind the line. But in all clubs in the 1930s and 1940s, players had to pay 5% vigorish to bet the numbers. I can understand why gamblers played 5% craps in those days. It was the only way the game was dealt. But today's crapshooters have been exposed to several forms of dice in other areas, such as Nevada where you can bet the numbers without giving up 5%, by making a come bet. Most world gambling centers haven't opened with strictly 5% craps, because in my opinion the owners didn't believe there were that many players in the world stupid enough to play at a strictly 5% game.

The Bahamas proved everybody wrong.

The sad truth is that in 5% craps you've got to be twice as lucky and win twice as much just to break even.

This next example should drive the point home. I worked in an Eastern club many years ago, a favorite haunt for a wealthy Oriental

who loved to shoot "claps" (as he called it). We dubbed him Charley
Claps. The game had a $300 limit on the numbers. Charley liked to
bet $300 on each number (4, 5, 6, 8, 9, and 10). This cost him $90 in
"vigorish" (5%) each turnover, and $15 each time a number was
made.

One night we decided to keep track of the vigorish Charley paid
during an evening. He played from 9 p.m. to 2 a.m., stopping only a
few minutes to wolf down some dinner. During those five hours he
lost $30,000 cash from his own pocket and during the play the 5%
came to $36,000. How could he win? In this type of game, the longer
you play, the more you lose as the 5% eats you up.

Charley, like his modern counterparts in the Bahamas and other
countries playing the same game, didn't have a chance for his money
unless he ran into a fantastic lucky streak. But Charley, like other
New York-trained crapshooters, returned week after week to take
another brutal beating. The 5% game proved so strong for the club
that even some of the most cold-blooded casino owners seemed to
feel a little guilty about taking the players' money. One boss actually
told us to "go easy" on the 5% players, because he felt sorry for them.

In his club, we would mark up the vigorish of each player as the
bets were being made. At the end of the hand, or when a 7 the loser
was thrown, we collected the 5% vig from the players in rotation.
Under instructions from the good-hearted boss, we often gave
players a little break. If a player owed $120 vigorish, we rounded it off
to $100 and told him to "call it even." The players were ecstatic. They
gladly gave the $100, because they felt they were saving $20. If a
player owed $60 or $70, we would round it off to $50. News of the soft-
hearted boss's tactics spread, and the club attracted big crapshooters
from across the nation. Players thought they actually were getting
something for nothing. But they didn't have a chance for their money.
They were the lambs and we were waiting at the door with the butcher
knives.

Some big players ran up such high markers (credits) they were
afraid to enter the club, because they knew their credit was zilch and
figured the boss would ask them to pay their markers. But the shrewd
boss knew the 5% game was so strong it wasn't even a gamble for the
club. All he needed was players. At Christmastime, he tore in half
several of the biggest markers owed by 5% crapshooters and sent the
torn marker to each player in a little Christmas package with a note.

It said the club tore up the marker as a Christmas gift, but "from now on when you come into the club, please play for cash, no more credit."

Several markers were worth tens of thousands of dollars and were owed by big businessmen. You would think they would question the boss's eagerness to lure them back to the tables. Instead, they questioned his sanity for tossing away what they considered thousands of dollars in debts. But through the years those players paid for the markers many, many times over.

It's no wonder that early casino owners promoted 5% craps. By the late 1940s, the biggest crap games in the world were the 5% games being held in the plush casinos that opened in Florida near Miami. The three most famous clubs were the Sunny Isles Club at 163rd Street and Collins Avenue, the 86 Club on Biscayne Boulevard, and the Colonial Inn in Hallendale north of Miami Beach. One of the biggest crap games—and I've yet to see one bigger—was held at the 115 Club on the highway north of Miami on the way toward Hollywood, Florida.

Millions in cash changed hands weekly across the crap tables in that club during the postwar years. It was a typical New York fading game where the players bet among themselves on the Pass line or main numbers; but if they wanted to bet any other number, the house booked the action for 5%. If the player called off the bet, he didn't get his 5% back. Many of these high rollers knew each other, so to speed the game they bet money "packets." They wrapped paper money in $5,000 and $10,000 packages with the value marked on each packet so other players would know instantly how much was there without stopping to count it. The packets would pile up around the table like play money in a Monopoly game.

The club took as high as a $5,000 bet on a box number. When you bet $5,000 on a number, that's $250 vigorish. It doesn't sound like much to a $5,000 bettor, but after several hours of play the vigorish paid often was more than many men earn in a year.

These big action games attracted many "desperados," those gambling hustlers with ice water in their veins who can walk into a casino with $100 cash and end up beating you out of $100,000 without blinking an eye. A desperado can thread a needle betting $1 or $10,000. One aspiring desperado was a chemin de fer dealer who worked at the Colonial Inn. He was a nice Italian boy from Brooklyn, but because he was dealing chemin de fer he had developed a phony French accent to help increase his tips, so we called him The Count. He hit the big fading games weekly with a few hundred bucks, or whatever he scraped up, and bet it up as fast and as high as other players and the clubs would allow.

One night at the 115 Club, The Count, betting that the dice would hit or pass ran into several good hands. He managed his money well and within a few hours he was $120,000 winner. The next shooter threw 4 for a point. The Count liked to bet the 4 and 10 because of the 2 to 1 odds. They were his favorite numbers. He bet around the table seeking other players to fade as much of his $120,000 as possible.

A fading game crap table in those days was much bigger than crap tables used today. Many more players could crowd around them.

All of The Count's $120,000 was faded on the 4 within minutes. Even for those big games, a $120,000 bet by *one* player in *one* shot was big action.

You could hear a pin drop as the shooter threw the dice. The two cubes sailed across the stacks of paper money and came up 7 the loser. A sigh swept the table. All eyes turned toward The Count. He didn't say a word, just smiled and borrowed cab fare home.

The next day I asked The Count, with whom I had worked for years around New York, why he had bet his whole bankroll on one number. I reminded him of the many times he had drilled into my head, *"Never, never break yourself on one number."*

The Count gazed out of his apartment window; his voice was a hoarse whisper: "Mike, you and I usually laugh when players say they have a 'feeling' they're going to win. But I swear I had that same feeling last night when the shooter rolled the four. For the first time, my stomach was tied in knots and my heart was pounding when I bet the $120,000, but I felt I couldn't lose. I planned to bet the $360,000 on the next number and not stop until I could quit a millionaire." He was silent for several minutes. Then he said, "Mike, you're going to think that I'm nuts, but I still have that same feeling, only now it's even stronger, I can't lose."

The Count was broke; I knew what was coming next. Before he could ask, I gave him the $600 I had in my pocket at the time and wished him luck.

That night he sauntered up to the crap table with my $600. Several players and kibitzers crowded around expectantly, but The Count lost the $600 in the first roll and left without a word.

It was the last crowd he ever attracted.

The Count never won anything close to that $120,000 score again, but he never mentioned it or showed a bit of regret. If he didn't make another big score, it wasn't because he had lost his nerve. He continued to act the same betting $600 or $60,000. As for the "winning feeling" that possessed him those two days, well, if he ever had that feeling again, he kept it to himself.

The Count died broke a few years ago, but at least for one brief moment in that Miami club he captured the admiration of the world's toughest gamblers.

They weren't an easy bunch to impress. I dealt to all of them in the biggest banking "paper" money, 5% crap game in the world in those years at the Sunny Isles Club. The game was so big that we opened with a $20 minimum bet, but after five minutes we jumped the minimum to $40 just to get rid of the small players. The club dealt a $1,000 limit and had many customers with $100,000 credit lines, plus at least fifty "open cards" where credit was virtually limitless. Other Miami clubs dealt a $500 limit. The 5% games were so strong and the clubs won so much money that they actually baled the money with wire. That's how fast they took it in. They just couldn't count it at the time. It was baled like hay and counted later.

We used to kid the bosses in those days that we were going to buy them hay balers for Christmas. I wonder if the dealers in the Bahamas and other 5% countries kid their bosses the same way.

The longer you play in a 5% game, the less chance you have. It's common sense. Giving up 5% on every bet means exactly that. Every time you bet a number, you pay for it. If the dice are making a couple of numbers and then miss out, as often happens, you get clobbered. A $5 bettor in this situation could wind up paying $25 an hour just for vigorish. And that's if you stay at the $5 bet. If you press your bet after a number is made, you'll pay about $40 an hour vigorish. By the end of the evening, often you have given up more money in vigorish than you started with in your pockets.

How to Play 5% Craps

The first rule is to play the *Pass line only* and take the odds. They're *free*. You must not make any other bet on the layout. I don't care how tempting it is to bet on a number. You must fight the temptation and stick to the Pass line. If crapshooters, whether they're beginners or veterans, follow my advice in this chapter, the casinos in the Bahamas and other countries with strictly 5% games would have to change their layouts or close their crap tables.

All Bahama crap games have a $5 minimum, and this simple betting and playing method for conservative and moderate players requires an investment of at least $100, so $2 type bettors with short bankrolls should think twice before taking the plunge.

Your first bet is $5, and $5 odds when a point is thrown; then $10 and $10 odds, and $10 and $10 odds again for one more bet. If you win, jump to $20, $20 odds; stay at $20 and $20 odds for one more bet if you win; then $40, $40 odds, and finally $50, $50 odds. That is high enough for the $5 player. If you lose at any time during the play, immediately revert to your original $5 bet. If a crap is thrown on the comeout roll, stay at the same bet you were making. If you were at the second $10 bet and a crap was thrown, your next bet still would be $10. If a 7 or 11 is thrown on the comeout roll, also stay at the same previous bet; consider it a bonus roll.

A conservative $10 bettor starts with $10 on the line and $10 odds; then $20, $20 odds; $20, $20 odds again; $40, $40 odds; $40, $40 odds again. If you win the second $40 bet, jump to $80 and $80 odds. Your next bet still would be $80 and $80 odds. Your last and biggest bet would be $100 and $100 odds. That should be your limit. That means a few numbers have been made and you've run into a little hand. As you should know, hands don't show that often, so take advantage of one by progressing as you win.

For the conservative $25 player, start with $25, $25 odds; then $50, $50 odds; $50, $50 odds again, then $100, $100 odds; $100, $100 odds again. The last bet should be $200, $200 odds on the line. Stay at $200 until you lose, then revert to your original $25 bet.

For the conservative $50 bettor, $50, $50 odds; $100, $100 odds; $100, $100 odds again; $200, $200 odds; then $200, $200 odds again; and finally $300, $300 odds. That is high enough for the $50 bettor, but don't be afraid to jump to $500 and $500 odds if the shooter makes a couple of $300 numbers. A $50 bettor is in a high enough bracket to make the jump to $500 without distorting the picture.

The conservative $100 player starts with $100, $100 odds; $200, $200 odds; $200, $200 odds again; $400, $400 odds; then $400, $400 odds again; and then $500, $500 odds.

The conservative betting progression method may not seem fast enough for players who like to bet the Pass line and then cover all the numbers or boxes. But remember, you have to fight the temptation to make number bets in playing a 5% game or you'll get murdered.

But here is a faster betting method which should keep even some of the most dedicated number players busy and out of trouble.

You can afford to play at this quicker pace, because you are not throwing your money away by buying box numbers. You'll now last much longer and will have a chance to win if a few Pass line numbers are made.

For the fast $5 bettor, jump your bet a little higher and faster after the first number has been made. If you have $5 on the line and a number is made, you next bet would be $15 and $15 odds. That's called "pressing" a bet. You have invested $20 in the shooter. Remember, a 7 or 11 is not what we call a number; it is a bonus for the player. If the shooter makes the $15 number, your next bet would be $30, $30 odds; then $30, $30 odds again; then $50, $50 odds; $75, $75 odds; and finally your maximum bet, $100, $100 odds. If you consider yourself a fearless player, then bet accordingly beyond the $100 maximum.

For the fast $10 bettor, your first bet would be $10, $10 odds; $30, $30 odds; $60, $60 odds; then $60, $60 odds again; $100, $100 odds; $150, $150 odds; and your last bet $200, $200 odds.

For the fast $25 player, the first bet would be $25, $25 odds; $75,

$75 odds; $150, $150 odds; $150, $150 odds again; and finally $250, $250 odds.

A fast $100 player would bet $100, $100 odds; $300, $300 odds; $300, $300 odds again; and the last bet $500, $500 odds.

A big player ($500-a-bet league) should not start at the maximum $500. You're going to be there all evening, especially if you're losing. Give yourself a chance. You cannot progress when your first bet is $500. You cannot go any higher, and if you get stuck right away you may never get out. By starting at a $100 minimum, you will reach the maximum fast enough if the dice pass, and you will not have missed a thing. And by dropping your minimum bet if the dice are cold, you still have the capability of winning big; but it will be tougher than hell for the club to grind you down.

The moment you lose control of your betting method and start chasing your money, you are at the casino's mercy. You are a cooked goose.

I realize many diehard number addicts won't change their betting methods no matter what I say about a 5% game. My heart goes out to these poor souls, for I know they exist in great numbers. They come into casinos day after day. I've even seen "number freaks" buy the numbers and pay 5% when they don't have to, like in Nevada where you can bet the numbers without paying 5%. That's how diehards were broken in to play and nothing will change them. It's this kind of player we want to pick up at the airport in a limousine. If he's wealthy enough, we'll send a plane to get him.

An old card hustler once told me that, if a person is determined to be a sucker, let him have his way. But I guess I'm turning into a softie. Against my better judgment, and with a conscience tormented by misgivings, I'm going to give the diehard 5% crapshooters a way to play the 5% game and still bet the numbers but, now at least, with a little chance for their money.

First, you must change your betting methods somewhat. I don't care how bad the withdrawal pains are. If you want to have a chance at the 5% game, you can't bet as many numbers as before.

Many years ago, shortly after the 5% game was created, some New York crapshooter got the bright idea that the more numbers you bet, the better chance you had. That theory must have been planted by casino owners. Nothing could be further from the truth, especially when you're betting the numbers with your own money.

The more numbers you bet, the harder it is to win. It's very simple to figure out. Even if you bet all the numbers and four of them are made, you'll be lucky to break even. One 7 the loser wipes out your winnings, and more.

You are beaten before you start.

It is fine to spread out and bet on a few numbers when dice are passing, but only when you are betting with the house's money. Betting all the numbers from the start is stupid even if you're not playing a 5% game, and it's idiotic if you are. The vigorish will eat you up unless you walk into a tremendous hand at the beginning of the play. That happens very rarely.

The second change is to forget about betting the 6 and 8. I realize they are very popular bets with number players, especially New Yorkers. But the percentage is too strong against the player. For example, the house percentage on placing the 5 and 9 in countries which don't deal a strictly 5% game is 4 percent against the player. So when you bet the 5 or 9 in the Bahamas, you give up an extra 1 percent. It's bad enough giving up the extra 1 percent on the 5 and 9, but if you buy the 6 and 8 in the Bahamas you give up additional 3.5 percent because the normal house percentage against you is 1.5 percent outside the Bahamas. You already are considered a sucker by betting the 5% numbers anyway, so please don't become a bigger sap by buying the 6 and 8.

At a 5% game the player must hit and run. He must take advantage quickly if the dice make a few numbers. If the dice are cold, he must leave quickly.

The first step for diehards is always to bet the Pass line. Then, if the dice make a couple of passes, look around cautiously for a number to bet in the boxes. Of course, now you will be paying 5%.

Pick out one or two numbers (4, 5, 9, or 10) and stick with them. Eliminate the guesswork. It does not make any difference what numbers you pick. Just pick one or two numbers that strike your fancy and stay with them. No one I've ever met knows what number will be thrown on the next roll.

Don't bet any more than two numbers. Remember, you are paying dearly. In fact, one box bet is enough for players with a small bankroll. You still have the Pass line bet working. Now if you should catch a few numbers, you'll be playing with the club's money; then maybe you can afford to make another number bet.

If numbers are being made, you must bet a little faster than normal. An ordinary $5 bettor must become a $10 bettor. Small players should invest a maximum of about $200—and that's quite a bit. Your first bet would be $10 in the box of the one number you picked.

Only bet each number individually, and only bet them up individually as the number shows.

Let's say you bet $10 each on the 4 and 10 (vigorish is $1), and the 4 is made. Your next bet would be $30 on the 4 only. That costs you $1.50 in vig. If the second 4 hits, then bet $70 (vig $3.50). At this point you have invested $6 of your own money. You are in the driver's seat. If another 4 is made, then bet $100. You have playing money for a few more bets. If you win, your next bet still is $100 (vig $5). If you win, your next bet is $200 (vig $10). Now add $50 more to each bet as long as the 4 is made, or until you reach the club limit.

Take ruthless advantage when your box numbers are hitting. It's the only way to beat a 5% game when betting the boxes or numbers. Bet it up fast, then hit and run.

Betting the 4 and 10

For the $25 bettor who likes the 4 and 10, start with $25, then $75, then $150, $250, then $250 again, and, if you keep winning, add $50 a bet until you lose or reach the club limit. Once you lose, always revert to your minimum bet.

For the $50 bettor, $50, $150, $300, $400, $400 again, $500.

For the $100 bettor, $100, $300, $400, $500.

High rollers have nothing to lose and everything to gain by starting at $100 instead of the $500 maximum. By starting at $100 and raising your bet when winning, *you* will be controlling your money instead of the casino. The player betting $500 from the start is in trouble if the dice are cold, while the $100 bettor can recoup and, by betting it up, can finish winner, even if just a few numbers are made.

Betting the 5 and 9

The player must alter his bets a little when buying the 5 and 9, because the payoff (3 to 2) is different than the 4 and 10 payoff (2 to 1). If you bet $10, for example, and the 5/9 was made, you win $15.

As for how to progress your bets, let's say you're a $10 bettor and you bet the 5. If it is made, your next bet would be $20. If the second 5 is made, your next bet would be $40, then $70, then $100 and $100 again. If you win, jump to $200 and add $50 to each bet as long as you keep winning. If the shooter throws a 7 immediately, revert to your original $10 bet.

For the $25 bettor, start with $30, then if you win go to $70, then $140, and jump to $200, and $200 again if you win. Now add $50 to each winning bet.

For the $50 bettor, $50, $120, then $250, $350, then $350 again, and finally $500.

For the $100 bettor, $100, $250, $400, $400 again, and $500.

Casinos will allow 5 and 9 bettors to put up an extra $5 on their odds if their Pass line bet doesn't match the 3 to 2 payoff.

For example, if you're betting $15 on the Pass line and a 5 or 9 is thrown, you can take $20 odds behind your Pass line bet.

If you were betting $25 on the line, you could take $30 odds, and so on.

Another tip: If you ever decide to take your bet off the box numbers, make sure the croupier gives back the 5% vig you paid. Some croupiers have a tendency to "forget" to return a player's vig, especially if that player didn't tip the croupier during the play.

You also can take your buy bets off the numbers and the odds behind the line at any time. The only bet you can't take off is the Pass line bet.

All this advice isn't worth a hoot *if you don't know when to quit.*

If the shooter makes several numbers or some of your box numbers, get ready to quit, but don't be afraid to give the next shooter a chance. You must raise your minimum bet to the next level as stated in the betting method. If you are a $10 bettor, raise to the $25 level and so on. The $100 bettor stays at the $100 level at all times. The most you can lose with the next shooter is a couple of bets, if he misses out. But he could be better than the previous shooter.

Once you get into the $100 bracket, when you're betting $100 and making two or three numbers, you can afford to give the next couple of shooters a chance before quitting. Play blackjack or roulette for a while. That's the only way to play 5%. Do not let the size of the bet interfere with your betting. Remember, if you do reach a $50 or $100 bet, it's not your money. It's the house's money.

The casino hopes you'll play "scared" and reduce your bets once you start winning. Casino bosses count on your being "chicken." By hedging or reducing your bets, you play longer, pay more vigorish, and fail to reap the advantage when the dice are hot. You must be alert in a 5% game, because if you miss one bet the club's edge is going to be very hard to overcome.

Many players also don't realize that a 5% crap game is much faster than the normal Las Vegas-style crap game, where you can make come bets to get on the numbers and where you can take the odds on the numbers but then can call off the odds if you want. But in a 5% game, most players make only two kinds of bets: Pass line bets and number bets. The game isn't slowed by players changing their odds or by constantly making come or don't come bets. The 5% game's faster tempo increases shooter turnover, thus increasing the 5% rake.

Most players don't realize that a casino has a strong enough percentage in its favor even if the player doesn't give up 5% "vig" on each buy bet. If crap games weren't in favor of the club, the casinos wouldn't have them. Casinos work on volume. The more bets made, the more cash goes into the money boxes. Contrary to the belief that bosses sweat out each big bet, modern casino bosses don't worry that much about big winners. They just want players to bet. Volume is the name of the game today. The percentage will overcome all. Bosses know that as long as there's plenty of business, the percentage will be there, and the boxes will be full of cash.

Most gamblers learn about percentages the hard way, like the three bosses of a Reno club who tried to overcome the crap table percentages a few years ago. Every day they ate lunch and/or dinner at their biggest competitor's, Harold's Club, and took an extra twenty or thirty minutes to shoot craps. They were $500-a-bet players. After playing $500 and $500 odds for several months, the three bosses, who had been losing consistently, convinced a Harold's Club boss to deal double odds to them. This meant they could bet $500 on the line and get $1,000 odds. By increasing the size of their odds bet, they lowered the percentage against them. They played this way a few months and lost another bundle.

But it was all part of their strategy. They would have preferred to win from the start, but their long-range plan was to con the boss into increasing the odds bet even higher.

It worked. The Harold's Club boss agreed to deal them triple odds if they played for cash. The three bosses were smart gamblers. By getting triple odds, they reduced the house PC (percentage) against them to less than 1 percent, about a half of 1 percent. That is a very small percentage to give up, but still it was too much. Also, dice still have to pass; and when you lose, you lose twice as much money.

To make a long and very expensive story short, during the two years they played "lunchtime craps" at Harold's Club, the three bosses lost an estimated $3 million among them. Even by playing $500 on the Pass or Come line and getting $1,500 odds, the house PC ground them down with only the 0.5% advantage. With that in mind, imagine what dismal chances the 5% crapshooter has over any length of time.

The classic example of a percentage victim was Nick the Greek, who liked to bet wrong and lay the odds. He was one of the biggest losers Las Vegas has ever seen around crap games. This is not just hearsay. I knew Nick, who died a few years ago, personally and for a long time. I've seen Nick the Greek stuck from $30,000 to $60,000 in a game and never change his expression. I've seen him winning $40,000 or $50,000 and never change his expression, and always chewing on an unlit cigar.

Nick's name was magic. Players from across town would crowd around a crap table just to watch. He was what we call a "pocket player." He kept all his money in his pockets, only using a small working bankroll to bet with. If he needed more money, he'd pull out package after package of $100 bills. Nick liked to play with cash only. When the dealers paid him chips, he would accumulate a few thousand, then he would exchange them at the casino cage for cash and stuff it in his pockets.

It was almost impossible to tell when he was winning or losing. He kept everyone guessing, sometimes even himself. Toward the end of his career, Nick just played to play. He didn't care if he won or lost. If his bankroll was short, he'd bet $50 and $100. When he was flush, he'd bet $500, always laying the odds. He had the lowest house percentage bet on the table going for him, but he still was ground out of his money. The house PC and Nick's countless hours of play broke him in the end.

The normal house PC is so strong that I think 5% clubs, like casinos in the Bahamas and on islands elsewhere that also deal 5% games, sometimes should, in all fairness, keep track of the players' personal cash losses for the evening.

And if the players finish losers, the casinos should return 20 percent of what they lost and let them start over again. The players still wouldn't win, but at least they could play a little longer with genuine enjoyment. The casinos would still get rich, and the delighted players would leave thinking they got something for nothing, already counting the days till their next visit. I'm not kidding. I'm being very sincere.

21 in the Bahamas

Read my betting and playing methods in the New 21 chapter on how to play against the shoe and you should be able to handle any playing situation in the Bahamas. The money management section should handle your betting problems.

A $300 maximum 21 limit is dealt in the Bahamas, which is fine for most good players. The game is dealt Nevada-style. Most games have a $5 minimum, but each club usually has a few tables with a $2 or $3 minimum. All games are dealt from the shoe face up. The croupiers are British subjects and speak English. This eliminates the language barrier. The only Americans are supervisors and executives. If you have any complaints, at least no one can claim "No speaka da English."

Bahamas 21 dealers are known for their inclination and ability to hustle or "break down" players for tips. But don't fall for the Continental soft tongue and accent of these cute croupiers. Supervisors pay scant attention to the tip hustlers, and they let the croupiers control the games. Don't worry about the croupiers and their sad looks as they shake you down for tips. I have several friends working the Bahamas and I can assure you that some of the croupiers make more than the guests. Tips are for service, so if you don't receive service you don't have to tip. Dealing the cards is not an extra service by croupiers; it is their job. Wait until you are through playing for the evening. Then, if you should finish winner, tip accordingly.

Roulette in the Bahamas

Roulette is dealt Nevada-style with all American wheels, no French wheels. The absence of French wheels is one break for the player (see French roulette chapter). All the wheels have "0" and "00," which gives the club a little stronger edge than French, English, and other foreign-style roulette wheels where the "00" is missing. The minimum buy-in is a $5 stack of 20 chips (25¢ each). Play the wheels for enjoyment only. Unlike French roulette, each player has his own color chip, so you don't have to worry about claim-bet hustlers.

Just bet one chip on four or five of your favorite numbers straight up in the center of each number. If a number hits, then bet 5 chips straight up on each number. If one of the 5-chip numbers hits, you'll receive 175 chips, which should last the evening. The average player should stay at 5 chips until he loses. Then start again with one chip on each of the favorite numbers. If you've got a little guts, add 5 chips to each number if a 5-chip bet hits. You'll then be betting 10 chips on each number. Now if you win, you'll have paid for your plane fare with plenty left over. Don't imitate other roulette players, especially those who spread chips all over the layout. It may seem as if they are always winning, but often they may be betting 20 chips on twenty numbers each time. The odds are 35 to 1, so if you bet 20 chips and your number hits, you've only won 15 chips—and that's only if the number hits.

We had a player who used to bet $5 every spin on each of the thirty-eight numbers on the roulette table. I asked him why he was betting on all the numbers each time.

He replied, "One's got to hit. I can't lose."

I said, "How can you finish winner? You only get 35 to 1 odds, so you lose $10 every time."

"That don't count," the player replied. "I just want to feel what it's like to be a winner. I used to bet only a few numbers, but I never won. They never hit. Now I win every time and people gather around to watch me. They think I have some new kind of system. My wife and I also get a lot of free booze out of the deal. Since I am spreading my money all over the place, the casino bosses and cocktail waitresses ply us with free drinks. By the end of the evening, the old lady and I are well oiled for free and everybody treats me like a big shot."

You know something; this player was right. He stayed at the club for several hours and during that time I bought him and his wife drinks and even treated them to dinner. Of course, it wasn't for free; he paid for the dinner and drinks many times over at the tables, but then so do many players who gamble just as stupidly and don't get drinks or dinner compliments of the club. I would not consider this player a mental giant, but, still, he had his own form of logic. He expected to lose in Las Vegas anyway, so while he was there at least he would be treated like a high roller.

Bahamas Casinos

There are two popular casinos in the Bahamas: the El Casino and the Paradise Island Casino. They are very pretty, and there are no entrance fees.

My main complaint about the Bahamas is the attitude of the local residents. The Bahamas have had trouble with locals, because they have been known to harass tourists and are envious of the casino help imported from other countries such as England. I don't advise tourists to stray too far from their hotels at night. The Bahamas is one place where you can truthfully say, "The natives are restless."

The first of the new casinos in the Bahamas was opened in 1964. It was the Monte Carlo Casino, now closed. Then the El Casino was opened in 1967, and the Paradise Island Casino opened in 1968. Before these clubs opened, there was only one gambling club in Nassau, the Bahamian Club. It opened seasonally for about forty years for just ten weeks each year. It closed several years ago.

El Casino—Located in Freeport. A very large club with six crap games, twenty-eight 21 games, five roulette wheels, a Big Six wheel, and about two hundred slot machines, each with a 25¢ minimum. The casino is across from the King's Inn Hotel, next to the International Hotel.

Paradise Island Casino—Located just over the bridge from Nassau between the Hotel Britannica and the Paradise Island Hotel. It is a very large, crowded casino with a tiny lounge at the entrance that seats three people and has very little other sitting space. If you want to sit down outside the bar area, you've got to sit at the tables and play.

The club has eight crap games, fourteen 21 games, six roulette wheels, plus about three hundred slots with a 25¢ minimum.

The future of gaming is up in the air in the Bahamas, because the islands have gained independence from British government and now are a commonwealth within the empire. The local politicians, with the coming of independence, have vowed to make several changes. Business dropped around 23 percent in the early 1970s. Some people have attributed this loss to the locals, who have harassed the British subjects and tourists. Hopefully, with this new independence, the Grand Bahamian leaders will modernize their crap games and eliminate the 5% game. But if crapshooters went to the Bahamas and played as I've advised, the politicians would have little choice but to eliminate the 5%, because their revenues would drop sharply.

How to Play Roulette in England and Europe

For tourists who want to spend a leisurely evening in an English or European casino and not tax their brains, I advise playing American-style roulette. But treat French roulette, which abounds in European and English casinos, as if it were fly paper and you were a fat, sluggish fly.

The percentages for American-style roulette are much better for the player in England than in most other world gambling centers. In Nevada, for example, "0" and "00" on the roulette table layouts increase the percentage for the club. But in England and in many European casinos, only "0" appears on the layout; the "00" has been eliminated. This practically cuts the percentage against the player in half, because most roulette wheels have thirty-eight numbers (1 to 36, plus 0 and 00). With the "00" gone, you have thirty-seven numbers, but you are paid the same odds (35 to 1) as if you were playing with thirty-eight numbers. There is one less number (00) on which you can lose your bet.

There is another important advantage in playing American-style roulette. Many players like to make wagers that pay even money if the right numeral or color shows. These "even money" bets include "odd" or "even," "red" or "black," and numbers "1 to 18" or "19 to 36." In many other gambling centers, such as Nevada, the Caribbean, or the Bahamas, if the "0" or "00" shows on even money bets, the casino takes all your bet. But in many European casinos, the club only takes half your bet or puts your chips in prison and gives you another chance.

These extra bonuses on roulette odds fit right along with the percentage advantages English casinos give in 21 and craps. Some of you cynics must be wondering why our jolly English neighbors are being so generous. It's simple. English casinos are trying to capture a bigger share of the global tourist gambling trade by advertising England as the best place in the world to gamble. But they aren't being completely honest. You don't hear foreign casinos announcing that some of their games, such as French roulette, aren't such bargains.

Even if you're an experienced American gambler, stay away from French roulette unless you have a photographic memory, can fluently speak the language where you are playing, and aren't afraid to raise hell in the middle of the most sedate casino.

Here's why. In American roulette, the dealers give you a chip colored differently from other players' chips when you buy in to play the game. The chip color you get is yours as long as you are playing, and there cannot be any mistake as to who gets paid when a number is hit. If you have a red chip with a green dot in the middle and you put that chip on number 6, and 6 hits, there is no confusion about who owns the chip.

But in French roulette, many players generally will get the same color chip. This leads to problems, especially for the poor bumbling American in a foreign country, equipped with only his vest-pocket dictionary and the half-dozen words he remembers from some high school language course.

Imagine a foreign casino with several American tourists and local residents clustered around a table. Spread over the layout are piles of the same color chips belonging to a dozen different people. The chips are stacked everywhere, on top of each other, and spilling over each other. Then a number hits that's covered with chips from a half-dozen bettors.

Chaos.

And who always gets the worst of the mad scramble that follows? The American tourist. He stands there fumbling through his dictionary trying to explain to the dealer that one of those winning bets was his.

But the dealer, who spoke English moments before, now can only mumble some words in his own lingo while he pushes the stacks of chips toward the locals. In my journeys through Europe, I've seen this happen over and over. Also, locals arguing with locals about who the chips belong to. I blame the French roulette croupiers and management. They are the creators of all arguments. Sitting on their buttocks must affect their brains.

If there is any action on the table, when a number hits the croupier will start pointing to the chips on the number with his rake and sort of look around like asking "Whose chips are these?" It seems that whoever raises his hand first has the best chance of receiving the bet. God forbid that two players should raise their hands at the same time. Then the argument starts.

Croupiers are given tips for the service they give to the players. They must have complete control of the game and have a good idea about who the bets belong to. But from what I have seen in my travels, all croupiers who deal French roulette should go back to school and be taught how to distinguish one player's bet from another's. Some acquaintances of mine, who would rather spend six months figuring out how to make $100 dishonestly, have used the American tourist and French roulette to make themselves a nice living.

One of the legendary masters, who has been bilking American tourists for years in Europe, is a man we shall call only "Kelly."

Kelly worked for me as a dealer in Las Vegas several years ago. Then he decided to take a two-month leave of absence for a European vacation. When he returned, he began enrolling in correspondence courses to learn foreign languages. We didn't see much of Kelly outside of working hours for about one year. Then one day he gave me two weeks notice and told me he was going to Europe with a "sure-fire money-making system." That's all he said. Then he vanished, until two years ago when he returned to Las Vegas and asked me to meet him for a drink. Instead of the pudgy, balding, pasty-faced dealer I had known for years, Kelly now was suntanned, svelte, with a beautiful mane of snowy white hair. His hair, of course, was a "rug," but with today's experts, you couldn't tell the difference. He looked as if he were a judge or banker, and that is exactly what Kelly wanted. It was the key to his success.

After several drinks, Kelly's tongue loosened and he disclosed how he was making his living off American tourists playing French roulette.

It sounded simple at first. The hardest part, Kelly explained, was finding the right partner. He needed an attractive American girl with style, class, and guts. That kind of woman (pardon me, ladies) would be hard enough to find in this country, but Kelly needed one who also was familiar with England and Europe, and who was living abroad. He advertised in several London newspapers for two months, and said he interviewed more than thirty girls. Finally, he found a pretty guide for a tourist agency who was bored with her job and who fit the bill. (He later divorced his American wife of twenty years.)

Anyway, after much coaxing and reminding Kelly of how I gave him his first job, and put him back to work after he first returned from Europe, the old con man reluctantly agreed to meet me when I went to Baden-Baden that spring and to let me watch him operate while I was surveying the casino there. A few days after I arrived, Kelly called me at my hotel, the Brenners Park, and told me to go to the casino, browse around until he arrived, but then keep a safe distance and give no sign of recognition of him or the girl.

Kelly entered the casino about an hour after I arrived. He bought several hundred dollars worth of chips and strolled around as if he were a big player, fiddling with his chips, making a couple of bets at different games, and moving on. He was impeccably dressed in a tuxedo, expensive patent leather shoes, modish glasses with sweeping gold rims, a large black sapphire ring, and a heavy gold watch.

About forty-five minutes later, the girl, whom we shall call Francine, arrived. She brushed by Kelly. He slipped her a stack of chips and later told me that he had whispered "goatee." Francine wore a simple, low-cut black dress with a strand of pearls that almost matched the two giant pearls her low-cut dress was trying to contain. Francine and Kelly acted like strangers after their brief meeting.

After cruising the casino for nearly thirty minutes, Kelly went to a French-style roulette table, with a 10DM (Deutsche mark) minimum (about $3.60), made a bet, and then walked away, but not too far away. That was the signal for Francine. The table was crowded with Americans and locals betting 10, 50, and 100DM chips, a nice big game. Kelly knew that the bigger the game, the better. All the players were big bettors. Typical was an American, a slender man with a wispy goatee, who was wearing a beautiful gray silk tuxedo. He obviously was a wealthy tourist out for an evening of fun.

The American was betting 50 and 100DM on the numbers. He would bet one number straight up, meaning he would get the full 35 to 1 odds on that number if it hit; he would also "star" the number with several chips around it, so not only would he get paid 35 to 1, but he also would get paid on the splits and corners if that one number hit. Francine also would bet one or two chips on the same numbers as the American, and they would have an occasional disagreement about who got paid when one of the fringe numbers hit. This went on for nearly fifteen minutes. Then the American hit the "star" number, which was covered mostly by his chips and a couple of Francine's. The American threw his arms into the air with excitement.

"I finally hit the big one!"

But Francine interrupted in a low, sweet voice: "That is my number. I have been playing my birthday all night."

The American looked stunned. He quite reasonably thought he was alone in starring that number (it was 23).

The two started arguing. The supervisors were at a loss. Rarely did two Americans fight with each other over bets. And as always happens at a gambling table, the other players were concerned only with their own bets, and the croupiers, until the shouting began, were more worried about rubbing their numb legs from sitting than watching who was betting on the different numbers.

Francine started crying, the American's face was turning purple, and the two supervisors were mumbling to each other, trying to figure out what to do.

Then, from the edge of the knot of people that had gathered, Kelly stepped between the two antagonists and began talking rapidly to the supervisors and dealers in excellent German. The two bosses looked at each other, shrugged their shoulders, and one nodded toward Francine. The color drained from the American's face as the dealer pushed the huge pile of chips toward Francine with the wooden rake. A supervisor tried to explain to the American what Kelly had said but he grabbed what was left of his money and stormed out the front door. The American had starred the number 23 with 100DM chips, one chip straight up, four on the splits, and four on the corners. The payoff to Francine was about $5,400. It was the biggest score she and Kelly had made that year.

I've seen this type of move hundreds of time during my forty years in the gambling business, but rarely in roulette. A "claim bet" artist usually works around crap tables, because players often lose track of their bets on the complex layouts, especially if they are novices or have been drinking. But I have to admit I never had seen the move performed with such finesse as Kelly and Francine handled it that night.

Later, back at the hotel, Kelly explained to me the only part I hadn't understood: what he said when he stepped in. Kelly said he told the bosses that he had been idly watching the game while waiting for his wife to come out of the rest room, and he happened to be watching that particular play. He said the American simply had not been on that number that time, and the girl had. He told the supervisors that yes, it was a confusing situation, but because of her attractiveness he had been watching her closely as she leaned low over the table to make that specific bet. Kelly asked me to keep secret how he identified himself to the supervisors, saying it had taken months of brainstorming to think up the "perfect" identity and he wanted to keep that to himself. The real clincher was his ability to speak the language and look as if he knew what he was talking about.

But Kelly also conceded that this was an exceptionally lucky "score" and often he and Francine would have to settle for $300 or $400 a week from several small scores. Kelly and Francine also didn't live as richly as they dressed. They had purchased a motor home, and that's how they traveled from country to country. They would spend their money carefully and frugally.

Kelly's main problem now, and it was becoming a serious one, was how to keep the croupiers and supervisors in the different clubs across Europe and England from recognizing him, because he had been to most of them several times. A change of disguise would ruin his stately image, although he had purchased a professional makeup kit, and both he and Francine were experimenting with different disguises. It's a problem that scores of slot cheaters, card hustlers, and 21 counters have experienced. Nevada casinos all have photographs and records of the known cheaters, and most bosses can spot them on sight. Once a cheater has been "made" by the club, he is doomed. No matter how good he is, he might as well learn to drive a cab. Many cheaters who are too well known in Nevada have tried other parts of the world, with varying success.

But Kelly is limited to those casinos which have French-style roulette and which are large, with a lot of American tourists. He and Francine now are trying to adapt some of their moves to craps, which is becoming more and more popular in foreign countries. If that works, and as long as new casinos continue to open in this global gambling boom, Kelly and Francine may continue for several years traveling the world in comfortable fashion, compliments of the gullible American tourist and inept foreign casino employees.

Kelly did most of his business during the high tourist season in Europe—from May to October when the American tourists are plentiful.

But don't let Kelly's story lull you into thinking that only big players such as that American in Baden-Baden can lose their chips to a claim bet hustler. It happens constantly on a much smaller scale to small bettors, such as the average American tourist is. I've seen it happen in London and in many casinos in Europe, including Baden-Baden, Monte Carlo, Cannes, Nice, Athens, Estoril, and several others.

When the arguments start in foreign casinos, it always will be the locals who win out, regardless of what the game is. Remember that.

Unlike American-style roulette, where your chips are worth only what you bought them for at the table and can be cashed out only at that game, the chips in French roulette, which can be round or square and different colors, are worth their face value in cash. They can be use at any game in the casino or can be cashed out at the casino cage. This easy conversion further tempts claim bet hustlers and grifters to operate around French roulette wheels.

So stay away from French roulette; but with a definite betting technique and money management system, you can have fun playing American-style roulette. When you buy chips at an American-style roulette table, you must tell the croupier what price chips you want. Signs above the wheel give the minimum and maximum bets.

Remember, these American roulette chips, unlike French roulette chips, are good only at the wheel where you're playing, and while you're playing. If you leave the table with the chips or take them out of the club, you may end up with some pretty expensive souvenirs, because if you return to the table to cash them, the croupier may give you a blank stare. Chances are he won't know or remember what you paid for them, and somebody else may be using your old color. Now you've got a handful of chips that aren't good for much, as hundreds of players have found out. They taste lousy, even with ketchup. They are too light for fishing sinkers, but they do skip across the water well, even better than a flat, smooth rock. I had one player tell me he and his son got fourteen skips from one chip, but he would have preferred rocks. They are much cheaper. These plastic chips cost the clubs about 14¢ each. In England, most clubs have a 25 pence (about 65¢) or 50 pence (about $1.25) minimum. Europe is the same, or higher. At that rate of exchange, the casinos don't care if you cart out the American roulette chips by the wheelbarrow.

But those minimums are pretty high for the average American wheel player, who likes to buy a stack of twenty chips for 10¢ or 25¢ each in the States and other parts of the world, and likes to spread the chips all over the layout. It could be an expensive or even tragic evening in London if you play this way, with each chip costing from 62¢ to $1.25, or more.

Here's a betting method so that you'll maybe last the evening and possibly even win a few dollars. First, pick out four or five numbers which strike your fancy, such as anniversary dates, birthdays, your wedding date (if you want to remember that) or, as is becoming more common, your divorce date. Then bet each one of those four or five favorite numbers straight up with one chip, meaning take one chip and place it directly on the center of the number.

If others are betting on the same number, put your chip on top of theirs. Now, if one of your four or five numbers should hit, meaning that the little ivory ball drops into the slot on the wheel that has your number painted on it, you'll receive thirty-five chips. Your next bet would be five chips on each number. Five chips is enough to bet on any one number each time, especially in roulette. If one of the five numbers should hit again, you'll have a hundred and seventy-five chips, but your next bet still would be five chips. Five chips is enough. Don't be greedy. Don't try to break the club. It hasn't happened very often, if ever. Stay at five chips until you lose, meaning until none of your numbers show up on the next spin. Now your bet would be one chip on each favorite number. That is the idea of money management in American-style roulette. Stay at one chip until you hit a number again. If you want to pray, then pray that two of your numbers hit in a row. With a hundred and seventy-five chips, you can play all evening with the club's money.

A minimum stack of chips in England would cost about $12.50 American, so roulette in England is not a cheap game. If you start going bad and lose two or three stacks of chips, you'd better call it quits and try something else that tourists do in England. Have a spot of tea, stand out in the fog and get mugged, catch a cold, drive around in a vintage Austin taxicab, listen to Big Ben tick, or watch the changing of the guard. Just call it a night at the gaming tables.

Roulette is strictly luck, contrary to what many people think. And obviously your luck at roulette hasn't been good that night. Roulette is not a game of skill. It doesn't make any difference what numbers you pick.

The only skill at playing roulette is managing your money and learning how to play with the chips in your hand so that everybody else at the table thinks you're an experienced gambler. Those are the only two ways to impress upon onlookers and traveling companions that you know how to play roulette.

Learn how to shuffle the chips like cards or flip the chips and cut and stack them into little stacks the way the dealer does. Then your loved ones, and those playing next to you, will "ooh" and "ah," because you have mastered the only skill attached to the game.

I have seen players make little houses and pyramids out of their chips, spin their chips like a top for several seconds, and flip-flop their chips along their fingers and knuckles like a card-trick magician. But if you don't manage your money, all the chip tricks in the world won't help.

Above all, don't pay attention to what European or English roulette players do at the tables. It seems that many European players like to keep track of the roulette numbers that already have come up during the evening or in past days. All foreign clubs even give players special roulette cards to keep track of those numbers. You will see this very often on the French wheels. But believe me, it's just a waste of time. Our most brilliant scientists, mathematicians, and professional gamblers have proved that a number that has just showed has the same opportunity to come up on the next spin as any other number, unless, of course, it's a crooked game. Every spin is a new spin, so don't waste your time keeping track of the numbers as you'll see many other players do.

Gambler's Guide to England

Casino owners and officials around the world, especially in Nevada, may howl in anguish, but the best overall casino percentage gamble for your money is in England. The percentages don't lie. It's the simple truth.

England's crap tables, for example, pay 9½ to 5 on a place bet on the 4 or 10. A place bet on the 4 or 10 in other countries and gambling cities, including Las Vegas, pays only 9 to 5. And England's dice and roulette odds are better on several other bets, which we'll discuss later.

As for 21, England is the only country I've seen with a law ordering casino owners to help the 21 player get the best bet for his money. Every club in England must display government-approved "suggestive rules" at each 21 table. The croupier must not allow the player to vary from some of the rules, which is a lucky thing for most 21 players.

England also is one of the few countries I've surveyed where dealers are forbidden to accept tips. Thousands of tourists, particularly tip-happy Americans, don't realize it, but this no-tipping law is a blessing. Night after night, year after year, I've watched untold numbers of players all over the world leave a table busted and disgusted, while the dealer they've been tipping lavishly all evening ends up with a pocketful of chips, their chips. Don't tip in any country unless you leave the table a winner. Only a sucker tips his money away before he wins. This no-tipping rule was started in June 1970 by Sir Stanley Raymond, the chap appointed by the Queen to keep England's gamblers honest and on their toes and to clean up the country's tarnished gambling image. I must say that he is doing a very good job.

Widespread gambling started in England in the early 1700s, long before the Monaco or Monte Carlo casinos existed, and when the residents of Las Vegas were a couple of Indians who probably gambled only on who could catch the most jackrabbits each day. But England was governed by men who loved to play cards and dice. Englishmen still talk about the fourth Earl of Sandwich (1718-92), who was so busy gambling that he hated to leave the tables for any reason, so when he got hungry he had his favorite cook slice two slabs of bread from a loaf, put some mutton or cheese between the slices, and bring it to the gambling tables along with a tankard of ale. Hence, with a slurp and belch, sprang the word "sandwich."

But when Queen Victoria took power in 1837, she banned gambling. Barmaids and tavern owners were arrested if a dice cup or cards were even shown. The gaming ban continued until 1960, when Queen Elizabeth approved the Gaming and Betting Act for licensed clubs and their registered members.

Clubs sprang up across England, especially in London, but the English hadn't been active in casino-type gaming for more than a hundred years, and they were babes in the woods.

Cheaters from all over the world came to London to test the ability of the English casinos to catch them. These cheaters showed the casino owners how little they knew about protecting the games. It cost English casinos millions of dollars to realize what was happening to them, especially when it came to the 21 "counters" and dice cheaters.

Some cheaters I know said they made enough money to retire for life. But through the years, the English casinos have gradually learned how to protect themselves. The lessons were painful.

By 1968, the English Parliament realized that legalized gambling had turned into a monster. There were more than 2,500 gambling licenses issued in England with no real control over the clubs. It was a nightmare for the honest casino bosses, players, and tourists, but the cheaters, crooked bosses, and con men were in seventh heaven. Then a high Member of Parliament pushed through a tough reform bill giving complete control to the gaming board. Some say this MP was a big punter (big gambler) who had argued with a casino owner over a bet and pledged that he was going to get even and teach the clubs a lesson. But whatever the reason, the casino owners didn't know what hit them.

One of the few smart things the newly empowered gaming board did was to journey to Nevada and learn how the games are policed, and how to keep tight security in the casinos. Now, under Sir Stanley's iron rule, some casinos are doing very well, though many owners have told me they are scared stiff of the gaming commission because it can shut them down for little or no reason.

In London, in 1972, while I was writing this book, I called on a few clubs. Some, such as the Palm Beach Club, Playboy Club, and the International Sporting Club, said they didn't want me to check their clubs. They didn't even want to admit me. The bosses said they were afraid that I might write something derogatory about the club, which might cause Sir Stanley to swoop down on his white horse and close the place. I hope that was their only reason for barring me. I would hate to think I was banned because those casinos were up to some skullduggery and that I might spot it. I got into those casinos anyway by applying through proper channels for membership and paying the admission fee. The club owners probably knew I was coming, but there was little they could do to stop me. I gave the games close scrutiny and I must say they were very well run casinos.

They have good reason to be scared. The gaming commission, with its new dictatorial powers, has revoked more than 1,500 licenses. To get a license now, you must be a combination of Abe Lincoln, J. Edgar Hoover, and Billy Graham. Casino employees also now must be licensed, and there is an unwritten law that any casino employee caught gambling in any club will be fired. Suggested betting rules were ordered to be displayed at all 21 tables, and the commission directed the clubs which survived the purge to give players better odds at the crap tables, especially on proposition bets. I guess the vindictive MP who started the whole thing was a proposition player.

But the new law that really zapped the casino owners and dealers was abolition of all tipping in casinos. In the past, the club owners had been keeping 80 percent of the dealers' tips. The dealers would split the leftovers each week. This was great for the casino owners because their lion's share of the tips paid for much of the casino overhead. The rest was gravy. But that gravy train is finished now. No tips for any dealers in England. But in Europe, casino owners still can skim their croupiers' tips, so if you are a softy and like to tip the croupiers, just remember that most of that tip will go to the bosses.

And, unfortunately, some of England's other gaming laws have backfired. These laws have cost casino owners millions of dollars in revenue, and have caused thousands of tourists to leave England, fuming. The 48-hour law is typical and one of the silliest. It requires a foreign tourist to register with each club he wants to visit and then wait 48 hours before he is allowed to enter that casino so that British authorities can check out the tourist to make sure he is not a "gangster." I'm afraid that Sir Stanley has been watching too many American movies. What really happens, of course, is that the average American tourist visiting England for the first time, or for just a few days, doesn't have the foggiest notion about the 48-hour rule and is shocked to learn he can't visit or spend his money in the clubs. He usually finds that out during the last days of his visit, when it is too late to register. I watched one New Yorker beg the guards at the Playboy Club to let him in. He reached into his pocket and pulled out a thick book of American Express traveler's cheques.

"My money's good all over the world," he yelled. "What do you mean I can't come in? What do I have, bubonic plague or something?" He was not admitted.

Even if you survive the 48-hour quarantine, 99 percent of the clubs charge an admission fee ranging from $10 to $25. If you are a good player or you know one of the casino executives in a London club, then you might be able to get around the admission fee. Phone ahead to the club and mention that you are coming over. The casino executive can invite you in as an "honorary guest." That way you don't have to pay the admission. Or if you have played heavily in a club, don't be afraid to ask the boss to phone ahead to the next club so that you might be able to beat the admission price. In Nevada we call this using your "juice" to ease the way.

Nevada still has the finest casinos, entertainment, atmosphere, and style of handling players in the world, but the major clubs in London run a close second, though you, the tourist, still must take precautions that you wouldn't have to worry about in Nevada.

Once you have decided that you're going to gamble in England, you must quickly but very carefully choose the clubs where you want to register.

As I have advised for most non-Nevada gambling, stick strictly to the major clubs. Don't venture off the main trail into the small hit-and-run joints. They have small bankrolls and can't afford for you to win much. It is very tempting for them to pull a few shenanigans. And the limits in most small clubs are low (about $50 tops), so you can easily lose a lot of money but you would need a fantastic lucky streak to win very much; and if you get stuck, the low limits may prevent you from ever getting even.

Just stay with the major clubs in the London area.

Another thing, in America and in most other gambling centers, the slang expression for a big bettor is "high roller." And a small player is called a "small player." Makes sense, but in England they call big bettors "big punters," and small bettors "small punters." So don't be surprised if you hear yourself, or some other player, referred to as a punter of one size or another. But the nickname for American tourists hasn't changed, no matter what casino you enter in any part of the world. We still are called "suckers."

Here are ten tips before stepping out on the town to gamble in England:

1. Don't worry about dress. Wear the same clothes you would during an evening of night clubbing in the States, but don't get too casual: tie and jacket for the man (or for the women, as the case may be).

2. Major clubs are open from 2 p.m. to 4 a.m. on weekdays, and to 3 a.m. Sunday beginning Saturday nights.

3. Don't cash traveler's cheques or American currency for English money in the casinos. Banks generally give you a better rate of exchange, so there's no sense getting the worst of it before you even make a bet.

4. If you just like to play slot machines, then you might not want to waste money spending the entrance fee in London because major clubs are allowed only two slot machines, which take only a 6-pence coin (about 12¢), and often the two lonely machines have lines of people waiting to play them.

5. Expect to pay an entrance fee of up to $25 at each club, except a few. If you just want to tour a casino, it might save money to phone ahead and check if there is a fee.

6. London casinos aren't for boozers. No drinks are allowed near the gaming tables, and the bars close by 11:30 p.m.

7. Don't worry about addresses because cab drivers know the locations of the major clubs. But be careful, because the cabbies and bellhops in some hotels might try to steer you to smaller, outlying clubs so that they can get kickbacks from the club owners as a reward for luring tourists off the beaten track to the boondocks.

8. English casinos are very strict on credit. Don't expect credit

unless you have impressive references and credentials. For example, you can't make "call" bets (a spur of the moment bet without immediately putting up cash), but must play with cash or go to the cashier's cage and get some, if you can.

9. Minimum and maximum bets vary among the clubs, but generally speaking you can usually get by with a minimum bet of 50 pence and £1 on 21 and craps in most games at most major clubs.

10. A final bit of advice: There's an English law that you can't be taxed for the money you win, but our Internal Revenue boys consider that to be a valid law only if you live in England.

21 in England

There's no question that England gives you the best deal in 21 for your money, and that's good. But the English also give you the fastest deal, and that's bad. In England, the dealers, whose salaries range from $65 to $185 weekly, aren't allowed to accept tips, so they don't waste time with small talk or in slowing down to kibitz or help a potential tipper. Most English dealers don't smile, or even yawn. They deal the game as if somebody had a gun stuck in their backs and their lives depended on how fast they flipped the cards around the table and scooped in the money.

This attitude startles Americans, who are used to the friendly dealers in Nevada and other gambling centers. American players, who are not known among professional gamblers for their brilliance, don't realize that 99 percent of the friendly dealers in the world are just hustling the players for tips. But in Merry Olde England, often you are just another lump of flesh sitting at the table, whether you bet £1 or £100. If you aren't prepared mentally when you sit down, English 21 dealers will run over you, so here's a money management and playing method to slow them down and give you a chance.

First, watch the game for a while and become familiar with the cards, which are different than American cards. Make sure you know the value of the chips. Most 21 games in England have a 50-pence minimum (about $1.25). Some clubs also have £1 minimums (about $2.50) and tables for big players with £5 minimums. You also should know the maximum bets, because they can range from £50 ($125) to £200 ($500) in a few clubs which cater to high rollers. It is important to know the maximum bet so that you don't get stuck and suddenly realize that the club limit isn't high enough to let you get your money back unless you win fifty hands in a row.

Once you sit down, don't let the dealer buffalo you. Don't be afraid to hold up your hand and say, "Just a minute, please. I haven't made up my mind." If you make a mistake and the dealer scoops your money into the tray, you can't promise him that it won't happen again and ask for another chance. Speak up. Dealers are not ogres or wizards. They are human beings.

But don't be a jerk, either. Casino dealers have it rough enough. Many people think that being a casino dealer is a glamorous, "swinging" profession where you "frolic" to sleep every night with the young jet-setters who have been hanging around the tables. Many young dealers break into the business thinking about the glamour of the casino, but soon they realize it can be a dull, tedious job. The only guarantee is that you'll get plenty of abuse. Being a dealer probably brings more abuse from customers than any other job there is, except maybe being a doormat. A dealer's only defense is to tune out the player mentally and just deal the game, unless, of course, the player is tipping, in which case the dealer is tuned in and is all smiles. But usually the player is losing and the dealer gets the blame, not the cards or the casino. I've heard dealers called every foul name in the book, plus a few new ones, and sometimes all in one evening. You name it, a dealer's been called it, especially after a player has had his courage bolstered by a few drinks. If a player had a fight with his wife, or if his wife has a sunburn, it's the dealer who gets it in the end. Even when some players start winning, they still give the dealer static. Sometimes it sounds like a personal victory over the dealer with remarks such as "Now I've got you on the run, you son of a bitch. Ha ha ha. Ho ho ho. Hee hee hee." I've seen players go on and on, cackling with glee for several hands. Of course, the dealer looks at them as if they've lost their marbles. Dealers in most legitimate clubs outside England want players to win, otherwise they won't get any tips.

Of course, a dealer has to be very careful about his facial expressions. I had one dealer we called "Smiley" because he grinned all the time, regardless whether the players were winning or losing. Smiley couldn't help it, and occasionally a player would ask him why he was smiling. Smiley always answered that it was his birthday and he was thinking about the party his wife and two lovely children were planning.

That answer always satisfied the customer. One night an elderly woman wearing a mink stole and an impressive array of finger, neck, and arm jewelry sat down at Smiley's table. She was friendly and polite until she lost eight hands in a row. Naturally, Smiley was smiling. After losing the ninth hand, the woman got up and asked, "What are you smiling about, schmuck?"

"It's my birthday," Smiley replied, "and I'm thinking about the little party my wife and two children are planning for me when I get off work."

"Isn't that sweet?" said the woman. She motioned for Smiley to lean forward and she whispered into his ear. It wasn't happy birthday.

Smiley quit smiling until she left the table.

But sometimes a dealer will try to be a wise guy, too. Usually that backfires, as one rookie found out a few years ago. It was in the Sheraton hotel-casino in Aruba, a tiny island eighteen miles off the Venezuelan coast. I was casino consultant for Sheraton Hotels at the time and was in charge of the casino. We were closing for the night when one of our regular customers, a Venezuelan bush pilot for some American oil exploration firms, came in with two of his "lady" friends. The dealers groaned, because this bush pilot, who was as wild as the jungles he flew over, could gamble and drink American Scotch all night, and he never tipped the Aruban dealers. Venezuelans and Arubans have no love lost for each other.

The pilot started betting $100 a hand at 21 for himself and $50 for each girl. He couldn't win a hand and lost several thousand dollars very quickly. The dealer was smug and started jabbering to the other dealers in Papiamento, the island language that few outsiders understand.

The pilot, now very drunk and very mean, muttered under his breath in Spanish, "Talk so I can understand, or keep your mouth shut."

The dealer, a young hothead, short on brains but long on guts, snapped back, "What's wrong—you a bad loser?"

With a flash of his hand, the pilot reached over the table, grabbed the Aruban by his tie, pulled him across the table, and slashed off the tie right below the knot with a straight-edge razor he had pulled from a jacket pocket. "The next time it will be your throat," he said and flipped the table over on the terrified dealer, grabbed his two girls, and stormed out.

The five Aruban dealers still working that night were incensed. They jumped up and down in a frenzy, but not one ventured out after the bush pilot, who had headed for the casino across the street, apparently already forgetting about the incident. The bush pilot, always loud and boisterous, lost thousands of dollars in the club every month and never really bothered anybody. The only damaged items that night were the dealer's pride and his two-dollar tie. And most important of all, the dealer had asked for trouble with his big mouth. The bush pilot was back the next night, loud and boisterous as ever, but not a dealer uttered a peep to him in Spanish, Papiamento, Yiddish, Pig Latin, or any other language.

The pilot incident is an extreme case, but it shows what can happen when people are gambling with their own money, whether it be $1 or $1,000. Their whole personality can change.

A Midwestern American rabbi who has been visiting Las Vegas for years is an example of this Jekyll and Hyde syndrome among players. The rabbi would come out twice a year. It was a standing rule that "Mr. B" did not want anybody to know about his rabbinical background, and for good reason. It was obvious that he came to Las Vegas to release some of the frustrations and aggravation that his congregation had been heaping upon him all year. The dealers, who didn't know he was a rabbi, feared him because he was especially obnoxious when he was losing, and that happened quite often. He was such a big player that the dealers knew they couldn't say much for fear of losing their jobs.

On his latest trip, it got unusually bad the first evening he arrived. He had been losing and drinking for three hours. It got to the point where every time he lost a hand he would call the dealer, male or female, a "son of a bitch" or worse. Finally, I gave him a polite warning. He laughed, and after the next hand, which he lost, he promptly called the dealer a son of a bitch. I walked over to the table, took a $25 chip from his stack, and dropped it into the dealer's pocket. "There's a $25 fine here for swearing at the dealers, Mr. B, and it doubles each time," I said, and walked off. Mr. B did not utter another foul word that evening, or for the rest of his stay in our casino, but every time I sauntered by his table, his lips would move silently in what I am sure was a prayer wishing me the best of health and happiness.

These incidents happen constantly to casino bosses and dealers around the world, but I doubt if you will witness them in England, because they're very restrictive about liquor in English casinos and many Americans appear subdued by the sedate atmosphere of English and European clubs, and the gentlemanly, sometimes stuffy, attitude of English and European gamblers.

Money Management and Betting for English 21

If you're a small player ($1 to $2) or just want to experiment, your first bet would be 50 pence. If you win, your next bet would be £1½. You're betting faster because you're playing against the shoe in most cases (see Shoe chapter), and you must jump one bet to give yourself a little edge. Now let the £1½ ride. Your next bet would be £3. (£1 is about $2.30.) Your next bet would be £3, and you scoop in £3. Then if you win, bet £5 and, if you win that one, bet £8. That is high enough for the 50-pence bettor.

If you are a £5 player (about $12.50) your first bet would be £5. If you win, then bet £15. If you win again, jump to £30, then £30 again, then £40, and, if you win, then £50. That is high enough for a £5 bettor. It's like betting $125.

For a £10 bettor (about $25) jump to £30 after winning the first bet, then £60, £60 again, then £90, and finally £100 maximum. At this point, a player must know the table limits, which are shown at each table. Make sure you know what they are, especially when you start betting £50 to £60.

A £10 bettor cannot play at a £50 maximum table, because he may never get even if he gets stuck. You must play at a £100 or £200 maximum table. Some clubs, like the Victoria Club in London, which has a £50 maximum, sometimes will raise the limit for a big bettor. If they don't, then you must use the £5 betting method.

As for doubling down or splitting a hand, there is no law that says you must do either. Let's say you are a 50-pence player who has reached a £3 bet and you catch a 10 or 11. If you don't have enough money in front of you, you do not have to double down. Just hit the hand as I have advised earlier in my chapter on 21. This also applies to splitting a hand. You do not have to split two 7s against a 5 or 4.

Just hit. You don't have to double down on your first big bet, like £3. If you keep winning, then you can double or split if the hand calls for it. Don't wipe yourself out on the first big bet simply to split or double down. Those are not cinch bets, and there is no guarantee that you are going to win. Just try to analyze the hand and don't try and push yourself into saying, as so many players do, "I have 11, so I should double down." It's fine to do that when you are winning and going good; *then* take advantage of every play.

The most common bettor I noticed in England was the £1 bettor. The £1 bettor is similar to the $2 bettor in Nevada, the most common bettor there. In England, if you win your first £1 bet, then wager £3, and, if you win, bet £6. The next bet would still be £6 so that you can have a little playing money. Then if you continue to win, bet £9; your next bet is £12, and your highest bet would be £15 (about $37.50). Stop there. That is high enough for any £1 player ($2 bettor). And, as in playing any other casino game, the moment you lose a hand, you immediately revert to the minimum bet with which you started.

For example, if you're a £1 bettor and you win the first bet, your next bet is £3. If you win that bet, your next bet is £6. But if you lose that bet, go right back to £1 as the next bet.

While playing 21, you must remember to play the cards and not the amount of chips in front of you. If the hand calls for a hit, then you must hit. Don't let the amount of chips bet play the hand. Just close your eyes and say, "Hit."

Gamblers in foreign countries often look awkward when they play because they are unfamiliar with the chips, or some of the games, and often the rules. This especially applies to 21 where kibitzers can hang around the table to see how you play your cards. Don't let anybody play for you at any time wherever you go. This can easily happen in a foreign casino where one of the locals, whether it be in England, France, Germany, the Caribbean, or any other foreign gambling center, might offer to play for you. Just tell him to get lost, despite such phony pitches as how great he can play or that he knows the local dealers and can speak the language. Just ask this wise guy, "How come you're not playing with your own money if you are such a good gambler?"

Don't worry about this problem much in England because the rules are listed at each table. It is difficult for someone to suggest that he play the game for you when the rules are in front of you.

Why is England the only country that actually gives the players good, intelligent instructions to play 21? Well, my investigation shows that when England first opened up, the counters and cheaters had a field day. They really took the clubs to the cleaners. The English were new at modern gambling, but in time they learned by asking questions, by losing untold sums of money, and by visiting Nevada officials to learn how they stopped counters and cheaters. Englishmen learned that counters, for example, will play 21 erratically and not according to the best way to play the game when they have determined that the cards are going in their favor. So mandatory rules at each table hinder counters. In the old days, if the cards were going good for the counter, he might split pictures or 10s against a high card. Also, he might split 9s, possibly double down on soft hands, like an ace and 5, or even an ace and 8, against certain face cards. But with the new rules, the counter can't do this. The new rules make the counter play like everybody else, and he doesn't like that.

Each blackjack table in England has a printed card with the rules. I have devised a better 21 playing method in my 21 chapter, but when playing in England you should be familiar with their rules.

The rules include:

1. A player can take insurance only when he has a blackjack, not on any other combination of cards. The insurance bet must be placed before any player can draw a card, though I advise to never take insurance.

2. A player may double down only when his first two cards total 9, 10, or 11. The player is advised to double down only when the dealer's card is a 2, 3, 4, 5, 6, or 7.

3. If a player's two cards have the same value, he may split, receiving an extra card face up for each hand, subject to the following rules. The original bet goes on one hand and he has to put an equal amount on the other hand. The rules state that 10s, 5s, or 4s may not be split, but other pairs may be split. Players are advised to split aces and 8s always, and other pairs only if the dealer's card is 2, 3, 4, 5, 6, or 7. A player may split only once. One additional card will be dealt to each hand before a third card may be drawn if required on the first hand. A player may double down on either hand after splitting, with the exception of splitting aces.

4. Players are advised to stand with a hard total of 12 or more if the dealer shows 2, 3, 4, 5, or a 6. The player should stand with a total of 17 or more if the dealer's hand shows 7, 8, 9, 10, or ace. A player always should stand with a soft total of 18 or more.

5. A player having a total of 11 or under must take a card.

6. If a card is dealt and is in excess of the player's requirements through a misunderstanding, that card shall not be used in the game. The inspector's decision shall be final in any dispute.

My 21 playing method is much simpler and stronger for the player, but if you get confused don't be afraid of these posted rules. They are in favor of the player, and they make it very difficult for the player to make a mistake.

If you had read my book *How To Win,* you would have noticed that quite a few of the rules were from my book. But my hitting and stopping is for a single deck, *not* for a shoe as is dealt in Europe.

How to Shoot Dice in England

Near the entrance to the Las Vegas airport, there is a sign declaring that dice and other gaming odds are better in England than any other place in the world. The sign is correct to a point. All crap odds are not better in England, but some bets, such as the propositions, are better. But remember, a proposition bet is one of the worst bets on a dice layout. Proposition players pay for the overhead of the gaming casino and the employees' salaries. Propositions are displayed invitingly in the middle of the dice layout. They include "two aces," "two sixes" (which is 12), "11," "ace-deuce," "any craps," and all the "hard ways," such as the hard 4 and 10 and the hard 6 and 8. English propositions do pay more than Nevada clubs and other clubs around the world. In England, two sixes (12) pays 33 to 1, while in Nevada most clubs pay 30 for 1 and some pay 30 to 1. On the hard ways, English clubs pay more than Nevada clubs. A hard eight pays 9 to 1 in Nevada, compared to 9½ to 1 in England. A hard 4 or 10 in England pays 7½ to 1 compared to 7 to 1 in Nevada, and placing the 4 and 10 pays 9½ to 5 compared to 9 to 5 in other casinos.

But stay away from propositions and place bets and stick to the Pass line. On most English layouts, the Pass line is called the Win line. This is where the player betting to win places his money. This means you the player will be a right bettor, or a win bettor. Don't worry about other bets on the layout, such as the hard ways, crap, eleven, aces, or sixes. Those propositions are for the sucker players. The smartest and toughest player at a crap game is the one who makes one bet—I repeat, one bet only—and takes the odds on the number. Also, he bets more when winning and less when losing.

American crap shooters don't like to play this way. Americans gamble like they have only five hours to live. They are always in a hurry. But remember, you're on a vacation and you must play wisely or else you won't have a chance for your money in a foreign country.

Enjoy your vacation. Pay heed to what I say and you'll become a tough player. The gaming clubs will respect your ability, and, best of all, you might win some money.

The first thing to learn is that you must bet on the Win line and you *must always* take the odds. That is very important. The odds are the only thing you get free in a gambling club. By betting on the Win line (Pass line), you are making the smartest bet for your money. You don't have to just bet on yourself when you throw the dice. You can bet with any other shooter. Betting on another shooter is the same as you shooting the dice. If a 7 or 11 is thrown on the first roll, you win. Then make the same bet. Don't raise your bet. If a crap (2, 3, or 12) is thrown on the first roll, the croupiers will take your money but then you still make the same bet. Don't raise it.

The only time you raise your bet is when you win after a number is thrown on the first roll. These special numbers are called points. They are the 4, 5, 6, 8, 9, or 10. When one of these numbers is thrown, take the odds on the number. That is a must. Always take the odds. By taking the odds, you're lowering the percentage against the number and it's a free bet. Place your odds bet a few inches behind your Win line bet. This tells the croupier that you're taking the odds. If you're ever in doubt on the odds, don't be ashamed to ask the croupier what odds to take. He must tell you.

Here's an example of using odds. Say you're betting £2 (around $5) and the first number rolled is a 5 or 9. You then put another £2 behind the £2 on the Win line. If the point is made, you'll receive £3 for the £2 you had behind the line, because the 5 or 9 pays 3 to 2 odds. You also would receive £2 for the £2 you had on the Win line, because that was an even money bet. The same method applies to 4 and 10 which pay 2 to 1. You are allowed to put up as much behind the line for odds as you have on the Win line. This also applies to the £1 bettor in betting the 5 and 9 or the 4 and 10.

The 6 and 8 pays 6 to 5 odds, so if you had £2 on the win line you can put up £2½ odds behind the Win line. You will then receive £3 for your odds bet behind the line if 6 or 8 is made. This simple playing technique will keep you out of trouble. And if a hand shows (by "hand," I mean that numbers are being made and the dice are passing), you should make some money.

Casino owners do not relish the player who bets only the line and takes the odds, because he is giving up the least possible percentage on a crap table, less than 1 percent (about 0.8 percent).

But just as important as betting is money management. Proper management of money in gambling is the difference between a winner and a loser. Many players recklessly gamble their money away early in the evening, so when the big hand finally shows, they have nothing left to bet. You can't play without money and you must be especially careful to limit your losses when you're gambling in foreign countries. You must quit after you lose the amount you decided to gamble. Under no conditions dig into your pockets to try to get even. Just quit for the evening. Tomorrow's another day. The downfall of thousands of tourists is trying to get even the same night. I'm sure you've heard players say, "Maybe I'll get even if I try another $100." That comment has ruined many marriages and vacations. Once you start gambling in a foreign country, you must stay on your toes. Remember at all times the value of the money compared to American dollars, because when you're going good the croupiers will convert your £1 chips to £5 chips, then to £25 chips. That's done so you will bet more, and most players do, so you had better know what you are doing.

A friend of mine, playing in London last year, bought in for $500 in English pounds at a crap table. He likes to place the 6 and 8. He gave the croupier two £25 chips and two £5 chips. The denominations on the chips made my friend think he was betting $30 on the 6 and $30 on the 8. It wasn't long before he lost the first $500, so he bought in for another $500 and lost that. Then he bought in for another $500 and lost that. He could not understand why he was losing so much money. Finally he asked a croupier the values on the chips he had been scattering across the table.

"Are these $25 chips?"

"No," said the croupier. "It's a £25 chip. You are betting £30 on the 6 and 8 (around $75)."

My friend bet slower and more carefully after that.

Money Management

The best way to gamble at a dice table, especially in a foreign country with foreign currency, is to use a money management system. Let's say you're a typical American tourist making a £2 bet at a dice table in a London casino. Your first bet is £2 to win. If a 7 or 11 is thrown, you'll win, but still only bet £2 on the win line. If a crap is thrown, you lose, but your next bet still is only £2. Increase your bet only if a number (point) is made. If a 4, 5, 9, or 10 is thrown, you put £2 directly behind your money on the Win line for the odds. If the point 6 or 8 is thrown, put £2½ behind your money on the Win line for the odds. If the point is made, your next bet is £6. Now you're betting a little more, not much more, but it will give you a better chance to win faster. This is called "jumping" a bet. Every time a 7 or 11 is thrown, always make the same bet. And every time a crap is thrown after you have made a £6 bet, then, on the next bet, bet half. For example, if you had bet £6 and the shooter threw a crap, your next bet would still be £3. If a point is thrown (4, 5, 9, 10), take £3 odds. (If the point were a 6 or 8, take £5 odds.) If the number is made, your next bet is £6 and £6 odds. If the shooter makes this point, only two numbers have been made, but now you're in a very good position to win a few dollars. You've invested around £7. Your next bet is £10. If a point is thrown, you take £10 odds on the number. If the number is made, your next bet is still £10 and £10 odds. That will leave you with some reserve to bet with on the next shooter, if the present shooter should "miss out" (throw a 7).

Now you are playing with the club's money and that's the best way to gamble in a casino, with somebody else's money. If you win the second £10 bet, your next bet would be £15 and £15 odds. And that is high enough for £2 bettors. You're now betting around $37.50 on the front line and $37.50 behind. If a few numbers are made, you could win enough to pay for part of your vacation. After two numbers have been made, you should be in good shape if you bet properly. Every bet you win after that is with the club's money. Now if the shooter continues to make numbers, the real gutsy player won't be afraid to bet it up (progress at £5 a number) until he reaches £25 and £25 odds. Do not flinch. You're only playing with chips. And do not take any money down as long as the dice are passing. Remember, every roll is a new roll. Nobody can foresee when the dice will pass or miss. So don't be a guesser. By managing your money at the crap table, you will last much longer, and you will be respected, especially after a few numbers are made. Don't be a hit and miss player. Those are the ones who use crystal ball, tarot cards, and guesswork to make their bets. And those are the players gambling clubs wish would come in more often.

If you have enough guts to reach the £25 bet and the shooter does finally miss out, then start with a £5 bet with the next shooter. You now have enough money to win a possible big score. If the next shooter does not make a number or just makes a couple of numbers and misses, revert to the £2 bet. I repeat, go right back to the original bet and, this way, you'll always have a chance for your money. Never bet more unless you win. Nobody knows what the next shooter is going to do, so you have to manage your money and hang in there. If the dice are cold and are missing, just walk away from the table and go play blackjack or watch the girls (or men, as the case may be). Give yourself a chance to cool off. Don't let the dice take advantage of you. Don't pay attention to what other players are doing. You won't be as busy as they are because you have only one bet to watch. Let the wise guys who think they know what's going on make a lot of bets at the table. If all American tourists practiced money management, took the odds, and made only one bet at a time, then London casinos would have a harder time beating us out of our money.

The limits in most clubs in England are high enough for most players. The major clubs have from £100 to £200 maximum bet. But not everybody bets the same, or wants to bet the same. So here are different ways to manage and progress your bets depending on the size of your wallet.

For the £1 bettor (about $2.50): begin by putting £1 on the line and £1 odds behind. The next bet would be £3 and £3 odds (take £5 odds on the 6 or 8); next bet £3 and £3 odds, then £6 and £6 odds, and finally £10 and £10 odds. That is high enough for the £1 bettor. Stay at £10 until the shooter misses out (throws a 7), then start over again at £1.

For the £2 bettor: begin by putting £2 on the line and £2 odds. After the point is made (if 6 and 8 is thrown, take £2½ odds), the next bet would be £6, £6 odds, then £10, £10 odds; £10, £10 odds again; £15, £15 odds; raise £5 each number to £25, £25 odds.

For the £5 bettor: £5, £5 odds; then £15, £15 odds; £25, £25 odds, £25, £25 odds again; £40, £40 odds, and finally £60, £60 odds.

For the £10 bettor: £10, £10 odds; £30, £30 odds; £50, £50 odds; £50, £50 odds again; £75, £75 odds; and £100, £100 odds.

A £15 bettor: £15, £15 odds; £45, £45 odds; £75, £75 odds; £75, £75 odds again; £100, £100 odds; and £125, £125 odds.

A £25 player: £25, £25 odds; £75, £75 odds; £125, £125 odds; £125, £125 odds again; £150, £150 odds; and £200, £200 odds.

If you're a big player, I don't believe you should jump right to the maximum £200 bet as you might do in Nevada with a $500 bet. Do not get involved so quickly in foreign countries. If you've got plenty of time and plenty of money, that does not mean you should give it away by betting fast. In England, they call big players "big punters," and many clubs will raise the limit for a big punter. But that isn't done for the ordinary player who bets £5 and £10 at a time. If he gets hooked and wants casino bosses to raise the limit, they will not do it. They'll use the old expression. "Get out the way you got in." You have to be very careful. It is very important to know the limits of the game before you start playing. Even a big punter should play conservatively and use money management. I advise that he use the £25 betting progression. He'll get up to the £200 limit ($500) fast enough if he makes a few numbers. Also, he won't get hurt if the dice miss. He can recuperate much faster.

I realize that many big punters and experienced players who are used to a lot of action, especially with a few drinks under their belts, are not going to be content with making just one bet at a time. For these players, it is okay to make a come bet or two after a point has been made on the Win line. This will allow a little more action; and if a hand shows, you'll make more money.

In making a come bet, you are in effect trying to make two numbers instead of one: the Win line number and the come bet number. You play and manage your money on the come bet the same as you would on the Win line. Increase your bet when you win and revert to your minimum bet when you lose. By making one or two bets, shooting craps becomes very relaxing. You'll get much enjoyment watching the exasperated and confused expressions and gestures of the other players who look like octopuses as they move all over the dice layout with their chips. Actually, 90 percent of the crap players don't know how to play and are trying to figure out what to do next. But you don't have to worry about that. Every move is planned in advance and it will show in your playing. You won't be classed as another American sucker.

As for the proper time to quit, well, if a few numbers have been made and the chips are piled in front of you, then start thinking about going back to the hotel. Give the next shooter a chance in case the dice should continue to pass, but quit if the next shooter misses out. Do not wait for another shooter. Cash out and leave the club.

Players that club owners would like to hang by their thumbs are the players who bet one number, take the odds at all times, bet it up when winning, and stay at the minimum bet when losing. Those players are the toughest crapshooters in the world. But if you remain an ordinary crapshooter, you will be in the same category as millions of other players—you will be called a "live one," which means a chicken ready to be plucked. Take your choice.

Wrong Bettors

There's nothing wrong with a wrong bettor, who is a person who bets against the Win line (with the house) or on the Don't Come line. There are quite a few players who bet that way. If you are a wrong bettor in England, just make one or two bets and *never* lay the odds. I've seen dice go completely around the table with not one shooter making the point. The trouble with wrong bettors is that they like to lay the odds, especially laying 2 to 1 against the 4 and 10. And this has ruined many of them. My money management system is applicable to a wrong bettor. Just don't lay the odds.

Nick the Greek, the famous American gambler, was strictly a wrong bettor. He never bet right in a crap game in his life. But Nick lost millions of dollars betting wrong. Shortly before he died, he admitted to me that laying the odds ruined him when he was betting wrong. So take it from Nick the Greek, there's nothing wrong with betting wrong, but don't lay the odds, especially when you're on vacation and on a short bankroll.

Guide to London Gaming Clubs

There were hundreds of gaming clubs in London in the late 1960s, but the government closed most of them during the "purge" years after the 1968 reform bill passed. Now there are about thirty in the London area.

Here are a few major ones I recommend:

Playboy Club: Park Lane area. Membership £10 ($25) per year. Most popular club in London, but stay away on a Saturday night because it seems as if half of London's tourists and lords and ladies are climbing over each other to get inside. Playboy bunnies dressed in blue velvet with white bunny tails check credentials at the door. There are bunnies running all over the place as dealers and other club workers. They have specially designed little bunny outfits that push their bosoms up toward their faces and they all but fall out whenever they move around. Club is five levels high: first level—orchestra, dancing, drinking. On the second level, a special VIP room done in blue with blue velvet furniture and fixtures, soft lighting with crystal and gold chandeliers. 21 and roulette games are scattered in little alcoves as you wander up through the different levels. The third and fourth floors contain most of the casino games, including French and American-style roulette, craps, punto banco, and 21. Fifth floor has plush VIP apartments. All gaming rooms narrow and crowded, a good spot for pickpockets, so sew your bankroll to your undershorts or panties. Some casino rooms only about 20 feet wide and about 150 feet long with games lined on one side. Can get crowded as hell; skinniest casino I've ever seen. Betting limits vary. French wheel: £1 to £10 on straight up bet or star bets; £200 maximum on dozens and column bets, and £500 maximum on even numbers. 21 bets vary greatly and are labeled at each table, ranging from 50 pence to £100. Craps £1 to £200. Punto banco, £2 to £300.

Ladbroke Club: Berkeley Square. Membership fee about $10 per year. Originally a card room and home of the fourth Earl of Sandwich. Beautifully decorated. The Ladbroke organization have been London bookmakers for over a hundred years, and they seem to have spared no expense in redoing the house as a casino. You enter into a softly lit, thickly carpeted, paneled foyer. Three "charming" gentlemen in tuxedos check credentials as in most other clubs. Walls covered with expensive brown embossed suede from Spain. Crystal chandeliers; atmosphere quiet and sedate. Small restaurant and cocktail lounge. Soft lighting. Walls decorated with horse paintings valued at more than $500,000. Dinner superb, wines excellent, about $10 a person for full-course meal, plus wines. Gaming is in two different sections with main casino on second floor and crap game on third floor. Standard casino games, including American-type wheels, baccara, punto banco, and 21. Dealers very cordial and dressed in tuxedo-type outfits. Most croupiers are English. Standard minimums and limits on games. 21, for example, 50 pence (about $1.25) to £200 (about $500).

Victoria Sporting Club: 150 Edgeware Road. Only London club really resembling Las Vegas type casino, but on smaller scale. One of biggest London clubs, and one of most popular and busy. Not as fancy as others like Playboy Club and Ladbroke; about $10 admission fee for foreigners. Just fill out application and wait the mandatory forty-eight hours unless you are invited as a guest by a member. Locals pay membership, about $10 a year. Bright lighting. Entire club done in red carpet and walls. Three floors. Large, busy casino. First floor has restaurant. Whole place has Las Vegas look and feel about it. Service not too good. It took two hours to get a spot of tea in restaurant until employees found out I was studying their casino. Then bosses and waiters swarmed all over me. Casino has men sitting on high ladder above each game. Best method to protect crap game, from above. Standard limits on most games. Deal £50 limit on 21; but if big punter comes in, club will raise limits, say, to £200. Several wheels, one punto banco, one chemin de fer. On fourth floor is large card room with about forty tables, plus a bar and lounge. Here they play kaluki, the most popular game in London, especially among women. Also popular with American ladies. Have a room curtained off where they play stud poker. Games have £10 stakes, also a £25 stake game. With kaluki and these other games, you must put name on a waiting list similar to busy Las Vegas pan parlors.

International Sporting Club: Berkeley Square. Membership £3. Shabby gaming equipment, small club. Don't think they do much business, was closed a few years. American wheels, three 21 games, one crap game, one punto banco, no French wheels. Once called the Colony Club, which was first club opened by Americans in London, about six years ago. Did a booming business and was run like a Las Vegas casino. George Raft was the host, and celebrities visiting London would drop by. But after a few years, the government closed the club over suspicions of possible underworld affiliations. The goverment then decided that no Americans should be running English casinos and kicked them all out, apparently on the premise that all Americans are gangsters with "rods" in their jackets and a "gun moll" nearby. The law in England now is that you have to be an English subject to be an executive. That law will keep most Americans out, because who wants to be an English subject? Bosses are trying to rejuvenate this club, but they aren't doing a very good job of it. All male dealers. Owners apparently under the impression that women do not belong in gaming casinos, but there still are plenty of girls working in some clubs. As you enter this club, you walk down three flights of stairs on a spiral staircase as if you were going into a basement speakeasy of the 1920s in America. Small casino, restaurant, and cocktail lounge. Trying to make club different by spreading women's jockey uniforms, hats, and blouses all over the walls. When women's horse racing began in England, International Sporting Club owners were trying to capitalize on it, but decorations look ridiculous, unless you like to look at ladies' jockey outfits. Then it's a great place to go. Has standard minimum and maximum bets.

Knightsbridge Sporting Club: 163 Knightsbridge; five-minute ride from Playboy Club. Caters mostly to locals, but I recommend it highly. £5 membership charge. Large, square gaming room, very pleasant, but not expensively decorated. Gaming area similar to Las Vegas with crap table, four wheels, three 21 games, and one chemin de fer which converts into a punto banco table. Cordial atmosphere. All female croupiers, very pretty and very sociable. The boss personally interviews, selects, and trains them. He seem to be doing an excellent job. I wonder what his secret is. Girls dressed in white blouses and long Scotch plaid skirts. Player can feel at ease in this club. Has standard minimum and maximum bets.

Parklane Casino: Park Lane area. Membership fee $10 American. Entrance richly carpeted and paneled. Looks like a foyer in a home, and it was. Employees cordial. Enter casino via beautiful winding marble staircase surrounded by mirrored walls. Club has gorgeous Oriental wall-to-wall rugs. Atmosphere quiet, subdued, elegant. Has full range of games. Equipment and gaming area in good condition. Uses standard foreign cards, which are large Spanish cards with large numbers, easy to distinguish; sort of a cardboard card that is worn out after one night's use. Much easier to read than our Bee cards in the states. Drinks are typical prices: Scotch 25 pence, 35 pence with soda, liqueurs 50 pence.

Palm Beach Casino Club: 30 Berkeley Street. Gaming in one large room with a full selection of standard games. All male croupiers. 21 table betting prices vary sharply. You can bet 25 pence to £50 on some tables, with other minimum bets of £5 to £50. Punto banco minimum is £2 to £1,000; crap limits: the Do and Don't line, 50 pence to £200; field, 50 pence to £200; hard ways, 50 pence to £20; propositions: ace-deuce and 11, 50 pence to £12; aces and sixes, 50 pence to £6; any crap, 50 pence to £24. This club has the largest French wheel limit in London, £2 to £100 straight up and star bets; £200 on splits, £400 on corners. American style roulette games, minimum bet 50 pence.

Crockford's: 16 Carlton House Terrace, SW London. $26 membership (entrance) fee. One of Europe's and England's oldest and plushiest casinos. Closed since 1970 when French-Algerian owners were run out of the country, along with many other foreign casino owners, under England's new gambling rules. Club, reopened in late 1972 at a cost of $2.6 million, was founded in 1828 by William Crockford after he won $100,000 in one night playing hazard, so the publicity agents claim.

Wide range of games, including American-style and French roulette with a 50-pence minimum bet and a maximum of about £100. Standard 21 and dice limits. Also has punto banco, draw and stud poker, and kaluki, plus slot machines. The club's restaurant and main bar are on the ground floor, gambling on the second, third, and fourth floors. Normal operating hours. Whole casino is elegantly furnished down to its four hundred handsomely upholstered chairs and stools; has crystal chandeliers, paneled walls, cheery fireplaces; beautifully decorated ceilings. New members must play with cash. Other facilities include a racing room where members may make their own bets over telephone. Casino buffet on the second floor which offers quick service and light meals, and an after-midnight breakfast.

Downtown Clubs—If you are staying in the downtown area, the Golden Nugget is near Piccadilly Circus; The Sportsman's Club is on Tottenham Road, a couple of miles from the Circus. These clubs deal all games; not lavishly furnished. But if you are interested just in gambling and not scenery, the clubs will accommodate you. They deal the same limits as the plush clubs.

The Continent

I must tell travelers this: If you make advance reservations in European hotels you are usually requested to pay one day's rent in advance. You must make sure on leaving the hotel to double-check your bill. I have had a few occasions where the advance deposit was *not* deducted from the bill. I'm sure it is an honest mistake at most hotels, but *check!*

My advice to the American tourist playing in European casinos is not to do what the European players do. You do not have to throw your money away by tipping as often as they do, because after a couple of hours play they are broke and croupiers and casinos wind up with the tips. Do not worry what they think of you, the croupiers or anybody in the casino, when you do not tip if you're hitting a number or playing blackjack and win a couple of hands. The only time to tip is when you are through playing. If a person kept track of the tips that he gave up during the course of his play (and remember, some people play for quite a few hours), he'd find he'd have enough money left to try to get even or else maybe play a little longer at the end of an evening. Play your own way; do not play the way the Europeans play.

Also, take my advice and speak up when you think something not right is happening. Do not be bashful; it's your money. When you think you're not getting the right payoff, you have an argument; argue about it. You paid your entrance fee, and you paid for the privilege of playing in their casinos. That is sufficient.

If you should be a winner at the end of an evening, cash out and leave a tip accordingly. But don't be over-extravagant. The croupiers just deal and are not worried whether you come back or not. They feel about tipping that's the way it's supposed to be, because it's been that way through the years. But I don't think that American tourists, who maybe play only once a year in some of these casinos, have to be forced into giving tips every time they hit a number. Yet it happens in 21 and even crap games in certain countries. Don't do it.

Baden-Baden Casino, Germany

Baden-Baden has the most magnificent casino that I've seen in the world. I urge you to visit it, but please don't necessarily gamble there, because some of the games are designed for people with a lot of money who want to get rid of it in a hurry.

The gambling complex is in the center of town, in a huge marble building, and was opened more than two hundred years ago. Admission is 4 Deutsche marks (DM) (about $1.44) for one day and 7 marks for two days. You must show passports, as at most other European clubs. Attire is dressy. The main casino, called Salle Louis XIII, is gorgeous, done in crystal, gold, marble, and gilt-edged wallpaper. Paintings, tapestries, hand-painted and antique playing cards, and other historical objects line the walls. Furnishings in the Salle Pompadour room are from the Louis XIV period. Years ago gold and silver jetons were used as chips at the roulette wheels in this room. Murals cover the ceilings as in the Sistine Chapel in the Vatican in Rome. Richly decorated salons and alcoves are scattered through the casino complex. Cocktails and pastries are served in small bar areas, but not in the casino. If you want to drink and gamble, you have to grab a drink, sip it in the bar area, then run back to your table and play. Or, have your girlfriend or wife (or both) hold the drink behind you at the table so that you can turn around and have a taste while playing. Also, there is no restaurant in the casino complex. If you're hungry, eat before you go inside.

The casino has three chemin de fer games, four American 21 games, where you must reserve a seat (big deal), two American-style roulette wheels, and nineteen French wheels, including one with a huge double layout in a beautiful room by itself, called Salle Pompadour (or Salle Louis XIV). Limits range from a 2DM minimum (about 72¢) on some games to a maximum of 9,000DM on even money bets on one high-roller French roulette game. The 21 games always are crowded. Sometimes you even need a reservation to get a seat, mainly because the other games are strange to tourists, or else they have been reading my French roulette chapter.

The croupiers run a poor second compared to American and English dealers of either sex. In Baden-Baden all croupiers are men and slow, sloppy, and inaccurate. The 21 dealers actually sit in chairs while they deal, which might be a good idea, because some croupiers looked too old and rickety to stand up for more than ten minutes. They are in no hurry here. They have been playing and dealing this way for two hundred years and the razzle-dazzle of the Western gambling craze doesn't seem to faze them. Even the playing cards are old and ragged, and the croupiers shuffle them as if they were paper plates. They use the cards for weeks on end and often these pasteboards become unreadable. Apparently they can't afford to buy new cards. The cards are French, and you have to become accustomed to the numbers which are shaped differently from those on American cards. I suggest you watch the game for a while, and watch the cards.

Baden-Baden has a 10DM minimum (about $3.60) on 21, and a 250DM maximum (about $90). They don't deal in odd amounts, only in sequences of tens (10, 10, 30, 40). You cannot bet 12 or 13 marks; and if you are normally a $15 to $25 bettor in America, don't bet too highly at the Baden-Baden 21 tables or in the rest of Germany. The low limits there can hook you. And if you should get hooked, pardner, you'll never get out. I advise to stay at the minimum bet and move up very slowly if you are winning, and don't move up at all if you are losing. I don't care if you are a multimillionaire and are used to betting $500 right from the start in Nevada, because if you start immediately betting 250DM in Baden-Baden, your multimillionaire days may be over. Just relax, enjoy yourself, and save your heavy betting for a casino with decent limits.

Also, do not tip or make a bet for the croupier while you are playing. Wait until you are through and you're a winner. Only suckers, novices, and greenhorns who don't understand the game tip while losing and playing. The games are tough enough to beat without giving your money away. I've sat down and played in Baden-Baden and watched the other bettors give the croupiers 10DM or more every time they won a hand. Of course, during the play they are also buying more chips. So the croupier winds up with all the tips and the Americans wind up with empty pockets. Croupiers in Baden-Baden are very sly at weaseling tips, but they're certainly not as brazen as some of our Nevada dealers. In Baden-Baden the dealers do everything with their eyes; they try to outstare you. I've noticed that when big numbers hit on roulette, or somebody wins a big bet at 21, the croupiers spread the chips out very slowly in stacks of five and count them as if they were worth a king's ransom, explaining to the player very meticulously and slowly that he has won. As they count and explain, they stare at you with puppy dog eyes as if they each had a wife and 36 kids at home to feed and you are Mister Scrooge. It's what I call the "soft hustle," and many players I watched turned out to be soft touches. All the croupier has to do while he pays off a big bet is to outstare the poor player, and out of guilt the croupier often will receive a tip. But many times these same players will lose the next ten bets. I wonder what would happen if they asked the poor, watery-eyed croupier for their tips back?

What you need to play 21 in Baden-Baden is a simplified system so that you can relax. It's a beautiful place, and just for a few drinks and the admission, you can stroll around and admire the opulent surroundings. But if you want to play, take it easy, don't double down on any hand regardless of what it is. Just hit the hand and don't look for trouble. You won't have to worry about putting up more money, especially when doubling down on a big bet and losing. Just use the simplified betting method explained in the 21 chapter. And don't split any pairs except aces. There's no reason to spread your money thin. But don't worry too much, because the dealers are so slow in Baden-Baden that after several minutes you'll probably become bored and leave the casino or go to another type of game. The dealers aren't too accurate with their counting either, so be alert. Baden-Baden is what we call a "grind store" in 21. They just want to grind everybody out of their money because the limits are too low for you to win much.

But there is one bonus in Baden-Baden 21. They call it the "five card trick." If a player draws five cards without exceeding the total of 21, he can be beaten only by a blackjack. Also, don't be surprised if someone puts money alongside your bet. In Baden-Baden an onlooker is allowed to make a bet in a box on a strange player's hand, but the total bets cannot exceed the table limit. At least the standing player, who may be a complete stranger, can't give advice to the sitting player on whether to draw or stand, or how to play the hand—

or bawl you out if you lose. The rule states that only the player sitting can act on the hand.

After watching the 21 action for the past few years on my trips to Europe, I've come to the conclusion that Baden-Baden casino bosses never wanted to put in 21 tables because it detracted from the glamorous European gaming atmosphere. But they had to put it in because their customers, many of whom are Americans, have played the game in other parts of the world and have demanded it. Even the sleepy Baden-Baden casino operator couldn't pass up more money. But the 21 tables and the two American-style wheels are set off in a separate room as if they were some kind of bastard child who showed up on the doorstep. It looks like an old storage room they re-decorated.

Stay away from the French roulette wheels which are all over the place in Baden-Baden. They're poison, as I've explained elsewhere in this book. Fortunately for Americans, in June 1972 Baden Baden installed two American-type wheels with different colored chips. Just stick to that game. One night I acted like a typical American tourist and began playing French roulette. Within four plays I had eight contested claims on chips I had bet on the layout. Of course, most of the other small players were betting the same colored chips. In the eight disputes I won six and lost two. The others didn't speak English and I didn't speak German, and it is a known fact that American tourists have rarely won an argument on a French roulette bet.

On the American-type wheel, progress the way I've suggested that you play in England. You bet the minimum amount, making four or five bets straight up. If you win, then bet five chips on the same number straight up, and that is the biggest bet you make.

You'll have an enjoyable evening playing that way, and one thing is for sure: nobody can make a claim against your chips.

They have three chemin de fer games in Baden-Baden casino and, as I've explained in previous chapters, they are strictly for the suckers.

Don't look for slot machines in Baden-Baden or other German gambling casinos, because they just don't have them as yet. Why, I don't know. Often American tourists will play the slots heavily because they don't know how to play the foreign games.

But it seems that even outside the casino many locals consider the Americans to be suckers. There was a newspaper stand near the club, and I went there one evening to buy an American paper. A little old lady runs the stand. I gave her a 10DM bill, which is worth about $3.60. She said she didn't have enough change, and offered me two little Chiclet gum boxes, those tiny little boxes that hold two square hard pieces of white sugar-coated gum. Shrugging her shoulders, she gave me some change and the Chiclet boxes as if the gum were supposed to make up the difference. She was short 8DM, which is about $2.88. I guess she figured I was a sucker American; but in the nicest voice I could muster, I told her to give me all my money back and I would go elsewhere. She shrugged her shoulders sadly again; but then, fumbling through a little pocket in her apron, she pulled out some crumpled bills and lo and behold! by some magic, she had discovered she did have the correct change. And she was such a sweet-looking old lady, too. Shame, shame.

Austria

Austria has seven casinos all owned by a private organization, the Austria Spielbank Co. The government is Spielbank's partner and controls the gaming.

The two most popular casinos are the Cercle Wien in the heart of downtown Vienna, and the Baden spa about thirty minutes drive from Vienna. The Cercle Wien is the classic casino of Austria. (Wien, pronounced "veen," is the German name of Vienna—and German is Austria's language.) The daily entrance fee is 100 schillings, which is about $5. No weekly fees in this casino. After buying an entrance ticket you are given a 50-schilling "jeton" (like a chip). This eases the pain of paying the 100 schillings, which is the highest entrance fee of any casino I've been to in Europe. This jeton is the same as a free play in Nevada. You must bet the chip because they're not cashable. If you win, you receive one 50-schilling jeton which *is* cashable—a much better deal than many other casinos in Europe where you pay an entrance fee and receive nothing in return.

Inside, the Cercle Wien is an ordinary little casino with three French wheels and a 21 game in a small room. A chemin de fer table is in a side room. The sign states "baccarat" but it is really a chemin de fer game. I do not advise Americans to play chemin de fer—leave it for the foreigners or the locals.

The minimum bet at all games in Cercle Wien is 50 schillings, (around $2.50). That is a pretty strong minimum, especially on the roulette wheel. Don't play the French wheels. The prices are too high, and there's always tension. I didn't play; I just watched the arguments between the players—mostly locals. They fight over who wins the bet. During a two-hour visit I counted twelve arguments. The decision is up to the supervisor as to who won the bet.

Owners of the casinos have what we call a "soft touch." First, the entrance fee is the highest in Europe. It pays the rent. Second, the croupiers do not receive a salary. They depend on tips for their salary. (Or so I was told.) And, of course, you pay for all drinks and snacks at the bar—even if you're the biggest player in town. The croupiers do not like living on tips but they have no alternative.

This system is hard on players, too. When they realize that the croupiers work for tips only, they feel obligated to tip every time they hit a number—which is not good for the player.

There is only one 21 game in Vienna club. It has a 50 schilling minimum ($2.50) to a 2,000 schilling maximum (around $100 American). The 21 game is dealt like it's dealt in England. If you're any type of a fair bettor you cannot play high because of the limit. A $2 or $3 bettor, however, can play at this game. Just use the betting method for a $2 bettor explained in my 21 chapter. Progress as you win, and check my betting method for a $10 and higher bettor. I must warn you: if you are betting a $10 and get up to a $50 bet, you must not let anyone else bet in your box (bet on your hand). The house limit applies to the total bet in the box so that way if you let people bet on your box and you're up to the $100 limit, you cannot bet any more. You must push any other person's bet out of your box when you are winning. Do not be embarrassed or ashamed: just tell them to bet in some other box.

The Baden spa is about fifteen miles from Vienna. Do not take a cab; it will cost you about $30 round trip. The best way is to go by bus, which takes about 35 minutes and costs about $1.75 round trip. Or you can take a surface train which takes one hour and costs a little less. The bus gives you a sightseeing trip through the wine country. The Baden Wien casino is much larger than the Casino Wien and the grounds are beautiful. It is a large complex with a theater, opera house, restaurant, band stand, and picnic grounds in a nice little park. The entrance fee is 50 schillings for the day and you get one 20 schilling jeton for a free play. Or they will charge you 120 schillings for a week and give you two 20 schilling jetons free play.

It is a narrow-shaped casino with nine French wheels, including one "quick wheel," which is a smaller wheel where you play faster and spin the ball faster—no seats. Two 21s, one chemin de fer. Baden Wien opens at 4 p.m., with a 20 schilling minimum on all games.

They have a peculiar 21 rule in Baden Wien. Two players must play before the croupier will deal the cards. One player cannot even play two or more hands to start a game. If you are playing and losing, and the other player (or players) quit and you are left alone, the croupier will stop dealing. There you are, holding your chips in your hand like a dummy, trying to hustle people walking by to play so that you can try and get even.

Belgium

There are a few clubs in Belgium, well spread out, like the Casino Kursaal D'Ostende, Casino Ostend, Casino Kursaal. All have French wheels and chemin de fer.

Do not play at all. At the wheels the club takes 5 percent on all winning bets, which is too strong for the player.

In some clubs the casino takes 10 percent of every winning roulette bet. They call it a state tax. That, of course, is besides tips. It's just plain impossible to win.

The Netherlands
(Holland)

In the very near future the Netherlands (Holland) will have a limited number of casinos in the Amsterdam area dealing French- and American-style games. While waiting for the green light, there are a few small clubs operating on the sneak. When gambling is legalized, it should pick up the tourist trade in the beautiful city of Amsterdam.

France

France has many gaming casinos, and Cannes has two of the prettiest and largest. They are well worth seeing. Just watch your money carefully. What happened to me in Cannes is typical of what is facing American tourists around the world.

I gamble in every casino I visit to see if the player is getting a fair shake for his money. On my latest trip to Cannes, I went straight to the central casino, the Municipal de Cannes, because it had been closed during an earlier visit. It was on a weekend and the casino was jammed. I began checking out the roulette wheels. At the first wheel I put two-franc chips (each about 46¢) on 19, 24, and 28, my three‐children's birthdays. On the third spin, 28 hit. Then I bet five chips on each number again, as I advise in this book on European roulette, money management, and betting. On the next spin, 24 came up. There were about eight chips on the same color 24 when it hit, and five were mine. The croupier paid off the other bets and turned toward me. Immediately I knew something was wrong. The croupier was spreading the chips in rows of five each, as is done in French roulette. I had won 175 chips. No honest, competent dealer in his right mind would count out 35 rows of 5 chips each. It would take too much time, and the player would need a bucket to carry the chips around. Normally, a croupier will give you larger value chips, such as three 100 franc chips, and then twenty-five 2 franc chips to play with, because the total payoff was 350 francs. As the croupier counted out my stacks, he looked at me sadly and counted very slowly as if it were a small fortune and he just needed one or to chips to replace his well-worn shiny pants. But when he got to 7 rows of 5 chips he stopped counting, separated the chips into two stacks, and pushed them toward me with the wooden rake. I gently stopped the rake with one hand, politely put up five fingers with the other, and pointed to the number 24. The dealer looked at me in wonderment. He shook his head and held up one finger. I help up five fingers again. He held up one. I held up five. He held up one and started to make the next spin. I put both hands across the layout so that nobody could make a bet and asked him to call an English-speaking supervisor. The two conversed rapidly in French. Then the supervisor turned to me and I explained how I play, that I bet three numbers with one chip each, and when I win I bet five chips on the same three numbers. So, I said, the croupier owed many more chips. I added that possibly he might have given them to some other player or "locked them up" for the club. I was a little hot under the collar.

The supervisor smiled at me patiently as if he were a kindergarten teacher and I were a naughty child who didn't know any better. He said that I had made a mistake and would I please take my hands off the layout so they could continue the game. I said that, yes, I had made many mistakes in my life, but when it comes to gambling, I rarely make any. I then gave him my card to show him I was a casino executive in Las Vegas and had been an international casino consultant, as well as the author of a best-selling book on gambling. Then I politely asked him again to pay me the total of 175 chips. The supervisor looked at my credentials and started to bawl out the croupier as if all of a sudden the croupier were the bumpkin. They paid me; I picked up my chips and cashed out. The supervisor followed me all the way to the door apologizing over and over. "Monsieur, monsieur, it was a mistake. It can happen, Mr. Goodman." I said, yes, croupiers can make mistakes all over the world, but it was becoming very discouraging to see it happen day after day even in many of the larger clubs, and almost exclusively to the American tourists.

The point is that if I had not been able to prove that I was in the gambling business, I would not have gotten paid.

But if you're in Cannes, at least visit one of the two beautiful casinos. Just keep my little tale in mind if you decide to do any gaming.

Trente et Quarante (30-40)

Trente et Quarante, or 30-40 as it's called by Americans, is very popular with the French people. Americans can learn to play it easily. It's not a thinking game. 30-40 is played with six decks of cards so small that one deck would easily fit into a matchbox.

The croupier deals a row of cards face up as you would in solitaire. He deals until the value of the cards totals more than 30 but less than 40. Picture cards (king, queen, jack) count 10. Aces are worth 1 point, and the other cards count their face value. After the dealer lays out the first row, which is called the "black row," he starts a new row directly under the first row. The second row is called the "red row."

The row with the smaller count of more than 30 but less than 40 is the winner. For example, if the count is 35 on the black row, but the red row total is 34, the red row bettors win.

There are only four bets you can make: noir (black), rouge (red), couleur (color), and inverse. Betting red or black simply means you are betting which row will win, red or black, simply a bet on which row will have the lower count over 30 but under 40. All bets pay even money.

If the count is the same, then it's a tie. You don't win or lose. The only way you can lose on a tie is if both rows have 31 at the same time. Then you lose half your bet. You can insure against 31 showing on both rows at once by putting up 10 percent of your bet as insurance. Then if 31 shows on both rows, you'll win your bet. I advise against taking the 10 percent insurance. Like most other casino insurance bets, the club has the strong edge.

If you put your money on color, you are betting that the first card turned over in the first row, the black row, will be the same color as the winning row. For example, if the markings on the first card are red (hearts or diamonds) and the red row wins, then you win.

If you bet inverse, you're betting that just the opposite will happen. For example, if you bet inverse, and the markings on the first card are black (spades or clubs) and the red row wins, then you win.

The minimum of most 30-40 games is 5 francs (about $1) to a 5,000 franc maximum. This game is played in casinos across France; it's the national game. It's as simple to play as the Big Six wheel in Nevada, where you just put your money on a color. There is no concentration or skill. I've noticed quite a few tourists playing the game, especially women who just want to relax and enjoy the casino and the Continental atmosphere. As for managing your bets in 30-40, just follow the English progression method in 21 and you'll stay out of trouble.

Paris

You can go to quite a few casinos in the metropolitan Paris area, but actually there are only around seven so-called plush private clubs in the greater Paris area. Membership only, and they cater mostly to local trade. Most business is done between 4 and 8 p.m. when businessmen are on the way home or going out to dinner. All a foreigner has to do is show a passport and indicate what profession he is in; no entry fee for foreigners. No women are allowed inside a casino, but some clubs have a card room where women can play card games.

Actually I don't call these clubs casinos, as the only games allowed are possibly one baccara and two or three chemin de fer games. By law, those two are the only games allowed within a radius of sixty-five miles of Paris. No roulette, craps, or 21.

The only casino that allows men and women to gamble together is Enghien les Bains, a large complex about six miles outside the city. They have a restaurant, with entertainment, very expensive, but the casino, which is quite large, only has chemin de fer tables.

One of the plushest private clubs is the Cercle Haussmann, run by a Lebanese group, very nice fellows, very cooperative in answering my questions. They deal $2,000 maximum (American dollars) at baccara, but of course nobody bets that high. Nothing elaborate; just a gaming room.

Most big casinos deal only two shoes a night. I guess this is to let the players keep their money so they can be back the next night. I do not advise Americans to go to these private clubs: in fact, I don't even think they're worthwhile visiting in the Paris area—a waste of time.

Cannes

Located in the heart of the city in a big, beautiful white stone building overlooking the marina is the Casino Municipal de Cannes. Admission fee, 10 francs, 14 francs weekly, 25 francs monthly, and 60 francs for the season (about 5 francs to the dollar). The casino opens November 1 and closes June 1. It opens every day at 3 p.m. and closes when the action stops. There is no official closing time. Like most European casinos, it has a large desk where you must check in and present your passport. Then the clerks check you out through their files, apparently to make sure you are not some American gangster or casino cheater. The casino deals only European games. The casino area is as large as most casinos in Las Vegas. "Elegant" is the only word to describe it. The tables are gold and white under dozens of enormous sparkling crystal chandeliers. The end of the casino area is a bar area with velvet lounge chairs and tables overlooking the marina. A beautiful view; a lovely little restaurant.

No matter how crowded the casino, there's a quiet atmosphere because there are no noisy crap games with Americans hollering for their numbers to hit. There are no slot machines, no drinking and boozing at the tables. Also, Europeans are quieter, and there is much less drinking in general. The casino has two large French double-layout roulette games and two large trente et quarante games in the center, several chemin de fer tables, and a large, beautiful room to the right of the casino with only one baccara table inside. It is roped off and seats are by reservation only. The baccara game is leased by a Greek syndicate. In this game the players play against the house, not like American baccarat. The club earns its rent by charging a 1.25 percent tax for every bet the bank wins. The minimum bet is 100 francs and *no* set maximum bet. Players can bet any amount within reason. The syndicate will book whatever your bankroll can stand to bet. The bank has much more than 5 percent the best of it; and by giving up 1.25 percent, the bank (the Greeks) still has an earning power of more than 5 percent, which isn't bad. It's a great gamble for your money if you're a baccara player. The game is exciting because there is no limit, and there's a lot of big action.

In a rear room there are five chemin de fer games. The house takes a 5 percent rake of the game. All they do is run the game. The minimum bets vary, depending what the banker must start with. One "chimmy" game has a 50 franc minimum (about $11.50); another has a 100 franc minimum, and the largest one has a 400 franc minimum. The gaming equipment is in good condition. The croupiers are all French, and they will speak a little English until an argument starts, at which point they mysteriously forget all languages but French. The four French double-layout roulette wheels have different minimum and maximum bets ranging from a 2 franc minimum to a 20,000 franc maximum on even money bets.

Dealers can accept tips, but remember that the owners keep most tips. The dealers all wear tuxedos and are very cool and aloof. The French government doesn't actually own the casino, but by charging high taxes they rake in 75 percent of the profits of every casino in France. The rest goes to a group of Frenchmen who lease the casinos. The only game I advise playing in the Casino Municipal is 30-40 (see the earlier section on 30-40). It's simple and relaxing.

Palm Beach Club: A beautiful white building surrounded by flowers and plants located on the edge of town toward Nice. Overlooks the marina. The club opens from June 1 (when the Casino Municipal closes) until October 31. Attire is dressy. Admission is 14 francs weekly and 60 francs for the season. Casino opens about three p.m. and stays open until the action dies. It is much larger than the Casino Municipal and has a wide variety of both American and European games. They are located in two separate rooms, and there is a special room for a high roller baccara game. The Palm Beach Casino is beautiful and one of the most exclusive in the world, but the minimum bets on all the games except roulette are very high for the American tourist on any sort of tight budget.

All the games except roulette deal at least a 50 franc minimum bet (about $11.50). That's pretty steep for the average tourist. To make matters worse, most crap and 21 dealers in the Palm Beach Casino aren't very good and usually their mistakes favor the house. So with an $11.50 minimum and sloppy dealers whose mistakes tend to favor the house, don't take a chance and gamble very much in this casino. Don't invest more than $50. If you like to gamble, wait until your last day in town, then go to the casino. That way you won't be able to lose too much, because you'll have to leave town the next day. Remember, a 50 franc minimum is five times more than the typical $2 player in Nevada bets.

The casino has fifteen French wheels, eight chemin de fer tables, the high roller baccara game, two American crap games, eight 21 games, and one American wheel. But the American wheel has "0" and "00" on the layout so nobody who knows what he's doing plays it (see chapter earlier on European roulette). I asked one supervisor why the casino had such stiff minimum limits, higher than almost any casino in the world. He replied, "We're open during the height of the tourist season, and if the tourists want to gamble, they must come here, so we've got to get it while we can." Then the supervisor added, "Stick around and you'll see what I mean." This supervisor was a character. He looked and acted like a "Continental" Frenchman with his tiny little pencil mustache. But whenever he talked about gambling, he sounded like a Las Vegas pit boss. Obviously my French friend had been watching a lot of American movies. He knew all the gambling jargon, mannerisms, twitches, and furtive glances. He would have been a perfect Damon Runyon character.

But he was right about one thing. That night and every other night during several trips I've made to the Palm Beach Club in the last couple of years, the place has been jammed with American tourists, Frenchmen, and others who couldn't wait to get to the tables. But, of course, many times I would watch the Americans—and other tourists unfamiliar with the high limits and strange chips—lose far more than they would have lost in an American casino where they could have made a $1 or $2 bet just to enjoy themselves and see the sights.

Play 21 in the Palm Beach Club as I advised earlier in my 21 chapter; but here there are different betting rules to follow because of the high minimum bets. If you are an average $2 bettor in Nevada or elsewhere, your first bet would be 50 francs. If you win, your next bet would be 50 francs. If you win, your next bet would be 100 francs and 100 francs again. If you continue winning, double it to 200 francs. That is $45 American, which is high enough. Stay at 200 francs until you lose, then drop back to 50 francs. This will keep you out of trouble, for a little while anyway.

If you are a $5 or a $10 bettor, then you can bet a little faster at the Palm Beach Casino. Your first bet is 50 francs, next bet 150 francs, and then 300 francs. Level off with a 300 francs bet again; but if you continue to win, bet 400 francs and 400 francs again. If you win that hand, then bet 500 francs. Now you are betting about $115 American, which should be high enough. Of course, once you start winning, don't let me try to limit how much you should bet. If you've got the guts, then go to 600 francs or 700 francs if you keep winning. But the moment you lose, revert to your original bet of 50 francs.

If you're a $20 bettor, which is a minimum of 100 francs, first bet 100 francs. Then jump to 300 francs and then 600 francs and 600 francs again. Then you can jump to 1,000 francs and 1,000 francs again if you continue to win. Your next bet is 1,500 francs, which is about $340 American.

A $50 minimum bettor should start at 250 francs. Then 750 francs, 1,500 francs, 1,500 francs again, and then 2,000 francs. If you win that hand, bet 2,500 francs (about $550). Of course, revert to your original bet of 250 francs when you lose. A $100 minimum bettor should bet the same as a $50 bettor.

As for the crap games, which also have a 50 franc minimum, I advise the $1 or $2 player just to make one bet only, on the Win line. Many small players like to bet on the come; but with this high minimum, just stick to the Win line. Remember, you are betting $10 and also taking $10 odds. And if you try to get into come bets and take the odds, you'll have $100 scattered across the layout before you know what happened. Your first bet would be 50 francs; and if the number is made, take 50 franc odds. If you win your next bet, your Win line wager would still be 50 francs and 50 francs odds if the number is thrown. Your next bet would be 100 francs and 100 francs odds. If you win that, still bet the 100 francs and the 100 francs odds. If you continue winning, your next bet would be 150 francs and 150 francs odds. Now you are betting $30 on the win line and $30 odds. I advise staying at this limit of 150 francs and 150 francs odds until you lose. Then revert to your minimum bet.

Even if you should lose your money, at least you can say you played at the famous Palm Beach Casino in Cannes.

And by making one bet you do not have to worry about any other bets on the table. Your money will be in front of you if you have to move quickly.

A $10 player should start off with 50 francs and 50 francs odds; then 100 francs and 100 francs odds, 100 francs and 100 francs odds again; then jump to 200 francs and 200 francs odds, and 300 francs and 300 francs odds if you continue to win. If the streak continues, go to 500 francs and 500 francs odds, which means you're betting about $115 on the line, and $115 odds. That's pretty good for a $10 bettor.

For a $20 to $30 player, stay low at first. Your first bet would be 150 francs and 150 francs odds, then 300 francs and 300 francs odds; 300 francs and 300 francs odds again, 500 francs and 500 francs odds, and 500 francs and 500 francs odds again. If you continue to win, then 700 francs and 700 francs odds, and then 1,000 francs and 1,000 francs odds. Stay at that level for the next few bets. Of course, you can go as high as you want to, but be careful.

For the $100 player, I advise dropping down to a $50 minimum in the Palm Beach Club. Your first bet would be 250 francs and 250 francs odds. Then 500 francs and 500 francs odds, and then 1,000 francs and 1,000 francs odds, and repeat that bet for a couple of hands. If you continue to win, your next bet would be 2,000 francs and 2,000 francs odds, and then 2,500 francs and 2,500 francs odds. You're now betting about $550 and $550 odds.

Probably the best game to play in this casino would be roulette, which deals a minimum of 5 francs to a maximum of 10,000 francs. The 5 franc minimum is safe enough for you to enjoy yourself. The maximums on the 21 games range up to 4,000 francs, and there is a 10,000 franc maximum on the crap games.

Nice

Comparing the casinos in Cannes to the casinos in Nice is like comparing Beverly Hills to the Bronx. The main casinos in Nice remind me of the old "sawdust joints" in which I worked many years ago on the East Coast. Those were what we called "come as you are clubs," with no rugs on the floor and a very casual atmosphere. If you want to visit a beautiful French casino, go to Cannes and forget about the casinos in Nice, unless you're bored to death and have nothing else to do. They really aren't much. The casino owners seem to know this because they promote people to come into the casinos by slipping free passes under hotel room doors or by giving them out at the hotels. So if you ask around a bit, you may be able to get into a Nice club free, but even then there are much prettier things to see than the not-so-nice Nice casinos.

The two main casinos also charge a 7 franc admission, if you can't get a free pass, and they do require a sports coat and tie at night. The clubs are the Casino Club and the Palais de la Mediterranee.

Palais de la Mediterranee: a large white marble building with large pillars in front. Looks like a government building. There are seventy-one marble steps up to the casino. Each step is large and wide, and they seem to get bigger and bigger as you near the top. A power lift is available if you have a weak heart or weak knees. The main casino, which looks like a big marble barn, has two American 21 games, two American crap tables, two American wheels, two French wheels, and five chemin de fer games. Much larger in space than most Vegas casinos. The 21 dealers are inexperienced and deal out of old, beat-up wooden shoes. The cards are French cards and look as if they were made when the Roman Empire was still controlling the world. Some of the cards looked like the soles of an old pair of shoes I bought before World War II.

Ten franc minimum on 21 and 1,000 franc maximum. On craps, the minimum bet is 10 francs on the Win line, Don't Come line, Come line, Don't Pass, and Field. The maximum bet is 1,000 francs. Maximum for the Big 6 and 8 is 1,000 francs; any seven 250 francs. A "horn bet" has a maximum of 250 francs and it pays 4 to 2, which is outlandish because in most other casinos you get much higher odds. It shouldn't even be on the layout. 100 franc maximum on 3 and 11, 100 franc maximum on any crap, 150 franc maximum on hard ways. Other proposition bets have maximum bets ranging from 100 francs to 150 francs. Place bets have 1,000 franc maximum; placing the 4, 5, 9, and 10 has a 1,000 franc maximum, and placing the 6 and 8 has a 1,200 franc maximum. The American wheels have a 10 franc minimum.

On the lower level, there are three 21 games, two 30-40 games with a 10 franc minimum and a 10,000 franc maximum, and three French wheels which average from a minimum of 5 francs to a maximum of 5,000 francs. The two American-style wheels have "0" and "00" on them, which the French people don't like. This club is strictly what we call a "grind store." A player shouldn't spend too much time or money here, because if he gets hooked he'll have a hard time getting out.

Casino Club: About a twenty-minute drive by taxi from hotel row. It's not worth the trip. Much smaller than the Mediterranee Club and not too many Americans go there. They have American-style games if you want to spend twenty minutes riding a cab just to see a bunch of old gaming tables.

The croupiers in both clubs speak little English, and the ones dealing the French games hardly say anything at all, either in English or French. If you have a question, it might be easier to hire a French interpreter to take along.

Nice is nice, but stick to Cannes for your gaming in that part of France.

Casino d'Evian

You can either drive around Lake Geneva to Casino d'Evian from Lausanne, Switzerland, or take a boat. Your best bet is the boat—driving takes much longer. Besides, night driving is risky on the small winding roads, especially for Americans. The boat ride takes about 35 minutes on a nice day, 50 minutes if it is stormy like one day I went. The fare is $2.75 round trip. It is a nice ride and they serve drinks, coffee, or light snacks on the boat, which seats around 500 people in the upper and lower decks. Take the boat ride even if you do not go to the casino.

On the boat I saw men and women studying pads and ledgers in which all the numbers that showed on the roulette wheels on their previous trips to the casino were listed. They would compare numbers with each other, why I don't know. What happened on preceding days or weeks has nothing to do with what is going to happen the day they are playing.

Casino d'Evian faces the lake as you enter the town of Evian in France. This casino depends on Swiss trade off the lake. With some 200,000 people in the area, it's more like a local casino.

The town of Evian's claim to fame is its water, which is considered the finest in the world and is bottled and shipped everywhere. But the casino is the main attraction. It was built around 1860 on a smaller scale and later expanded. It is not open year round. This casino includes a large complex with a discotheque on the ground floor. Entrance fee is three francs. They also have a boule room (a French game) next to the dance floor, but this is *not* a game for Americans.

If you have Swiss or American money, you should exchange it on the Swiss side for francs before leaving or taking the boat. This can be done at the ticket booth at the boat dock. Ten Swiss francs equals around 13 French francs.

If you are wanted by police anywhere in the world, don't go to Casino d'Evian. Your passport will be scrutinized very carefully. They have a filing system in the back room on wanted persons and also on counters and cheaters. I had to wait five minutes to be okayed; I guess my Nevada address caused the delay. They have tip boxes when you sign in and more tip boxes before you enter the casino. It seems like everyone has his hand out.

The 21 tables open around 9 in the evening, with a 10-franc minimum up to a 2,000 franc maximum, about $500.

When you enter the casino, there is a large room on the right with four French wheels, four chemin de fer games, and one baccarat game. The baccarat opens at 10 p.m.; they deal two shoes and then close. But they do not open every evening, as most of the local players will play the wheels or 21. This casino closes at 3 a.m. but, if the players want to play chemin de fer among themselves, the club will keep a table open and the players can play as long as there is a game.

There are no slot machines in France, so if you are a slot player intending to go to a casino to play slots, just forget about it.

The restaurant is very small, but the food is good and not too expensive and they have a new menu every evening. It is worth taking the boat ride and having dinner to spend an enjoyable evening. There is no rule stating you must gamble. Just make sure about when the next boat leaves for Lausanne; it usually leaves at 1 a.m., but you'd better check to make sure.

Divonne Casino

Divonne Casino is about eleven miles from Geneva on the autobahn (freeway). You can rent a car and chauffeur for about $33 for the evening. They also have buses that leave from Geneva at 2:30, 6:30, and 9:30 p.m. The last return bus would leave Divonne around 1 in the morning. The fare is about five francs, and in most instances it is returned by the casino. Divonne opened about 1954 and is one of the most successful casinos in France. Of course, the simple reason for its being so successful is that it's so close to Geneva, the heart of world banking trade, whereas a club like Evian depends mostly on Swiss nationals. Divonne is open all year and will usually stay open 24 hours. Tourists should buy French francs in Geneva because the casino will take the breakage on the exchange of money. Also, it is wise to have the right amount when paying your entrance fee, which 4 francs—per person.

The Divonne casino is a large, white, L-shaped complex with gardens on both sides. Concerts are held in June or July. This club makes plenty of money and the tips to the help are enormous. Europeans learn at an early age that you must tip quite often.

There are twelve French wheels in the casino, ranging from a 5 franc minimum to 600 francs straight up, about $150. Compared to Nevada, this is a steep game for the 25 cent wheel player. If you decide to play the French wheel, be careful how you bet your chips. You're betting $1.25 on each chip instead of 25 cents.

In back of the club is the American casino that opens around 9 each evening. The croupiers dealing the American wheels are very slow, but the 21 dealers are fast and accurate. They deal a six-deck shoe with a 10 franc and 20 franc minimum and a $250 to $500

American maximum. The 21 game is dealt similar to 21 in England, so read the chapter on the new 21.

Supervisors there are very worried about counters and do not hesitate to cut the deck or shoe in half. And they will keep cutting until they either tell you to leave or they have you arrested. They can cut the shoe as far down as they want to with no questions by the players.

Monte Carlo

Princess Grace is one of my favorite actresses and Prince Rainier looks like a splendid fellow, but the casino that has made their little kingdom of Monaco famous and has helped pay the grocery bills for eighty-nine years has deteriorated into one of the sleaziest tourist-trap casinos in the world. The casino, which is called the Casino de Monte Carlo, was built in 1884, and through the decades its international fame as a hangout for royalty and celebrities grew with the help of movies and books and, of course, that famous old-time song about "The Man Who Broke the Bank at Monte Carlo." But I doubt if you'd find any movie stars or royalty there anymore. The casino looks elegant from the outside, with huge marble columns and stairs, but you'll be shocked when you walk inside. The barren, drab walls , worn and scuffed floors, cold atmosphere, gloomy lighting, shabby uniforms, run-down equipment, and aloof, robot-like dealers make Monte Carlo about as appealing as a concentration camp. And the irony of it all is that they make you pay, not once, but *twice,* if you want to see the whole place. They should be paying the tourists to come inside.

The forty-three battered, ancient one franc slot machines crammed into a dirty little room at the entrance to the casino are reported to be so tight that some of the younger employees don't even know what the cry "Jackpot" means. The crap table layout went out of style fifty years ago. And whoever designed the table did an excellent job of making one of the most confusing layouts I've seen, with some of the worst bets in the world for the player. In 21, all casinos deal four decks at a time from the shoe, but in France and Monte Carlo they deal six decks, which gives the casino a little stronger edge. I'm sure they would deal fifty decks if they thought they could find somebody with enough strength to shuffle them, and if they were convinced that that would give them an even stronger edge. And unlike many other casinos, the Casino de Monte Carlo does not offer any help or explanations from the dealers on how to play the games. The only way to get some of the Monte Carlo dealers to answer questions is to put a gun to their temples. Then you might get some answers.

It costs 7 francs to enter the front part of the casino, and, unlike other casinos, there is no dress requirement during the day. It's come as you are and everybody does. Don't bother wearing nice clothes in Monte Carlo. You'll feel out of place in such a dumpy atmosphere. Back of the front casino area is the Salon Prive, which costs 9 francs extra to enter. Don't waste your time or money. There's nothing in the privy salon other than more gaming tables and a chemin de fer and baccara game but, of course, nobody tells you that. It's supposed to be more private and exclusive back there, but you'll find that the privy salon crowd is no different than in the front casino. They were just curious or stupid enough to pay the 9 francs extra. Stick to the front casino area and another room, which is the so-called "American" casino, though that is a joke, too.

The front casino has six French wheels, one 30-40 game, and several slot machines with a 2 franc (about 46¢) minimum. The French wheels deal a 5 franc minimum to 10,000 franc even money maximum, and a 300 franc maximum on a straight-up bet on dozens and column bets. The 30-40 game is a 10 franc minimum to 10,000 franc maximum.

At the rear of the front casino, a neon sign advertises "American Games" down a paneled hallway. I don't know why they call it an American casino. I once worked in a garage that was more appealing. It is a large, barren room with eleven slots, three 21 games, one crap table, and an American roulette wheel with 0 and 00 on the layout. Nobody plays it. (See the chapter on European roulette.) The 21 minimum is 10 francs (about $2.30) to a maximum of 500 francs (about $115). The crap game bars the "ace-deuce" bet, if you want to bet wrong. That bet went out with high-buttoned shoes (which are coming back). Also, you can't make a place bet against any numbers. You can't bet on the come—place bets only. I don't care for a game where you can bet only one way. Any crapshooter who knows what he's doing won't bet Don't Win because it bars the ace-deuce, which makes it too strong against the player. So Monte Carlo forces you to bet one way, that is, to Win only. The crap game has a minimum of 10

francs to 1,000 francs (about $230) maximum. Just make your small
bets (10, 20, or 30 francs) and don't try to bet too high and take the
odds. Bet on the Win line only and don't make any other bet. That's
the only way to play at the crap game in Monte Carlo. The craps and
21 dealers sit on chairs at the gaming tables and pay bets out by
throwing the chips at you, because the chips are plastic and slippery
and can't be cut into little stacks as is done in many other casinos.

If you're going to play 21, and I don't care how big a player you are,
you should set a minimum of 10 francs to 30 francs and progress as
you go up. Don't start with a higher minimum because you won't
have a chance against the $115 maximum bet. The maximum is fine
for $2 or $5 bettors, but the limit is too small for a fair bettor. Monte
Carlo has some of the worst limits I've ever seen in a gaming club in
Europe.

The dealers at Monte Carlo are what we call wind-up dealers. They
act just like wind-up toys or robots. They say they don't speak any
English, only certain phrases like "split," "double down," and "men's
room two doors to your right." That's the extent of their English
conversation, though usually the casino's clientele is largely made up
of American tourists. Don't expect any help from the employees in
Monte Carlo.

I finally cornered one casino executive in the Privy Salon and
asked him some questions. He said that many years ago there was a
rich clientele. Princes, kings, queens, oil tycoons, rich Greeks,
starlets, the "beautiful people," and jet setters flocked to Monte
Carlo. Now, the boss said very sadly, Monte Carlo attracts only what
we in Nevada call the "Greyhound bus" tourist crowd. The high-class
clientele has drifted to other parts of Europe, especially nearby
Cannes (about forty miles from Monte Carlo). This boss, a man in his
late 50s or early 60s, wore a tuxedo with a seat shiny enough to blind
you in the sun. He's probably been there forty years and feels that
everything is going downhill. He and other older employees think
that maybe the proposed new casino will never reflect the grand old
days of Monte Carlo. At least this boss was talkative. Most of the
casino help won't bother answering your questions at the tables; and
if a mistake is made and you try to argue with them, they'll often just
ignore you and continue the game.

In back of the privy room was a curtained-off area. I asked one
executive what was behind the curtain. He said it was a private
baccara game for high rollers and big players. Later, I peeked behind

the curtain. Instead of the high roller baccara game, a bunch of croupiers were practicing how to deal. But I imagine years ago it was a private baccara game.

The area in Monaco outside the casino has shopping centers, stores, and a large hotel. The hotel has a dining room which is very expensive, so I advise you to eat at the smaller restaurants. There is no food in the casino. There are dining tables in the privy room, but nobody serves food. I suggest that you eat in Monaco or in the surrounding area.

Monaco is about 25 kilometers (about 15 miles) from Nice. Buses run from Nice about every 15 or 30 minutes during the day. It's a 3 franc charge one way. A taxi will cost you 100 francs and the driver will wait for you. That is routine. When you take a taxi, they charge you for both ways, regardless. The same applies if you leave from Monte Carlo. If you took a bus to Monte Carlo, missed the bus, and wanted to take a taxi back, it would cost 100 francs anyway. The cab has to come back to Monte Carlo, and they charge for the return trip whether you like it or not.

Believe me, at this point, the Monte Carlo casino simply is not worth visiting unless you have nothing better to do.

Monaco has added a new summer casino, The Sportsmen Club. From what I hear it is a very beautiful club overlooking the sea. Top stars are booked to perform in the show room.

But, in all fairness to Princess Grace and Prince Rainier, I must say that Monaco's new hotel and casino have just opened. Reportedly, business had fallen off to the point where they had to do something. Cannes, with its beautiful casino and view, has been taking away much of Monte Carlo's business. The gaming limits in Monte Carlo are too low for big players, and any tourist in his right mind might visit Monte Carlo once out of curiosity, but I doubt if he would ever waste time and money visiting it again.

The new hotel, Loew's Monte Carlo Hotel, has 650 rooms. No European games, such as the French wheels, boule, 30-40, baccara, punto banco, and chemin de fer, will be allowed in the new casino. The reason is that they do not want to detract from the old Casino de Monte Carlo, though that outlived its glamour years ago. This new casino, with four crap tables, twelve blackjack tables with a $500 limit, two roulette wheels (0/00), and one hundred and twenty slot machines, is the only complete American casino in Europe. The only thing European in the casino is the betting chips; you play with French francs.

The local croupiers speak English. The executives are Americans. At least, if you have a complaint, the executives cannot say they do not speak English. I am sure the casino will be run much better than some of the casinos I have run into in Europe.

Malta

The Dragonara Palace Casino is situated on the furthest point of the peninsula. Once the private residence of the first Maltese banker, Marquis Scicluna, it's a beautiful building with a pretty casino inside. Also on the grounds is a first-class hotel, the Dragonara Hotel. There is a gourmet restaurant inside the casino. It's a very relaxing part of the island, a good place to spend a couple of days.

They have six 21 tables, six French roulette wheels, eight American roulette wheels, one crap table, and two chemin de fer games; there are no slot machines. The betting limits—currency is English pounds—are very, very low. On 21 and the crap table they deal a minimum $1.25 American to around $25 American maximum. At the roulette wheel there's about 60 cents minimum to a maximum of £5 (around $12.50) on a number.

Portugal - Estoril

The Casino Estoril is beautiful to look at, but as is true of so many other foreign casinos, the tourist must be very wary of what games to play, how to play, and how much to bet. Estoril's casino is strictly a nickel-and-dime grind operation designed to milk the tourist out of his last escudo, as I'll explain later. Leave your money in the hotel safe and visit Estoril for the beautiful tourist attraction that it is. It's located in the heart of Portugal's most fashionable and finest bathing resort on the Atlantic about thirteen miles west of Lisbon. Cabs are available, but buses are much cheaper and leave daily from Lisbon.

Casino admission is 30 escudos (about $1.35) for two days. This is another casino that charges you to come in and lose your money. Men should wear ties and coats. It has a large combination theater, night-club, and restaurant, with floor shows Las Vegas style but not as big.

A modern airy building with floor-to-ceiling glass windows ringing the marble column entrance and mezzanine houses the casino. More than a dozen flags flutter along the roof overlooking beautifully landscaped grounds and the broad walkways leading to the casino.

At night the casino glows like a beckoning beacon as you approach the luminous red, gold, and yellow fountain displays. Inside, a variety of glass-walled shops surround a softly lit fountain, and the light from the huge overhead chandeliers shimmers off the polished marble floor. Casino Estoril has more shops and facilities than any other casino operation without a hotel that I've seen. It's well worth a visit.

Crammed into a small room near the casino entrance were 180 new slot machines for the Portuguese peasants. Poor people are not allowed into the casino. Only persons earning more than 15,000 escudos a year can play with the tourists. If you look Portuguese, make sure you wear your fanciest clothes and jewels; otherwise you might find yourself out in the slot room with the peasants, though sometimes I wonder if they aren't having more fun. The machines are all the same, with the same payoffs, and take coins equal to 10 cents and 20 cents. Every night the peasants crowd into the tiny room dressed in their Sunday best and pull the slot arms with both hands, chattering all the time in Portuguese. They usually leave broke, but at least they were near a gambling casino. The ten slots *inside* the casino are ignored by the wealthy Portuguese, but Americans, like the peasants, often crowd around them.

Casino Estoril also is the only casino I've seen in my travels where you can't buy in at the tables. They do not have a money box at the games; I guess they don't trust the dealers. If you want to buy more chips, the supervisor rings a bell and a little man runs over, carrying a large black shoulder bag with money compartments in it. You give the runner escudos and he gives you chips. Maybe this is where shoulder bags for men started.

The main casino features six French roulette games with the largest layouts I've ever seen. You have to walk around them to bet, or use a carrier pigeon. I advise Americans to stay away from the French wheels. I have seen as many as twenty-five persons making a bet at the same wheel with chips that were generally the same color. It was very difficult to watch a bet and, as usual, the foreigners always lost the arguments, of which there quite a few. It takes the fun out of gambling when you have to concentrate on bets as if your life or bankbook depended on it. But it doesn't seem to bother the local players. The tables are close together, and I saw some players bet on one wheel while the ball was spinning and quickly bet on another wheel at the same time. I wouldn't advise trying that. The locals looked as if they knew what they were doing, but closer scrutiny indicated that the Portuguese players were as confused as the Americans. Minimum bets on some wheel games range from 10 escudos minimum to 7,000 escudos maximum. The maximum straight-up wheel bet is about $7 American. French roulette also has tougher odds for the player in Estoril. In most other European casinos, they'll take only half your bet or put your money "in prison" if the single 0 shows on an even money bet. But in Estoril everybody loses when a 0 shows on the roulette wheel, except the person who bet on 0. It also is the only casino I've seen where the players stand and the croupiers sit at roulette.

As for 21, the six games in Estoril have a 100 escudos minimum (about $3.50) and a 3,000 escudos maximum (about $105). The limits aren't bad for the small player who uses the betting and money management rules I lay out earlier in this book in the 21 chapter. But if you are a big player, be very careful playing 21. The limits are too small. You must bet a minimum of $5 or $10, and use the appropriate money management progression system described in the 21 chapter.

Even if a big player should lose $100, he must leave the game. Don't try to get even. In Estoril, 21 is strictly a grind game, and the casino will wear your bankroll down to nothing if you bet too high at the start. Even a $100 bettor must start at the $5 or $10 minimum.

At the crap tables, just bet the line only (Pass or Don't Pass).

Estoril, like a growing number of new foreign casinos, has eliminated come bets from its crap layouts. If you want to bet the numbers, you must place them. This is great for the club, but suicide for the player (see my chapter on place bets).

The maximum line bet isn't bad though, about $245. The minimum is 100 escudos. The field pays 2 to 1 on aces and sixes, with a minimum 20 escudos bet to a maximum of 2,500 escudos.

Estoril also has baccara, punto banco, and chemin de fer. These are more grind games; don't play them. At punto banco, for example, the club takes 10 percent of each winning bet by the banker—highway robbery. Most other casinos rake only 5 percent, and that's high enough.

Don't even go near Estoril's chuck-a-luck game. It's one of the oldest hustle games around. The percentage is too strong. You'll need a miracle to win if you play for any length of time.

There is one foreign game here, called "banca francesca," that's fun to play and simple to learn. It's played with three tiny dice. A croupier scoops up the dice in a little cup and drops them down a large tube. The dice bounce and rattle through the tube and out onto a small rubber mat. There are two bets: "small total" and "big total." A small total bet means you're wagering that the dice will add up to a total of 5, 6, or 7. A big total means the dice will add up to 14, 15, or 16. The croupier throws the dice until he hits a small or big total. If any other total shows, such as 8, 9, 10, or 11, nobody loses and the croupier throws the dice again until he makes a big or small total. The big and small total bets pay even money. If three aces are rolled, then everybody loses except the club, because it wins both sides. This is the club's edge, the house percentage. You can protect yourself by betting that three aces will show, but I wouldn't advise doing so. The three aces bet pays 60 to 1, but the payoff should be 213 to 1—another robbery. Stick to the big and small total bets and you'll find that banca francesca isn't a bad risk for your money and it requires little thought. Minimum bet is 20 escudos to 3,500 escudos maximum (about $120).

Estoril's casino games are so strong for the house that it is little wonder the Portuguese government taxes about 74 percent of the casino's winnings. The casino seems to do a tremendous business. It is surrounded by plush tourist hotels and is the only game in town. Another Estoril-type resort is being constructed several hundred kilometers to the south.

Portugal can't get on the international gambling bandwagon fast enough. The way they deal the games, I really can't blame them.

Algarve along the sunny southern coast will soon become the new Riviera. There are three casinos in the southern area, Penina, Vilamoura, and Monte Gordo, close to the border of Spain. In 1976 these casinos will be replaced by three palatial Casinos do Algarve; style similar to the casino in Estoril. The same limits as Estoril will apply in Algarve.

Italy

The Casino Municipale in San Remo is very popular with the natives. San Remo is a resort area and the casino is open all year. It has sixteen French wheels, nine chemin de fer tables, and four trente-et-quarante (30-40) games. They should have American games soon.

Yugoslavia

The main Yugoslavian resort area fringing the Adriatic Sea is beautiful, with its turquoise waters, craggy cliffs, mountains, and quaint little villages. But the gambling is second-rate, if that, and has proved to be very risky for both the player and the casino owner. They don't charge admission to enter Yugoslavian casinos, and that was a very smart move; otherwise, those casinos would quickly become bowling alleys, because few persons in their right minds would pay to visit them. Visit Yugoslavia for the scenery, not to gamble.

I would not advise tourists to gamble in this country until the government wakes up to the fact that it must hire gambling experts to keep the casinos operating in a straightforward manner.

It's a very picturesque county, but it's also a very poor country, and that's why I think the government allowed outsiders to set up casinos in the resort towns of Split, Bled, Maestral, Cavtat (fifteen miles south of Dubrovnik), Malinska on the island of Krk, Dubrovnik and other towns along the Adriatic, and even in the capital, Belgrade, in its largest hotel. Most of the casinos are small, with generally American games and Yugoslavian or English dealers. Most of the owners are Americans who lease the casino space from the hotels.

Yugoslavia is typical of the risks tourists face when gambling in small foreign countries new in the gaming business. Few, if any, officials are qualified in these countries to police or check the games to make sure the tourists, or the casino owners, aren't being cheated.

In Yugoslavia, 99 percent of the peasants and townspeople still think a crap table is a giant wooden washtub, and 50 percent probably still put money in the slot machines and wait for gumballs to come out. Yugoslavians aren't even allowed to gamble in the casinos. They can only play slot machines in a separate area, which might be an indication that the Yugoslavian government doesn't trust its own people in a casino, or doesn't trust the casinos. I am advising the American tourist to be especially wary when gambling in countries where there are few qualified persons to keep the casinos honest. I am not accusing anyone in particular of cheating. Gambling is just like any other business; skullduggery often occurs when there's little fear of being caught.

Take what happened to Harold Smith, Jr., a veteran Nevada gambler and son of the founder of Harold's Club in Reno, the oldest major casino in Nevada.

Without ever seeing the hotel, Smith entered into an agreement to run a casino and bar at a brand new resort in the Maestral Hotel in the town of Maestral near Sveti Stefan on the Adriatic Sea. Smith took over three rooms on the second floor. He installed the gaming equipment, built an elevator from the lobby to the second floor casino, and imported thirty Bally slot machines. They were beautiful machines, but they couldn't be played because none of the Yugoslavian coins fit. Smith was undaunted. The club opened with a bang. Well, maybe it was more of a "pop," but even that fizzled. The imported American supervisors told me (and I saw for myself when I got there) that instead of a first-rate hotel-club, it turned out to be a tenth-rate hotel-club, according to American standards.

Since locals weren't allowed inside to gamble, the club, like many others in Yugoslavia, had little walk-in traffic and had to depend on junkets. But some of the junkets cost more than what the junketeers lost at the tables. Smith also had imported English dealers to help out when the junkets came in. As the profits began diminishing, some of the English dealers suggested to Smith that he could make money by running a "flat store," or cheating the customer. The casino employees I interviewed said Smith would have none of that, but it doesn't say much for those English dealers.

My investigation, confirmed by news reports, also showed that some of the so-called peasants and hillbilly types in their quaint garb weren't as backward as they looked. A bottle of Russian vodka costs one dollar in nearby villages, but these so-called peasants sold it to the casino for three or four dollars. Who were the hillbillies in that case?

Smith finally lost the casino in the ill-fated venture and since has been planning other foreign casino adventures. I hope he checks them out a little more closely.

Yugoslavian casinos do get some action during the busy summer tourist months because of the Adriatic Sea, but, as in Smith's case, the casinos rely largely on junkets from America. Generally speaking, foreign casino junkets can be a gyp. The one I went on to Yugoslavia was typical. First, the junketeers had to put up $2,500 to $3,500 front money to insure they were going to play upon arrival. What many junketeers don't realize is that some casinos later charge players $700 to $800 extra if they don't play fast enough or don't spend enough. Other junketeers, after losing their front money, find out that they have to write a big check at the end of their "fun" visit to pay for their gambling losses. Often when you go on a junket to small countries, there is nothing else to do but gamble, and unless you want to pay your own plane fare out of town you either have to take a sleeping pill until the plane leaves or gamble at least until you have spent your front money. But often, after losing the front money, the player continues to gamble to try to get even.

On this particular junket, we were to spend four days in Yugoslavia and four days in Rome, all at the casino's expense. I was invited along as an observer.

It was a decision I have long regretted. First we were loaded like cattle six abreast on a chartered Jal Yugoslavian jet. The plane flew from Atlanta, where the junket originated, to Bangor, Maine. We were supposedly refueling but we were stuck in Maine for nearly three hours so I knew it was more than a gas stop. Halfway over the Atlantic, I found out the truth. The so-called airport near Sveti Stefan was nestled at the end of a gully between two huge mountains. Our pilots, who weren't too excited about landing there in the daytime, didn't have any intention of landing there at night, especially since the field wasn't lit, so we waited in Maine while the pilots gathered courage and while it approached daylight in Yugoslavia. Whiskey flowed like water as we flew over the Atlantic. The liquor was free, and the passengers had plenty of reason to drink.

It was a miserable trip. Sleep was impossible and there were only two stewardesses to serve 160 passengers. The stewardesses looked like refugees from the professional wrestling circuit and would have made a fortune as a tag team titled "The Balkan Bombshells." They were built like brick ??. Occasionally, one would elbow her way down

the crowded aisle and toss a customer a sandwich. I felt like a seal.
The aisles were crowded with people going to and from the restroom.
Many had one hand on their zipper and the other over their mouth. It
was a bumpy trip.

I took a commercial flight back.

When the plane touched down between the two mountains ·at
daybreak, the passengers, including myself, began applauding and
cheering. I even thought I heard some clapping from inside the pilot's
cabin. But upon our arrival at the hotel, there was pressure for the
junketeers to gamble because the casino owner didn't spend $90,000
to charter a plane and wine and dine the players to have them spend
their time strolling the beach photographing the cute little fishing
boats.

Many soon discovered that gambling isn't much fun with someone
looking over your shoulder to make sure you play a certain amount.

Those junketeers on the Yugoslavian trip were no different than
the thousands of junketeers I have talked to over the years across the
world. They all think they are getting something for nothing. That
may be true for some junkets to Nevada, because the casinos are
much larger, the accommodations are better, and the bosses don't
police the junketeers as closely to make sure that they gamble.
Nevada also is only at most a four-hour flight from anywhere in the
continental United States. But when you go on a junket to a small
foreign country, you pay for the junket many times over physically,
mentally, and financially.

It is much cheaper, and more relaxing, to visit countries such as
Yugoslavia as a regular tourist and gamble when and how much you
want. But again, the maximum limits are very low in most casinos,
except when the junkets are in, so be careful, bet low, and remember
you're on a vacation; enjoy yourself.

There are several casinos located in small towns and villages
surrounding Dubrovnik. The Maestral Hotel, which was owned by
Smith, was the largest in Yugoslavia before it closed. It might be a
good idea to check to see if it has reopened. It is about a ninety-
minute cab ride from Dubrovnik down a winding mountain road
across a fiord, and the trip includes a ferryboat ride. Very picturesque
to get there, but once you arrive, that's it. Not much else to look at.

Sveti Stefan: From what I have seen in Yugoslavia, this little castle
resort, about a mile from Maestral, is the country's prettiest hotel and

a great place to spend a weekend relaxing. The hotel, which was once a fourteenth century castle surrounded by water, is fronted by a beautiful park, has an excellent dining room and a marbled terrace dining area atop the castle which overlooks the Adriatic: a gorgeous view. On the second floor is a very small but very pretty casino with one 21 game and two French roulette wheels. That's all. No slots or any other games. The dealers are French, and the little casino seems to cater to its own guests. But don't worry; they will take anybody's money. They try to keep the casino in the European tradition, quiet and sedate.

In European casinos, when players get angry or aren't winning, they do not explode or throw their chips around, or raise little temper tantrums like players in American casinos. They get up like perfect ladies and gentlemen, leave their chips, and walk away from the game talking to themselves or whatever else they do to relieve their tensions. Nobody touches their chips. I'm quite sure many European gamblers have ulcers.

Albatross Hotel: A large, modern hotel, five hundred rooms, in a little village called Cavtat, some fifteen miles from Dubrovnik. It's about three miles from the airport, but you must take a long, winding road from the main road down to the Adriatic Sea, very tricky at night or even in the daytime. Very narrow. The casino is just off the lobby. You walk past twenty-five old slot machines, which take Yugoslavian coins between six and twelve cents American. Casino has four 21 tables, two American roulette wheels, one crap table, and one American-style baccarat. Mostly Yugoslavian dealers. Equipment is new and good, but croupiers don't speak English very well, especially when there is an argument or you have a beef against them. But the executives and casino management speak excellent English. Go directly to them if there is any problem. Minimum bet on 21 games is one dollar, with a $50 maximum bet. The wheels: $10 straight up, or any way you can get to it. Craps: on one side of the table you can bet a minimum of one dollar and a maximum of $100; on the other side, a minimum of one dollar to a maximum of $500. All games are American style.

Imperial Hotel: Located just outside Dubrovnik. Doesn't do much business. One 21 game with a $10 maximum; two French-style roulette wheels. Very small. Be careful in a place like this with the $10 maximum. No slots, no locals, just whoever or whatever falls into the place. It is not owned by Americans. My advice is to stick your head in the door, look around, and keep moving down the road.

Split and Bled: These towns along the Adriatic also have small casinos a few hours drive from Dubrovnik on a very winding road, about 225 miles. Don't drive if you have bad nerves or are in a hurry. It's not worth the annoyance, honking and praying that you are going to make it. Yugoslavian drivers are not known for their caution behind the wheel, as many of them haven't driven cars for too many years. They have a short plane flight from Dubrovnik to Bled and Split. If you can afford the plane fare, I advise taking the plane. But don't go to those little towns just for the casinos, because the limits are too small and it just isn't worth the risk that you might get cheated.

Yugoslavia is a cheap country for travel because food and rooms are most reasonable. But, like the casinos, the rooms and food can be disappointing to Americans who are used to fancy stuff.

I'm sure it won't be long before the Yugoslavian government starts taxing the casinos as other countries do. Maybe, with taxation, the government will be concerned enough to check the reputations and backgrounds of some casino owners. This will eliminate the fly-by-night operators.

Greece

The biggest casino in Greece and the only one near Athens is perched atop a 3,000-foot mountain, twenty-two miles from downtown Athens.

The view is breathtaking, the food passable; and it is almost worth risking your life to get there to watch the Greek gamblers play with their worry beads. There are three routes: the road, a skylift, or helicopter. Just make sure your insurance is paid before trying any of them. The road is winding and treacherous, especially in the winter. I wouldn't advise driving it unless you have suction cups for wheels. There were so many accidents after the casino opened in February 1971 that a cable lift was installed in April 1972, just a few weeks after the casino owner, F. Demetrius, was killed driving down from the club. The lift is no bargain either. It takes four minutes to reach the top. Just grab hold of something that won't get your face slapped, hold your breath, and don't look down.

Wind-alarm bells are at the top and bottom of the lift. If they ring, the lifts aren't supposed to go up or down. I asked our attendant what happens if the wind-alarm bells ring when you're between the summit and the ground. He shrugged and made the sign of the cross, which wouldn't do a Jewish feller from Brooklyn much good. One official joked, and it was a bad one, that it was safer to ride the lift than fly in an airplane because if the lift failed you would only fall 3,000 feet, while you might fall 20,000 feet in a plane crash. And if you get stuck in the middle, he said, they have a hand crank to wheel the cable car back down. Isn't that reassuring? The cable ride costs about 50 drachmas, about $1.75. The Swiss cable car company has assured the hotel they will replace the car for free if it breaks. How nice!

Once you swing and sway your way to the summit, it is about a quarter-mile hike through a drab building that looks like an airline terminal to reach the Mt. Parnes Hotel and Casino. The hotel was recently renovated. It has eighty-five rooms, fifteen suites, a small restaurant, a snack bar, a booze bar, a nightclub, and an orchestra. Men must wear coats and ties into the casino, and there's a 10 drachma entrance fee. Foreigners must show passports. The casino is open from 7 p.m. to 5 a.m. daily, except on Tuesday, the employees' day off. As is true of many other foreign casinos, the government owns a large piece of the casino (70 percent in taxes) and has guards in every nook and cranny to protect its investment. Some of the guards have big pistols on their hips, apparently to protect the government and casino owners against robbery. What they really need as protection is an antiaircraft battery nearby. Nobody in his right mind would try to rob the place unless he had a helicopter for his getaway. (Come to think of it, maybe that isn't so far-fetched, given the way movie plots have been picked up in real life).

The casino is split into two barn-sized rooms. One has American-style games, and the other, European. Stick to the American room for your gambling. You'll find ten 21 tables, eighteen American-type wheels, and one lonely crap game in the back.

The adjoining European room has a game called "boule" at the entrance. It is played on a very large table, twice as big as a normal roulette table, and has a miniature roulette wheel in the middle. In boule, a little rubber ball rolls around the mini roulette wheel, which has numbers from 1 to 9 on it. If you bet and your number hits, you get paid 8 to 1. Boule doesn't do much business, and I don't advise anyone to play it. The percentage against the player is three times stronger than in other similar roulette-type casino games. Behind the boule game are two French wheels, which get plenty of action, three chemin de fer games, and a baccara game which usually opens around midnight. Many local Greeks eat a late dinner and then head for the Mt. Parnes casino and the baccara table. It seems to be a popular late evening game for the locals. But the American games are crowded all the time.

Mt. Parnes is not a fancy casino. In fact, many layouts are worn and patched. The cards are washable and they have been scrubbed over and over. The kings, queens, and jacks look like they have a severe case of dishpan hands. Most of the croupiers in the European room are French, and the American room dealers are 98 percent

English. Girls dressed in drab sweaters and mini-skirts deal 21 and roulette. I don't know where they got these outfits, but they are about as colorful as gunnysacks. There is a supervisor at each roulette game, and at each wheel a man in a tuxedo stands next to the money box. He has a clicker and clicks it as the money goes into the box. I wonder who's clicking each time the clicker clicks to make sure the clicker is clicking honestly. He also writes down each winning number and payoff.

But the government and the casino owners shouldn't have to worry very much, because this casino should make a fortune. If you want to gamble and you're in Athens, the only place to go is the Mt. Parnes Casino. It's the only game in town—or even near town. The Greeks love to gamble and apparently don't mind risking their lives every week on the cable car, or the road, to venture up to the casino. Hotels in Athens now are organizing daily bus tours to the casino for tourists who don't know any better. For a nominal fee, the bus tour includes the lift price, casino admission, and a dinner. Parachutes and tranquilizers are extra.

The bus tours are a good deal for the club, but a poor deal for the tourist. The buses drop you off about 8:30 p.m. and pick you up at about 1 a.m. That gives you plenty of time to lose your money, because there's little else to do but gamble. How long can you look at the panoramic view of Athens and the Acropolis? The twinkling lights of Athens look like the twinkling lights of Cannes, or San Francisco, or Rio de Janeiro, or any other big city where you can still see through the smog. I watched one tourist who, apparently tired of gaming, bounced olives off the rocky cliffs at the edge of the hotel grounds as some kind of diversion. It wasn't long before he returned to the casino.

Many Greek gamblers solve their gaming worries by carrying their own worry beads, which are strung on thread and carried in the hand. You're supposed to fondle, caress, and rotate them in your hand to relax. Try it; you might find that it works. Some Greeks bring their favorite color beads to the casino one night, and if those don't prove lucky try another color the next night. When I was introduced to the casino manager, he had his worry beads in his hands while we were talking. Believe me, he looked worried. Why, I don't know; the casino was jammed with customers. But maybe, like all casino managers, he wanted to look worried in case the owner was around. I became so worried watching the Greeks with their worry beads that I bought a set at the gift counter. I immediately felt better, until I started thinking about the cable ride back down.

An American dollar is worth about 30 drachmas, so you need a portable adding machine to figure out some of the bets, payoffs, and limits. The American wheels deal a 50 drachma minimum (about $1.75) to a 12,000 drachma maximum. On even money numbers, the wheel heads have American-style numerals. But the numbers and sections are spaced differently than in Nevada. And, as at all European French wheels, the ball is spun in one direction during one turn and then in the opposite direction the next roll. Why they do this, I don't know. Maybe they think that by spinning the ball in opposite directions they are confusing the numbers, or the ball, making the game more honest. Or maybe they think they are mixing up the odds more by spinning the ball in different directions around the wheel. But I can assure you it makes little difference how you spin the ball, or in what direction. The odds aren't going to change unless the ball is made out of iron and your favorite numbers have magnets. American-style wheels have a faster track, the ball is also spun both ways, and you get more spins.

Most of the 21 games have a minimum 50 drachma bet to a maximum of 10,000 drachmas (about $335). They have two high roller 21 games with a minimum of 500 drachmas to a maximum of 10,000 drachmas. The crap game, which is quite new to Europe, gets its share of business, but not too much big play. It has a minimum of 100 drachmas to a maximum of 10,000 drachmas. French wheels have a minimum of 100 drachmas to a maximum of 12,000 drachmas. Baccara has a minimum of 500 drachmas to a maximum of 10,000 drachmas. The three chemin de fer games do very little business. Don't play them.

If you're a slot player, forget the Mt. Parnes Casino. They don't have any slots. But I predict that slots will be installed as soon as the new American owners who are trying to buy the club realize what money-makers they are.

There are a few other casinos in Greece that have been there for many years. One is in Corfu and the other is in Rhodes. They're both about two and a half to three hours from Athens by plane (in opposite directions) and offer American-style games through the summer tourist season. I haven't checked them out, so if you gamble there you're strictly on your own.

Istanbul

There's a casino in the Hilton Hotel in Istanbul with around twenty-five slots. The other games are dealt in lira or lyres; a lyre is about 8¢ American. They have two crap games, about ten 21s, and three wheels. They deal in one-dollar minimums. There is a private back-room casino featuring roulette for the rich Turkish merchants. Locals are not allowed into the main casino. They deal place bets only at the crap table—with a $200 limit. They also deal a $200 limit on 21 American style using shoes.

Puerto Rico

This island could have become the gambling center of the Caribbean. The only trouble is that the islanders did not go along with the times.

The casinos deal Nevada style.

The main reason for American tourists leaving Puerto Rico in disgust is the way they are handled in the hotel and casino areas. Also, some of the government rules in the clubs are ridiculous. I don't know who their adviser was in setting up these rules but they had better look elsewhere for advice. Anyone with a fair knowledge of gambling could have told the government that many rules were outdated forty years ago. They went out with high-button shoes. Like the string in the middle of each crap table on Puerto Rico. Both dice had to go over the string and stay over. If a short person, who is fortunate enough even to reach the table, shot the dice a couple of times and the dice didn't go over the string, the dealers would bawl the player out and sometimes wouldn't let him shoot again. Another rule is that if one of the dice lands on a chip (cocked dice), it is "no dice." And if it's a close decision, a supervisor will come over with a flashlight to see if there is light between a chip and the die so that they are not touching each other. In Nevada and in other countries, there is no string and cocked dice are called on the high side, whichever way the die is supposed to fall.

In many island hotels a player risks getting his knuckles rapped if he plays with the dice before shooting. God forbid that he should turn them over by accident. I've seen stick men—who control the dice— look at such a shooter as if he were going to be hung. If a shooter throws a couple of craps, feels unlucky, and wants to change the dice in the middle of the hand, too bad. You must shoot with the same unlucky dice.

These are examples of what we call ridiculous rules. They close up the games and cause arguments.

Some clubs don't even have a casino cage. They have a desk in the middle of the pit. When players cash out at a table, a runner will deliver the money. But many people have to go through quite a hassle to cash personal checks or traveler's cheques. I've seen it over and over. And if a pretty girl walks by a dealer, he will stop dealing and make comments to other dealers in Spanish. That's what you call a strong union.

My impression of all this was that the Puerto Ricans felt they were doing the Americans a favor by letting them spend and lose their money on the island. It has taken Americans a long time, but they have finally come to their senses. Quite a few have realized they don't have to take the harassments in the Peurto Rican hotels and casinos. There are other islands in the Caribbean that are being tried by the Americans who formerly patronized Puerto Rico. As a result, tourism and gambling have dropped off quite a bit. The government has even had to take over a couple of hotels that have closed for lack of business and is investigating what caused the decline.

Outside of the outlandish rules, the crap games in Puerto Rico are similar to those in Nevada, with a couple of exceptions. They have come bets and place bets, but they pay even money on the 6 and 8, so if you are a place bettor you must not place either number. Also, do not play or bet on the field.

Read the chapter on craps in England and play that way in Puerto Rico.

Puerto Rico still deals a $100 betting limit. If they want to raise table limits to $200, they must declare to the government before they open how many tables will be raised. Also, when clubs declare what tables are a $5 minimum, they must continue the $5 minimum bet the whole evening and cannot reduce the limit—even if nobody is playing.

When quite a few boats come into San Juan, some clubs will only keep their maximum limit to $100. The tourists on the boats do not stay ashore too long and play heavily. The club operators know they can grind the tourists out of their money with the $100 limit.

The government has appointed a gambling administrator to look into the cause of the declining tourist and gambling trade. I would suggest that his first assignment should be a visit to Nevada to see how casinos are run and what the rules are. He also must get the idea across to the natives that the customer comes first.

Because most of the gamblers that come into Puerto Rico are Americans, the casinos in Puerto Rico and other Caribbean islands should deal their games as close to the Nevada style as they can. But instead of making it easier for the players, they confuse them with their outdated rules and limits on the games.

Some European casinos, for example, handle American tourists as if they are never going to see them again, which is true in a sense. But to make sure the Americans will never come back, they add a little coal to the fire. If there is an argument about a bet, all of a sudden nobody speaks English. And this is happening in some of the Caribbean islands—like Puerto Rico. This should not happen on islands that welcome American tourists and gamblers. They should give them a little consideration. They are their bread and butter.

Slot machines are being installed in the casinos to pump up the revenue at this writing.

Haiti

Haiti is about an hour's flight from Miami. It is a poor country and is progressing very slowly, but the American tourist is treated much better than he is in Puerto Rico or in the Bahamas. The main international casino is in Port-au-Prince near the wharfs facing the sea. The games are dealt Nevada style. Drinks are free in the casino. Haitian money is about 5 to 1 to the American dollar. But the casino will deal American dollars to American players.

The people of the island are very friendly, and you can walk anywhere and not feel uneasy. There are four 21s, three wheels, one Big Six, and one crap table. They deal a $5 minimum with a $200 maximum in craps and 21. On the wheels you can bet $25 straight up on a number, which isn't bad for an island game. There are about a hundred and fifty slot machines outside and inside the casino. If you are a 21 player, read the chapter on the New 21 and play that way in Haiti, because they deal Nevada style with four decks. High-betting crapshooters must start at a small limit—$25 minimum or less—then progress as they win. The $200 limit is okay for $5 and $10 bettors.

The Royal Haitian, which has just opened in Port-au-Prince, is a 200-room hotel, owned by Mike and Bill McLaney, who also own the International Casino in the same town. Eddie Arcaro, the famous ex-jockey, is president, and they have brought down to Haiti L. McWillie, formerly of Las Vegas and one of the top men in the gambling business. Since the supervisors are also from the States (dealers are local), this is a good club to play in, run by reputable people. The new gambling casino deals $200 on the line and $200 odds, and place bets only to a $200 maximum at the crap table, but will deal a higher limit to a high roller. Limit at 21 is $200. The roulette wheel will take $25 bets any way you can get to a number.

Netherlands Antilles (Curacao, Aruba, St. Maarten, and Bonaire)

These islands are about two hours from Miami and about four hours from New York. Bonaire is the smallest. It has one small hotel which opens and closes sporadically. They deal a very small limit on Bonaire, so you must be careful and check the limit before you start playing when the club is open.

St. Maarten has the Concord Hotel, the St. Maarten Isle Hotel, and the Mulletts Bay Hotel. A $100 limit is dealt generally in these casinos. Read previous chapters on small limits and play accordingly. When the casinos are open.

Curacao is one of the major islands and has four hotels with casinos: The Hilton, Intercontinental, Sands, and Holiday Inn. They deal a $100 limit at craps and 21, which is dealt Nevada style with four decks. Read the chapter on the New 21 and play that way at their 21 games. In craps, even money is paid on the 6 and 8. As they deal a $100 limit you must be careful if you are a bettor who bets a little fast, or a high bettor.

Of these four islands, I suggest Aruba, one of the prettiest islands in the world. It has white sandy beaches; the temperature is in the 80s all year. The locals are very easy-going and pleasant, and most speak three or four languages. The native language on all these islands is Dutch, and you can walk or drive anywhere on any of the islands without worry or fear.

In Aruba, there are four major hotels: Aruba Caribbean, Aruba Sheraton, Holiday Inn, and Americana Hotel.

Practically all major casinos on the islands deal a $100 maximum limit in craps and 21. Some clubs will deal place bets only, no come bets. Even money is paid on the 6 and 8. Read the chapter on place bets if you are going to play in a club that deals place bets only. Some clubs that deal place bets may have a $200 limit on placing the numbers, so you must check at a crap game before you start playing. There is a club in Curacao that has been known to change its dice layout from barring the two 6s to barring the ace-deuce, knowing that quite a few players on a previous junket were wrong bettors and that they were coming in that weekend. It's a very strong percentage against a wrong bettor.

At a $100 maximum limit game, a $25 bettor must start at a $15 minimum bet and no higher. You will be betting the limit of $100 before you know it if you win two or three hands. Read the chapter on the New 21.

At a $100 maximum at a crap table with come bets, the high players must also be careful with their betting. It is smarter to start at the $15 minimum bet and work your way up with the club's money. Use the money management method that I have suggested.

Some casinos are open nights only. During the day they allow slot machine play only. Casinos usually open around 9 p.m. and close around 5 or 6 in the morning.

Costa Rica

They have only 21 games in their small clubs and generally deal a $25 maximum limit, English style. There are no double-downs. Because the limit is so small, I advise Americans not to play. If you must play, don't bet more than $1. Just pass the time. Wait until they open some bigger clubs and deal a higher maximum limit before you go in for serious gambling in Costa Rica.

Panama

Panama's four major casinos are in the lobbies of the major hotels. La Siesta Hotel is across from the airport, about twenty minutes from the city of Panama. The other three major hotels are in town: El Panama Hotel, Continental, and Granada. They all have slot machines but deal a very small limit at casino games, $1 minimum to $50 maximum in 21 and craps. I do not advise anybody who bets over $2 to play at these games, because the limit is too small. They have 10 cent chips and up for roulette.

These casinos are on what they call the Pacific Ocean side of Panama. There are also a couple of casinos on the Atlantic side, in the city of Colon. They also deal the same style and same limits as they do in the city of Panama, American style, with American currency.

Cairo

My advice for Egypt is to gamble only at the Sheraton Hotel in Cairo. I say that with some authority because I set up the casino in 1969 when I was the casino consultant for Sheraton Hotels International.

I also got the Egyptian government to change their rules for declaring currency by tourists. They fought me tooth and nail at first. It was the law that a tourist must declare all his currency and jewelry when he entered Egypt and could not leave with more money than he entered with. That might be a great law to make sure the country isn't drained of its cash, but what gambler—or even casual tourist—wants to play at a casino knowing that if he does win big he can't take the money out of the country unless he spends an equal amount on something else.

The government officials hemmed and hawed but finally saw the light. The Sheraton in Cairo became one of the only overseas casinos where Americans can cash out in and get American money in return, an idea I advise other casinos to follow.

Several American and European games are available at the Sheraton, such as 21, craps, roulette, baccara, chemin de fer, and slots. A player who likes to bet $10 or above must be careful. The maximum limits on most games are $100. If you follow the English method for playing and betting on craps and 21 that I've outlined in this book, you should be okay.

If the club is still dealing 5% at the crap table, *do not play*.

Middle East

Iran, Syria, Jordan, Kuwait, and other Middle Eastern countries are opening casinos, but I haven't had a chance to inspect many of them yet. Nor do I really want to under the present shooting-gallery conditions. But several of my sources for gambling information who have visited these countries tell me that government policing is very spotty and a tourist really takes a big chance if he makes any kind of large wager. Save your big betting for the casinos I have personally inspected and about which I am confident there's no skullduggery taking place.

Lebanon

One of the finest casinos in the Middle East is in the small town of Maameltin, about fifteen miles from Beirut, Lebanon. It is called Casino du Liban and sits on a hill overlooking the harbor, with the mountains as a backdrop. The club deals both American and European games, including 21, craps, roulette, baccara, and slot machines. The minimum and maximum bets range from $1.65 to $330. It takes about 3 Lebanese dollars (Ls) to equal one American dollar. A cab from Beirut to the Casino du Liban costs about 15L, including a tip. The only Lebanese citizens allowed into the casino are those who earn at least 15,000L a year.

I advise that you stick to the American games here. The club has its own version of baccara, which involves a bidding system where the house gets 5 percent when a player bids for the bank and gets it. The player and banker also can stop on any amount they want to, or don't have to hit if they don't want to. This makes the Lebanese version a tough game for the tourist dropping in—almost like playing poker with strangers. You can be outfoxed very easily.

If you decide to play 21, play the same style that I advise for England, and use the same betting methods. For crap players, bet on the Pass line only and use the English method of progressing your bets. The maximum bets on the crap tables are a little low for the high bettor—maximum $165—but it is a good game for the $1 and $2 player.

But do not bet on the field in the Casino du Liban under any conditions. They pay even money on *any* number that shows and have taken the 4 out and replaced it with the 5. You are giving up a little over 11 percent each time you bet. The field bet is strictly a sucker bet in Lebanon.

My final warning for Lebanon is simple. Play only in the Casino du Liban. I'm not crazy about the way they deal some of their games but it's about the only casino in that country where you should have a fair chance of not getting cheated. Do not play in any little off-beat club a cab driver or bellhop might try to steer you to. Don't listen to any stories.

The Casino du Liban also has an entrance fee of about $1.66 a person. Here also don't let the dealers push you into overtipping. Dealers on the European games work for tips only, so they must try to hustle you or they don't eat.

It seems they try to break in new players to tip them every time the player hits a number. But what the player doesn't know is that the bosses are cut in on the tips. So, by overtipping the croupiers, you are enriching the bosses, who, if you don't know, don't need the money. This practice occurs in much of Europe.

Australia

The major gambling casino in Australia is the Wrest Point Hotel and its spacious casino in the state of Tasmania, a large island off the coast south of Melbourne. You step down into the casino. At the rear is a sunken area where they have punto banco and chemin de fer tables. They also have a show room, with stars from around the world. In fact, Jerry Lewis performed there on opening night.

The games are dealt the way games are dealt in England. They also deal in Australian dollars, each worth approximately $1.50 to our dollar. The limits on 21 range from a 60-cent minimum to $100 maximum. Some have a $5 minimum to a $150 maximum, and some have a $15 minimum to a $600 maximum. The crap game deals a $3 minimum to a $600 maximum. Tipping of croupiers is *not* permitted.

Macao

There are four major casinos in Macao, but the only casino I recommend is in the Hotel Lisboa, and even some games there are a rip-off. The casino has two floors, including a circular area with a punto banco game surrounded by six 21 tables. In punto banco the betting is done among the players themselves, as in chemin de fer. But the casino will book extra bets up to a $3,000 maximum—that is, if no bets are covered by player or banker, the casino will book the balance of the bets up to $3,000, and take 5 percent of the banker's bet. The 21 tables have a $2 to $200 maximum (American dollars). There is also a crap table on the lower floor, but don't make *any* place bets at the crap table. The casino bosses have created their *own* odds on the place bet. They pay only even money on the 6 and 8 when placing. And if you are betting on the line and the point is either 6 or 8 and you take the odds, you'll also be paid even money. If you are placing the 5 or 9, they do not pay 7 to 5, which are the standard odds, but 6 to 5. On placing the 4 and 10, the standard odds are 9 to 5 but this club only pays 8 to 5. You are taking much, much the worst of the deal. The minimum is $4 to about a $250 maximum (American dollars) at the crap table.

One of the most popular games is fan tan. It is played with a large number of beans or buttons on a layout. You bet 1, 2, 3, or 4. If you should win, the odds are 3 to 1. They charge you 5 percent if you win the bet. The dealer covers a number of beans and when he is ready to proceed he rings a bell. That signals everybody to quit betting. Then he uncovers the beans and counts them out in fours. When he reaches the last batch—four beans or less—the winner is paid. If there are four beans left at the end, No. 4 wins. If three beans are left, No. 3 wins, and so on. It is a very popular game and it seems honest. It will give you something to do. There are hundreds of slot machines around each casino, with a minimum 25 cents to 50 cents on the average.

South Korea

The main thing to remember about Korea is the 12 o'clock curfew. *Everyone* must be off the streets by midnight. If you are in a casino at midnight, you cannot leave. You're stuck there until early morning when the curfew is lifted. Either sleep in one of the hotels, where the casinos are usually located, or stay up until the curfew is lifted. But that last way can get expensive. Bring a reliable timepiece with you.

There are four main casinos in South Korea. The biggest one, the Walker Hill Casino, is about fifty miles outside of Seoul. There is one in Pusan, one in Inchon, and a smaller one on Cheju Island. The larger casinos usually have between thirty-five and forty 21 tables, 21 being the big game in South Korea. Admission is around $1 American. They deal in Korean money, the "won." The smallest bill is $500 won ($1.25 American). All deal the same limits ($75) on a crap table, which is dealt American style. Also, there's a $75 limit on the place bets. They pay 7 to 6 on a 6 and 8, which is the correct price. And you can double down only on 11 at 21. The wheels are dealt American style, with 0 and 00. You can bet about $6 straight up on a number. If you are a very high player, they may raise the limit to $100 or $125 maximum at craps and 21. They deal baccarat more or less as they do in Nevada, but they also deal a $75 maximum limit at baccarat. They have a ruling in baccarat that big players can bet $75 on each of the other players' seats (positions). The players in those seats, however, must let you bet your money there.

South Korean clubs usually have some slot machines outside the casinos but they take very small coins, maybe a penny. It's just something extra for customers to do. As you can see by the limits, you have to be very careful gambling in South Korea.